THE KEYS OF
THE KINGDOM

By the same author:

Les tendances nouvelles de l'ecclésiologie

The Relevance of Physics

Brain, Mind and Computers
(Lecomte du Noüy Prize, 1970)

The Paradox of Olbers' Paradox

The Milky Way: An Elusive Road for Science

Science and Creation: From Eternal Cycles to an Oscillating Universe

Planets and Planetarians: A History of Theories of the Origin of Planetary Systems

The Road of Science and the Ways to God
(Gifford Lectures, University of Edinburgh, 1975 and 1976)

The Origin of Science and the Science of its Origin
(Fremantle Lectures, Oxford, 1977)

And on This Rock: The Witness of One Land and Two Covenants

Cosmos and Creator

Angels, Apes, and Men

Uneasy Genius: The Life and Work of Pierre Duhem

Chesterton, a Seer of Science

Chance or Reality and Other Essays

Lord Gifford and His Lectures: A Centenary Retrospect

Translations with introduction and notes:

The Ash Wednesday Supper (Giordano Bruno)

Cosmological Letters on the Arrangement of the World Edifice (J. H. Lambert)

Universal Natural History and Theory of the Heavens (I. Kant)

THE KEYS OF THE KINGDOM:
A Tool's Witness to Truth

Stanley L. Jaki

THE FRANCISCAN HERALD PRESS
1434 West 51st Street   Chicago, Illinois 60609

The Keys of the Kingdom: A Tool's Witness to Truth by Stanley L. Jaki.
Copyright © 1986 by the Franciscan Herald Press, 1434 West 51st Street,
Chicago, Illinois 60609. All rights reserved.

Library of Congress Cataloging-in-Publication Data

Jaki, Stanley L.
    The keys of the kingdom.

    1. Popes—Primacy. I. Title.
BX1805.J34 1986   262'.13   86-7657
ISBN 0-8199-0898-3

MADE IN THE UNITED STATES OF AMERICA

CONTENTS

INTRODUCTION — 1

Chapter 1 A WORLD OF KEYS — 7
Keys as Key Words (7)—Keys and Modern Life (9)—Keys and Uniqueness (14)—The Antiquity of Keys (18)

Chapter 2 KEYS AND THE BIBLE — 25
Exploit, Rendez-vous, and Prophecy (25)—The Keys of Caesarea Philippi (31)—The Keys of the New Temple (42)—Key Acts in the Acts of the Apostles (49)

Chapter 3 AWARENESS OF THE KEYS — 53
The Age-old Question (53)—Spirituals and Spirituals Again (58)—A Champion versus a Savior (67)—Peter's Keys from Nicea to Augustine (73)—The Witness of the East (82)—Leo the Great and the Roman Centuries (90)—Twilight with a Dark Finale (96)

Chapter 4 PETER'S KEYS IN PROTESTANT KEY — 105
Two Reformers, One Inconsistency (105)—The Key to True Reform (116)—The Key to the Keys (129)—Caught in Worn Tracks (138)

Chapter 5 THE KEYS OF AN OPEN CHURCH 149
Peter's Keys at Vatican II (149)—From Broken Keys to Broken Catholics (153)—The Keys of Truth and Life (163)—Solidarity with the Keybearer (170)

NOTES 179

ILLUSTRATIONS 209

INDEX OF NAMES 223

INTRODUCTION

The expression "open church" is foremost among phrases that for the past twenty-five years have set the tone of much of what is being said and written about the edifice Christ founded two thousand years ago. While Christ's provision about a foundation for his Church is too explicit to be readily talked away, a flood of "theological" dicta has become quite successful in giving new respectability to the old and often condemned error that Peter's subjective faith and not his objective being was meant by Christ when he spoke of the rock foundation of his Church.

While the rock as foundation of the Church has at least remained a part, however spurious in connotation, of the new ecclesiological vocabulary, quite different has become the fate of the keys. That the edifice Christ had in mind was to be operated by a set of keys is hardly to be found in that new theology of the Church in which novel phrases have successfully expropriated the status of learnedness. A startling development, precisely in an age which has become utterly dependent on the most widespread use of keys in every facet of life. It is an age which expects key-makers to come up with the most ingenious devices to secure to each and every key the exclusive individuality that makes its abuse well-nigh impossible.

Expectations about keys were not essentially different at

the time when Christ entrusted to Peter the keys of the kingdom of heaven. By then, keys, with the specific individuality of modern keys, had been for at least two centuries a feature of daily life in the Mediterranean world. Chapters I and II are in part a reminder of this fact, indispensable for a proper grasp of what Christ meant when he designated Peter as the key-bearer of his kingdom.

The church of the Fathers, which has recently been held high as the model along which the Church is to be constantly re-formed, had a far keener awareness of her being a structure operated by Peter's keys than is suggested by the "new" ecclesiology (Chapter III). Medieval continuity of that awareness was the reason that in Reformation times the keys of Peter were a central point of dispute. Salient details of that dispute hardly support the modern ecumenical stereotype according to which learning, biblical and historical, was almost invariably on the Reformers' side. Their handling of the major biblical references to keys was in fact a startling inconsistency in hermeneutics which is still to be widely perceived (Chapter IV). The true character of the pseudo-ecumenical ideal of a Church without keys—and if without keys, also without a door, without walls, and even without tangible foundations—should then be obvious (Chapter V).

The spelling out of all this in a straightforward manner will, of course, be deplored by Catholic writers who hope for unity at the price of clarity and substance. They are mostly responsible for those painful disappointments which are increasingly voiced by prominent and rank-and-file Protestants who began to wonder aloud about the extent to which Rome can and will be ecumenical. Once more they are forced to register that Rome refuses to be ecumenical if this means to become just another piece, however large, in an ecumenical mosaic. In Rome's view ecumenical fulness ought not to lack the unity which is tied to one set of keys handed over to one single individual.

Many statements of John XXIII and Paul VI bore plain witness to that view. Papa Giovanni's contagious joviality and Pope Paul's unassuming profile provided unintended encouragement to not a few Catholics and Protestants who nurtured another and very different view about unity. An ecumenism whose protagonists banked much more heavily on personalities and psychology than on doctrinal clarity was destined to be caught in its own logic. The logic may perhaps be called semi-Pelagian as it seemed to divide the ecumenical problem in two halves: one where grace ruled, the other where human skill held sway. Whereas with respect to the breaking up of unity, the mystery of man's sinfulness was stated often enough; the restoration of unity was looked for above all in procedures that were so many ways of distracting from the primacy of God's grace, although it alone can break down the wall of division (Eph 2:14).

At any rate, it has become all too clear that even on the strictly doctrinal level (a relatively easy domain compared with the rendering of assent to unifying truth) the ecumenical meeting of minds will not be forthcoming by talking about fundamental issues as little and as vaguely as possible. The fundamental issue about the meaning of the keys would have been spared studied vagueness had attention been paid to the meaning of small but ubiquitous tools called keys. The keys dangling from the keyring of any janitor, homeowner, storekeeper, and automobile operator are so many reminders of valuables to be secured for the benefit of their owners. Among all valuables the kingdom of heaven should seem to excel by infinite measure. No wonder that the keys of that kingdom are of heavenly make, never to be duplicated in any other way or substituted by anything else. Truly, the broader meaning of any key is a tool's plain witness to truth.

This is not to be construed as a judgment on the conscience of anyone whose belief in Christ and church implies a different understanding of the keys of the kingdom from the one set forth in this book. Its author is all too aware of the exemplary dedication of many Protestants to the highest Christian ideals and is deeply indebted to not a few of them. Fortunately, they too acknowledge the obvious: the unity of Christians has to be more than the totality of individual consciences, however upright. That totality can only be a nondescript sum but never a specific and vivid unity which is the fruit of true cohesion.

It then follows that all concerned about the unity of Christians should contribute to dialogues on its behalf according to their most considered insights. The two insights developed in this book relate to keys as most specific items and to the very specific ties to be kept with their custodians or owners insofar as one depends on them.

The application of those two insights to the keys of the kingdom and to the tie they imply with the Christ-appointed stewards of those keys was not meant to issue in a systematic treatise. The aim, a very modest one, was to bring together data and texts—technical, scriptural, historical, and theological—as so many pointers toward a matter of crucial importance, the matter of solidarity. The solidarity which is to function in the Christian context was clearly meant by Christ to be a solidarity with a very concrete twelve. Only they were sent as ones who had to be listened to as if Christ himself were speaking through them. That among the twelve Peter had a special role should be clear by a mere look at the keys which he alone was to hold and use.

Being the very object of a divine utterance, those keys had to be put to real use for no word of God can ever fail to achieve the end for which it was uttered (Is 55:11). Moreover, those keys were to be used with an *unlimited* scope implied in the words, "*whatever* you declare bound on earth . . . will be declared bound in heaven." Before those words were spoken to the twelve, who always had Peter as their leader, they were addressed to Peter alone and right after he had been promised the keys. The spectacle of the unlimited power deposited in one single individual, or in a special group including that individual as its head, can only rankle modern Christians. Engrossed with the democratic process which makes and unmakes authority, they cannot help suspecting something impossible if not sinister in the power of the keys. It is, of course, a power which could be given and guaranteed by the incarnate God alone. His message was a chain of declarations of the possibility of impossibilities. Those seeing an impossibility in the power of the keys still have to come to grips with the very possibility which Christ attributed to his impossibly new ideals of marriage and poverty. . . . The power of the keys should seem a plain possibility compared with his very coming among us. One can never ponder enough the fact that the Incarnation, which is the very start of Christianity, was announced by a message that included the phrase, "for nothing is impossible with God." It has always been the privilege of prayer to help one come to grips with divinely decreed impossibilities. No different will be the case with the "impossible" ideal of the full unity of all those who fully believe in Christ.

CHAPTER 1
A WORLD OF KEYS

Keys as Key Words

Keys are among modern man's most widely owned possessions. Our world has become a world of keys, a fact so pervasive as to be no more noticed than the air we breathe. Of keys it is literally true that they play a key role in our lives on all levels. Such a remark would be a not-too clever pun had the word key not become invested with an additional meaning which relates to everything and everybody of pivotal importance. Understandably while a short word, like key, has a special appeal to editors in search for catchy headlines, shortness in itself would not do were that added meaning absent.

Key is truly a key word about which any issue of any daily paper provides more than one illustration.[1] Reporting the political life is well-nigh inconceivable without resort to key legislators, key votes, key elections, key foreign policy, key parliamentary debates, key lawmakers, key primaries, and keynote addresses. No area of public life is without a keen competition for key roles and key positions. Court procedures all too often turn around key witnesses and key evidence. Accounts of what happens in business hardly reach the second line without a reference to key indicators, key currencies, key lending rates, key money policy, and key federal regulations. Insurance agents offer their packages as so many keys to one's prosperity, security, and health. Stockbrokers lure their customers with the prospect of key investments. Scientists are in pursuit of key discoveries, investors of key commodities, economists of key statistics and of keys to recovery. Key highways, key railroad junctions, key battles, key maneuvers and, of course, key victories are the chief objectives for the military. Their critics do not cease claiming the key to disarmament as the key to peace. The net outcome is all too often "increased cost" which, according to another headline, arises from "delays on key missiles."

The intellectual growth of a human being is a series of introductions to key concepts, to key problems, to key solutions. Books serving that process all too often carry the word key in their titles,[2] such as *Key Problems in Physics, Key to Aquinas, Key to Ming Pottery, Key to Modern British Poetry, Research Keys to the American Renaissance*, and the like. *Key Words in Education* would seem an appropriate title for a book if a book on education could be called the key profession. Digests of information all too often invite the word key in their titles such as *The Book of Key Facts*. A now defunct review of reviews was called *The Lock and Key Library*. When a book is analyzed the word key is almost natural with, at times, such graphic result as *The Key to Uncle Tom's Cabin*. A title, like *Key to the Parochial Registers of Scotland* may be suggestive of an area resembling a labyrinth. *Key to Prophecy, Key to Dreams, Key to Occultism, Key to the Whole Art of Astrology* are undoubtedly proper for any arcane topic, especially if it is nothing but "unknown knowledge." But even when the topic is merely outlandish, as for instance, *British Brackish Water Gastropods, Shelterbelt Insects, Nasal Mites of*

North American Birds, and so forth, the word key almost imposes itself in the titles of treatises offered as clues.

Of course, this time-hallowed usage can be overdone, as it was, for instance, by that mid-seventeenth-century author who offered his introduction to mathematics as a *Key New Forged and Filed*. Ever since Alexander Pope had success with his "A Key to the Lock" (1715), lesser poets and novelists followed suit with such titles as "Key to My Heart" and "Key to My Prison." "Key to the Door" as a title may sound trite but not when enlarged to "Key to the Russian Door." Falling back on the word key is all too tempting for a novelist bent on analyzing the hero or heroine, be it Barbara or someone more identifiable like Napoleon. That the news magazine for Phi Beta Kappa is called *The Key Reporter* should seem a foregone conclusion. Nobody can, of course, object to keymakers calling *Keynotes* their monthly circular.[3] In a book on the keys of the kingdom mention should be made not only of the appropriateness of the title, *Keepers of the Keys*, for a book on the papacy, but also of the readiness of authors of books on religion to call their products *Key to Life, Key to Paradise, Key to Heaven*, and no less often, *Key to the Bible*, which can logically be improved only as *Key to the Key of Scripture*.

Keys and Modern Life

This perhaps drawn-out tune about key words should help turn the topic to musicians. Even the mediocre among them are alert to the subtle differences among the various keys, sharp and flat. Sad and sentimental tunes have their preferred keys no less than happy and heroic melodies. There is more to this metaphorical use of the word *key* than meets the eye. The steps from the keyboard of musical instruments through the keyboard of typewriters and huge typesetting machines to the keyboards of computers represent an ever vaster metaphorical significance of the word key. A book title like *Keypunch, Keytape and Keydiscs*[4] is an uncanny reminder of the information explosion made possible by electronic data processing and of the vast dimensions of knowledge as power. The clue, a derivative of *clavis* (the Latin for key), to puzzles and problems of a vast variety is now in that computer which within a decade will be as much a part of daily life as are automobiles, if not more so. Computer keyboards are now replacing books as chief means of information retrieval. Within a few years their presence has spread from universities to elementary schools, where children are nowadays directed from old-fashioned dictionaries to word-processors which give them the proper words "at the flick of a key." But when all the latest in technology has been tried, it is found, to quote another headline, that an old shoe, namely, the finding of dedicated teachers, is "the key to reform in education."

Thirty years ago, when computers were unwieldy monsters requiring tens of thousands of electron tubes (all prone to breakdown) and a host of technicians (not always reluctant to strike), nobody would have thought of putting into a computer the over 50 million book titles which form the *National Union Catalogue of Printed Books*. The foldout, which gives the guidelines for the use of the over 1000 huge volumes of that *Catalogue*, carries on its front the picture of a big key.[5] Today all that information is accessible through computer keyboards in thousands of libraries. Computer keyboards have replaced slide rules, which are rapidly becoming museum pieces, and have for some time been the indispensable tools for the working out of the most advanced theories in physics and cosmology. Business and banking are inconceivable today without computer keyboards which enable the airline industry to record and store simultaneously millions of seat reservations all across the globe. Computer keyboards make possible the shifting around in the USA alone of small and big transactions which every day amount to half a trillion dollars.

Since even international banking conglomerates use but the minimum of coding in their money transactions, all that information is highly vulnerable to illegal access and, what is worse, to split-second erasure by electronic means. Coding, which like keys stands for very restricted access, is now a major challenge posed by the computer industry to mathematicians specializing in complexity theory. The challenge is most urgent for two reasons. One is the immense number of keys or code-words needed in the most widely used coding system known as DES (Data-Encryption-Standard) code. There, in addition to the transmission of the coded text, a secret key or code, which permits its deciphering, has also to be transmitted. Since in computerized transmission of messages a separate key is required for every combination of users and receivers to assure privacy, the number of such keys is half a million for a thousand users. No wonder that a manager of a computer security agency exclaimed: "The big problem in data encryption is managing the keys. That's the thing that drives people crazy."[6] The second reason of the urgency relates to the recent breaking of what appeared to be the foolproof system in which the single key or code was replaced by two keys, connected by a complex mathematical formula, of which one could be made public. In this story, which is not over yet, the expression "public-key" system is certainly noteworthy because it stands, as do the best keys, for the greatest measure of specificity or limited access without rendering the system unmanageable.

The story of the breaking of the double key system represents for all its modernity a very old pattern and procedure in which the notion of the proper key as a tool of deciphering, that is, of access, is central. In speaking of the search for scientific theory which would yield in the long run the clue to all puzzles of the material world, David Hartley more than two hundred years ago made observations that have a truly modern ring:

> We admit the Key of a Cypher to be a true one, when it explains the Cypher completely; and the Decypherer judges himself to approach to the true Key in proportion as he advances in the Explanation of the Cypher; and this without any direct Evidence at all. And as the false and imperfect Keys, which turn up to the Decypherer in his Researches, prepare the Way for the Discovery of the true and complete one, so any Hypothesis that has so much Plausibility, helps us to digest these Facts in proper Order.[7]

As to daily life, car keys and house keys have become status symbols as well as basic necessities. The importance of keys can be gathered from their numbers alone. To be sure, the dozen or so keys carried all the time by the average individual rarely make him aware of the millions of keys produced each month all over the world. But even he encounters every day various facets which vary from key rings through key racks to strong boxes, made necessary by the number of keys he needs. One's livelihood almost hangs on one's key-ring; its loss can, as few other losses, disrupt the normal course of life. If there is an item available in the most varied shops from newsstands through souvenir boutiques to department stores it is a key ring. Keys grace the front of real estate agencies, their roadside signs, and their newspaper advertisements. In some countries the lapels of hotel managers are decorated by keys, almost invariably advertising car rentals.[8] Cadillac dealers offer, not unexpectedly, a "Gold Key Treatment" to their customers. If the presence at a housewarming party is impossible, a greeting card showing a big key with a house in the background is the most frequently chosen form of conveying the appropriate good wishes.

Keys can loom large in the rawest as well as the most refined contexts of life. The heavy ring of keys around the hip of a prison guard is no less the object of longing looks than the delicate key of a prestigious honor society lying across a necktie. The former means access to the wide realm of freedom, the latter to the no less wide area of influence and affluence.[9] Keys have an unfailing fascination for babies in an instinctive anticipation of involvement with keys for the rest of their lives. The children's world has already its own set of keys, one opening and locking their first diaries and scrapbooks, another for their lockers in the gym, and still another for their bicycles—so many steps in exercising more and more exclusive control.

Initiation into the responsibilities of adulthood is marked not so much by a driver's license as by a key to the family car. The key to the safety deposit box, to the attaché case, to the filing cabinet, to the jewelry box, and last but not least to the family home are so many reminders of the control which an adult can have over his life. The control which keys hold over daily life is brought home to anyone passing by the janitors of an office building or manufacturing plant. Keys also mean safety as amply symbolized by the heavy set of keys carried by security guards. The loss of one master-key can render necessary the re-keying of hundreds of offices. Few items are so closely guarded by makers of automobiles as the master keys to the locks of their various car models. The theft of one such key sends shockwaves of concern through tens of thousands of owners.

The greater are the values to be protected, the more elaborate are the keys or the system of keys needed to give access to them. Home protection with various automatic warning systems, so many variations on complicated key lock mechanisms, is one of the boom industries of our days and also a warning which literally brings home to anyone the measure to which security of daily life depends on ever more complicated keys. Miniaturization of enormous complexity is the hallmark of recently marketed keys operating with their specially designed magnetic field. The vastness of the national treasury stored in gold bars in Fort Knox has its matching part in the complexity of keys and locks that assure its safety and the safe livelihood of hundreds of millions. To what extent that safety can depend on keys has found in our times an awesome illustration in the set of keys which can unleash nuclear devastation. No wonder that holders of such keys must give ample proof of their reliability before they are entrusted with their staggering responsibilities. At the same time the greater impact the turning of a key may have, the greater is the measure of complexity built into it, lest it be duplicated or its lock be picked with no great effort.

Keys and Uniqueness

At times, the complexity of keys can be staggering, but the most widely used kinds are complex only in the sense that they allow a very large number of variations on fairly simple models. The locks they operate are indeed so simple as to embody principles that were known, as will be seen shortly, already in early antiquity. The prototype of such locks, often referred to as pin-tumbler locks, was patented by Linus Yale, Sr., in 1857.[10] He wanted to serve the security of banks and not of ordinary dwellings. Between 1852 and 1862 he produced several improved forms of his Bank Lock of which the last was a transformation of the pins into disks, which together formed a dial combination lock. While the mechanism itself was not overly complex, his four-dial lock lent itself to over one hundred million combinations. Even today this is the kind of lock usually found in the door of bank vaults, the only major improvement being the electrical alarm system attached to it. The pin-tumbler lock and key became a household item through the skill of Linus Yale, Jr., who started out as an artist before realizing his inventive skill. In 1861 and 1865 he patented what is today known all over the world as the Yale key.

What assures to these very simple Yale keys a high degree of complexity is the sequence of grooves and protrusions along their upper edge and two sides. That sequence allows varieties in the billions so as to make each key a genuine individuum, which—and herein lies the enormous success of the patents of Linus Yale, Jr.—can be mass-produced. A quick look at the sketch of that key (Illustration 1) should make immediately clear its enormous variability. First, the inner cylindrical part of the lock, which is turned by the key, can obviously be made shorter or longer. The number of vertical shafts in which the pins are moving can also be varied and so can, of course, their relative spacings. In some early Yale locks there were as many as forty pins which in themselves make possible an astronomically large number of variations. There is, furthermore, the large number of variations allowed by the relative lengths of the non-suspended pins, which are pushed upward by the proper key so as not to protrude into the shafts which in the non-moving outer ring, a hollow cylinder, are occupied by the pins suspended on springs. The width of the key, which in turn must correspond to the diameter of the pins, is also a variable magnitude. Finally, a large number of variations are allowed in the shape of the keyhole or, what is the same, in the cross section of the stem and nose of the key (Illustration II). Of these cross sections any of the key manufacturers that today have a right to the original Yale patent use only a few (Illustration III). A look at the diagram of a Yale key should also make it clear that, as an authority on the subject emphatically noted, in designing a lock the key comes first[11] and that in the key itself it is its "bit" that predetermines the structure of the entire lock mechanism. To recall this point is even more important because modern keys represent in that respect no change whatever in their prototypes used in classical antiquity and even before.

As was noted above, the enormous advantage of the Yale lock consists in making possible the mass production of countless locks, each with its own uniqueness. There are, of course, practical limitations on the number of variations that can be manufactured. Even with the latest technology no more than ten distinct heights, or vertical protrusions, can be cut on the edge of the key.[12] As a result, a Yale lock with seven pins (with a given spacing and diameter and with a given cross section of the key itself) can be produced only in thirty to forty thousand different variations, instead of the theoretical maximum of ten million. There is no need that the absolute individuality of a lock and its key be strictly obtained. Of the same specific variation even hundreds of copies can be safely produced because marketing would scatter them very widely. There are astronomical odds against the turning up of two copies of the same Yale lock and key in two neighboring homes or shops.

Uniqueness or individuality was the chief value of keys long before they could be mass-produced with such a feature. In fact, the hundred or so years prior to the patenting of the Yale key witnessed several feats in key-making which were so many advances in assuring them a very high degree of individuality. All those advances aimed at going beyond the so-called ward keys which were two thousand years old when they began to disappear from the scene in technologically advanced countries about a generation or so ago. The story begins in 1778 with Robert Barron's combining spring-sliders with the ward key. Six years later Joseph Bramah, also in England, introduced along the axis of the lock spring-sliders which were operated by the parallel cuts at the end of the key with hollow shank. Smallness was a further advantage of the Bramah key whose inventor boasted that it was as "impregnable as the Rock of Gibraltar."[13] The Bramah lock did not prove "unpickable," even with the additional improvements made by the three Chubb brothers and by Thomas Hart. An American, Alfred C. Hobbes, made quite a sensation at the International Industrial Exhibition in London in 1851 by picking all the best locks displayed there.[14]

By then the ward key reached its highest level of individuality. The shape of its "bit" was made of thin cylinders of various widths and diameters which could be rearranged. Needless to say this was an even more cumbersome procedure as the corresponding parts of the lock, too, had to be readjusted. An early fifteenth–century adumbration of these keys was the comb key, so called because the resemblance of its "bit" to the teeth of a fine comb.[15]

As long as the now obsolete type of keys, the so-called ward keys, were produced by hand, the uniqueness of each could easily be secured. This can be readily seen from the variety of figures that could be cut into the flat blank ward of such a key. The blank ward again could be made smaller or larger and also bent in a large number of ways. Each of these again could be given further variations through modifying the width, the angle, and the spacing of those bents.

Keys displayed in museums are mostly of that type and the enormously large variety, which their design allows, can be noticed in any collection of them. These were the keys that dominated the medieval, renaissance and baroque centuries, partly because not only their wards but even more so their plates (handles) lent themselves to artistic designs. Keys produced between 1550 and 1650 in France constitute a class known as *clefs de chef-d'oeuvre* or masterpiece keys. About medieval keys it is aptly noted that their makers took their inspiration from the intricacies of illuminated manuscripts.[16] In general, it could aptly be said of keys that their development mirrors "the development of the sense of property and the increased value placed on individual privacy."[17] In spite of its sarcastic provenance, the remark that "locks and keys are the distinguishing device of civilization and enlightenment,"[18] has an undeniably constructive aspect. In a more philosophical sense, keys are so many witnesses of man's recognition that the value of a thing increases with its specificity. The more specific the key, the more special and unique is the item, the property, the structure, the realm to which its user and owner can have access. Awareness of this can be assumed to be as old as keys are; and, as will be seen, they were very widespread in that antiquity which witnessed the most momentous utterance ever made about keys.

The Antiquity of Keys

Both the ward key (and the padlock, much less used in medieval times) owe their essentially modern form to the inventiveness of the Romans who could justly be proud of their locksmiths. Their productivity has its proofs in the lock parts and keys that hardly ever fail to turn up whenever an old Roman settlement is explored. Their artistry is witnessed by the key inlaid with silver which was found, together with many other keys and locks, in what obviously was a locksmith shop in Pompei (Illustration IV). The daily use of keys by the Romans of old is also attested by the loose finger-rings on which they carried their keys, as the typical Roman garment had no pockets. That the Romans of old had to coin the expression *adulterina portarum* (adulteress of doors), denoting skeleton keys used by thieves, is a further proof of the wide use of keys in the Roman Empire. The same is brought out by ancient Roman social rites and idiomatic expressions. The handing over of the household keys to the bride was part of the Roman marriage ritual and the surrendering of keys by the wife a formalizing of divorce. Those behind the bars were referred to as the ones under the key (*sub clavi*). Perception of power, domination, and exclusive right is clearly behind that varied and widespread reference to keys among the Romans of old. The same perception is the climax of the mythological origin of the god of sleep (Somnium) which Marcus Cornelius Fronto recalled in 162 A.D. to his one-time pupil, the Roman Emperor Marcus Antonius, seeking relief from sleeplessness. After begetting Somnium, so goes Fronto's account of the myth, Jupiter "enrolled him among the gods, set him in charge of night and repose, and gave into his keeping the keys of men's eyes."[19]

In the literary use of the word *key*, the Romans were, of course, preceded by Greek authors. One of them, Plutarch (fl. 90 A.D.) described clumsiness as an effort to open a door with an axe and to cut wood with a key.[20] The Greeks also showed the way to the Romans in the art of manufacturing keys. The rotary motion of a Roman (or modern) ward key, which operated a lock connecting the door with the doorpost, was an ingenious improvement on the Laconian key named after the Spartan city known for its mines and foundries. Manufacture of keys in Laconia may have been initiated by Theodorus of Samos, famed metallurgist of the fifth century, whom Pliny credited with the invention.[21] The Laconian key (Illustration v) resembled a human hand in which the palm is turned at right angles both to the wrist and to the fingers. The typical Laconian key had three fingers or prongs and is alluded to as a customary household object in Aristophanes' play *Thesmophoriazusae*, a parody on Euripides' tragedies. There the inability of women to have ready access to their "little special perquisites, the corn, the wine, the oil," is ascribed to the fact that their husbands have got "such keys . . . such brutes, Laconian made, with triple rows of teeth," a far cry from "old times when women only had to buy a farthing ring, and pantry doors flew open."[22] This indicates that Greeks locked not only their houses but individual rooms as well, which is also suggested by the small size, about 6 inches, of such keys. Most importantly, since the number and relative spacings of the teeth allowed not a few variations, the Laconian key embodied a distinct measure of that individuality which is the chief characteristic and usefulness of keys in modern times.

The Laconian key is a major advance over a much larger lock and key (Illustration vi), widely in use in Homeric times among the Greeks who seem to have learned it from the Egyptians.[23] The lock consisted of two beams.[24] The horizontal was held by slots fastened to the door and to the doorpost. The shorter and vertical beam, through which the horizontal beam slid, was fastened to the door itself. Into the vertical beam there were carved a given number of holes in which the pins, made of very hard wood such as teak, could slide up and down. The horizontal beam had its corresponding set of holes and, most importantly, a trough that ran from the holes toward the proper extremity of the beam. The key itself was a wooden rod bent at midpoint, with a typical width of three inches and with a length from one to three feet. At one of its ends the rod had prongs which made it into a key. The unlocking consisted in sliding that rod into the trough until its prongs were under the pins, and then in pushing downward the free end of the rod. This in turn pushed up the prongs and the pins at the other end so that the horizontal beam could be pulled out of the vertical beam. Needless to say, the door to be opened with such a key had to have a hole of about four inches in diameter (Illustration VII). The latter is clearly mentioned toward the end of Homer's *Odyssey* where Penelope's final scheme to thwart her suitors is described in a dramatic fashion. The scheme was an offer of marriage to the man who would shoot an arrow between twelve axes without hitting any of them by using Ulysses' great bow kept in his treasure chamber:

> So she ascended the high staircase of her own house, and in her solid hand took up the beautiful, brazen and artfully curved key, with an ivory handle upon it . . .
> When she, shining among women, had come to the chamber, and had come up to the oaken threshold, which the carpenter once had expertly planed and drawn it true to a chalkline, and fitted the door posts to it and joined on the shining door leaves, first she quickly set the fastening free of the hook, then she inserted the key and knocked the bolt upward, pushing the key straight in, and the door bellowed aloud, as a bull does, when he feeds in his pasture; such was the noise the splendid doors made, struck with the key, and now they quickly spread open.[25]

This kind of key was so well known to the Greeks of old as to be denoted by them with a special name (*balanos*) which evoked the *falling* of the pins into their slots.

Far less security was provided when the inside bar was moved by a plain long metal rod bent twice in the same way as the Laconian key but with no prongs. Such "keys," which Aratus found helpful to explain the shape of the constellation Cassiopeia,[26] were used for the ceremonial closing and opening of temples. Priestesses carrying them on their shoulder have found frequent representations in Greek sculptures and vase paintings (Illustration VIII). While these keys hardly needed inventiveness, even the Egyptian (or Laconian) rods with prongs could be invented and reinvented in more than one place and time. A very large lock corresponding to that type of key was found in 1842 by Paul Emile Botta, the French consul of Mosul, who excavated the city and palace of Sargon II at Khorsabad on the Tigris.[27] Similar lock mechanisms were found in the tombs of pharaohs from the middle of the second millennium before Christ. Archeological evidence attests the use of that lock and key in ancient times in areas widely separated from one another, such as the Faroe Islands, Japan, India, and Peru.[28] Late-eighteenth and early-nineteenth-century European travelers in the Mideast found such keys in actual usage and saw them carried on the shoulder (Illustration IX).[29] For Europeans, long since unaware of their existence, such keys were a source both of surprise and puzzlement. Or as an Englishman who traveled through Turkey in the 1790s put it:

> Nothing can be more clumsy than the door-locks in Turkey, but their mechanism to prevent picking is admirable. It is a curious thing to see wooden locks upon iron doors, particularly in Asia, and on their caravansaries, and other great buildings, as well as on house doors. The key goes into the back part of the bolt, and is composed of a square stick with five or six iron or wooden pins about half an inch long, towards the end of it, placed at irregular distances, and answering to

holes in the upper part of the bolt, which is pierced with a square hole to receive the key. The key, being put in as far as it will go, is then lifted up, and the pins entering the corresponding holes raise other pins, which had dropt into these holes from the part of the lock immediately above, and which have heads to prevent them from falling lower than is necessary; the bolt, being thus freed from the upper pins, is drawn back by means of the key; the key is then lowered, and may be drawn out of the bolt: to lock it again, the bolt is only pushed in, and the upper pins fall into the holes in the bolt by their own weight. This idea might be improved on, but the Turks never think of improving.[30]

Powerful additional proofs of the wide use of keys in antiquity are the numerous references to keys in a metaphorical sense. In ancient Greek literature it is easy to observe the gradual enrichment of the words *kleis* and *kleioō*. As a noun and verb they originally stood for *bar* and *to bar* and for the very similar *bolt* and *to bolt*. Subsequent meanings were *catch, hook*, and *key* properly so-called. Things similar to keys, such as collar bones, promontories, straits, and rowing benches, soon began to be called keys, a development which set a pattern for the English too. They and all modern nations merely imitate the Greeks of old in speaking of the key to a problem. This metaphorical meaning was one aspect of the Greeks' seeing keys as symbols of power over any enclosure or domain, from house through towns to kingdoms, earthly as well as otherworldly. Keys were put in the hands of the various powers of the netherworld, such as Pluto, Eache, Persephone, Anubis, and Hecate.[31] The latter was honored, in Lagina, every four years by a procession in which the sacred key was carried first around the sanctuary and later around the city itself. Major godesses often had a key as the symbol of their power carried by their minor counterparts. Io was the keybearer for Hera, Iphigenia for Artemis, Eros for Aphrodite. Athena carried a key as guardian of the divine nuptial chamber as well as of the city of Athens. Dikē carried the keys of the day and the night. Kronos in the mythraic rite always had a key in his right hand. Seraphis was represented with the keys of the oceans.

Keys were inseparable from the Roman deity, Janus, who as keeper of the heavenly gates was also the guardian of all doors on earth. The temple of Janus in Rome was closed only when no Roman legions were engaged in war, a rare event to be sure. It was in the context of the most decisive phase of Roman military history, the Punic Wars, that there occurred possibly the first recorded surrender of a fortress by the handing over of its keys. The fortress was the acropolis of Syracuse, the narrator was Livy, the most avidly read Roman historian. His story[32] may have set a pattern for similar no less dramatic acts by which keys literally opened new phases of history and bore witness to the power they could so aptly symbolize.[33] Long before the Romans conquered all the Mediterranean, their (modern) ward key operating with a rotary motion was in use in all lands along its shores. Such was the magnificent bronze key (Illustration x) which opened the sarcophagus of Ptolemy II Philadelphus (283–246 B.C.). He was a chief representative of Hellenistic culture which began to make its heavy inroads during his reign into the land of the Old Testament.

CHAPTER 2
KEYS AND THE BIBLE

Exploit, Rendez-vous, and Prophecy

When an object is referred to only a few times in a record written over a thousand years, such as the Old Testament, the small number of references may mean either its rarity or the very opposite. In fact, when the few references are casual, the wide and daily use of the object should seem assured. Had this not been the case, the author of the Book of Judges would have expressed admiration over the fact that the upper chamber of Eglon, King of Moab, not only could be shut but locked as well. It is certainly not the locking mechanism which is meant to evoke surprise in the story (Jgs 3:15–25) of the daring exploit of Ehud, the Benjaminite. Claiming that he had a secret message, Ehud was admitted to the upper chamber of the king who, after being told that the message was from God himself, dismissed his attendants to be alone with Ehud. Standing face to face to the king, Ehud pulled his dagger and thrust it with such force that it entirely disappeared in the king's fat belly. Immediately afterwards, so we are told in the Book of Judges, "Ehud went out into the hall, shutting the doors of the upper room and locking them" (3:23). The lock, which is not described, was most likely the cross bar with a vertical complement having a certain number of pins in its holes. Ehud had no time to waste in the study of that locking mechanism. Familiarity with it was the key to his escape from the premises. He had to be a good distance away before the king's attendants would realize that it was not the king's choice to remain closeted away for a while so that he might ponder the message.

Ehud's exploit, which took place in pre-Davidic times, is the beginning of the properly historical part of the Book of Judges which in the 7th century B.C. was embellished with references to the Mosaic law as contained in Deuteronomy. If the locking of the door by Ehud was such a late embellishment it indicates familiarity with some locks and keys on the part of Israelites of pre-Exilic times. By then, the century before the destruction of Jerusalem, a matter-of-fact reference to a locking mechanism was part also of the recital of an encounter very different from the one between Ehud and Eglon. The popularity among Israelites of old of the Song of Solomon was only matched by the resolve of rabbis to keep it from the young and to assure a spiritual interpretation to an amorous lyric. Interpretation was hardly needed for that part of a rendez-vous between two lovers where the young man, arriving late at night to the house of his beloved, puts his hand through a hole in the door, in a vain effort to unlock it without a key. Apparently not even the beloved had a key. By the time she had risen, put a frock on herself, come to the door, and finished fumbling with the pins of the lock, the young man, possibly afraid of being noticed by a passerby or by the watchman, had taken to flight. Or, as the maiden bemoaned, the rendez-vous did not take place:

> My lover put his hand through the opening;
>   my heart trembled within me,
>   and I grew faint when he spoke.
> I rose to open to my lover,

> with my hands dripping myrrh:
> With my fingers dripping choice myrrh
> upon the fittings of the lock
> I opened to my lover
> but my lover had departed, gone (SS 5:4–6).

Even if this section of the Song of Solomon is post-Exilic, there is uncontrovertible evidence of the familiarity of Israelites with keys already at the time of Isaiah, or the 8th century B.C. They must, indeed, have been very familiar with keys (*mepatha—im*); otherwise keys would not have been mentioned by Isaiah somewhat earlier in a metaphorical sense which, as already noted, presupposes the very use of a thing which eventually lends itself to a metaphor. Isaiah used the metaphor of keys to announce the transfer from Shebna to Eliakim of the office of the master of the palace (*asher al habbayith*).[1] By the time of Isaiah the office of the master of the palace was three centuries old and the highest of the royal administration which Solomon organized in full. The title with an incomplete name appears on a tomb from the Shiloam area at the end of the Kedron valley outside the walls of Jerusalem. Three such masters are named in the Book of Kings between Solomon and Ezekiah who ruled when Sennacherib laid siege to Jerusalem at the very end of the 8th century B.C. It was as master of the palace that Eliakim met Sennacherib's representative under the walls of the City. Two hundred years later the title appeared on a seal impression carrying also the office holder's name, Godolias. He was the master of the palace under Sedekiah, the last king of Judah, and was installed by Nebuchadnessar as governor of Judah after the destruction of Jerusalem.

Solomon set up the office in imitation of the office of the Pharaoh's vizier. Unlike in Assyria and Babylon, where the master of the palace was a mere administrator of the king's household affairs, in Egypt as well as in Judah and Israel the master of the palace was the second in command after the king. In Egypt he reported every morning to the Pharaoh, received his instructions, and by ceremoniously opening the gates of the palace he let the official day begin for the Pharaoh's highest administrative offices. He was privy to all the major transactions of the Pharaoh's kingdom, all important documents had to have his seal, all other officials were subordinate to him, and he governed the whole land in the Pharaoh's absence. It was precisely this function which was exercised by Joseph whom the Pharaoh put in charge of his house (Gn 41:40), made the keeper of the royal seal and the ruler over the entire land of Egypt. Similarly, the master of the palace of the king of Israel headed the list of royal officials (2 Kgs 18:18) and he alone appears with the king (1 Kgs 18:3). The importance of the title is particularly apparent when Yotham assumes it in his capacity of regent of the kingdom during the final illness of his father King Ozias (2 Kgs 15:5).

The transfer of the office from Shebna to Eliakim was not, however, an ordinary event in the eyes of Isaiah. Before he announced the transfer itself, he made Shebna the target of passionate rebukes. He did so apparently with great suddenness, prompted by his being seized with the conviction that he must speak out in Yahweh's name (Is 22:15). It seems that Isaiah encountered Shebna as the latter was inspecting the construction of his tomb carved in the rock, possibly in Shiloam. Knowing that he was to announce to Shebna his deposition, Isaiah could charge him with presumptuousness for constructing a burial place matching the dignity of his exalted office (Is 22:16). Shebna was not only to be deposed but to be turned into a mere discard, like lice to be shaken out of a garment, or like a ball to be tossed into the wasteland (Is 22:17–18). Such was not an ordinary deposition, let alone an orderly transfer of office. It would not have been called for even if Shebna's pro-Assyrian policy had been the cause for the wrath of the prophet who stood for caution since it was his expectation that Yahweh would eventually dislodge the Assyrian power. The vistas of the prophet transcended the actual political framework as he informed Shebna both about his removal and about his successor:

> On that day I will summon my servant Eliakim,
>   son of Hilkiah;
> I will clothe him with your robe,
>   and gird him with your sash,
>   and give over to him your authority.
> He shall be a father to the inhabitants of Jerusalem,
>   and to the house of Judah.
> I will place the key of the House of David
>   on his shoulder;
>   when he opens, no one shall shut,
>   when he shuts, no one shall open.
> I will fix him like a peg in a sure spot,
>   to be a place of honor for his family;
> On him shall hang all the glory of his family;
>   descendants and offspring,
>   all the little dishes, from bowls to jugs.
> On that day says the Lord of hosts, the peg fixed in a sure spot shall give way, break off and fall, and the weight that hung on it shall be done away with; for the Lord has spoken (Is 22:19-25).

The concluding verses of Isaiah's pronouncement are not a proof that Ezekiah's descendants were to inherit his office. Isaiah rather seems to refer to the fact that a master of the palace could readily secure special benefits for his children and for his children's children. To this he adds his dire warning that, like other benefits, these too can disintegrate as quickly as a string of pots hanging on a peg can break to pieces once the peg falls out of the wall. In spite of this very clear warning about the transitoriness of Ezekiah's dignity and of the benefits devolving from it to his descendants, the utterance of Isaiah contains elements with an unmistakably eschatological or Messianic perspective.

The perspective in question is embodied in references to God's servant, to the house of David, and to the implementation of authority in the manner of a true father. As to the notion of God's servant, it should be enough to recall the four servant poems in Isaiah. In the first (42:1–4) Yahweh announces his servant who brings forth judgment and righteousness on the whole world. In the second (49:1–6) the servant himself speaks of his calling and of the difficulties of his mission which consists in the gathering of Israel and in being a mediator of God's salvation. In the third (50:4–9) the servant speaks of his mission as a teacher, of the opposition to his teaching, and of Yahweh's assurance and assistance. In the fourth poem (52:13–53:12) the servant suffers and dies an ignominious death which is mysterious because of his innocence. The mystery is resolved when that death is presented as an atonement for others' crimes and as a preliminary to resurrection. In the Old Testament, references to the servant of Yahweh received their strongest messianic or eschatological touch in these poems written perhaps by Deutero-Isaiah in post-Exilic times. The same touch was in a less articulated form present much earlier. In sacred texts contemporary with him, David is spoken of by Yahweh as "my servant whom I have chosen" (2 Sm 3:18, I Kgs 11:34, Ps 89:4, 21), a phrase with messianic ring. The destiny, which the House of David has until the end of time, is too much a part and parcel of the Old Testament to call for documentation; and the same is true of true fatherhood to be exercised over the people.

In an eschatological context the transfer of power by

placing the appropriate keys on one's shoulder could hardly lack a messianic connotation which became abundantly clear in the New Testament. Isaiah's prophecy was indeed a key prophecy in more than one sense. Even in Palestine keys other than the ones that had to be carried on one's shoulder were in use in New Testament times. By then, the Romans and their Seleucid predecessors had set up many new non-Jewish towns in the land and Jerusalem itself had been heavily penetrated by Hellenistic culture. Commodious metal keys, that could easily be held in one's hands or even dangled from one's fingers, were part of that culture in which metaphorical references to keys were no less widespread. In a memorable and pivotal passage of the New Testament, keys are not spoken of as objects to be laid on one's shoulders. Those witnessing Christ's promise to give Peter the very keys of the Kingdom of heaven most likely thought of keys as shaped by the Romans to their time-hallowed form.

The Keys of Caesarea Philippi

The distinguished biblical scholar, O. Cullmann, was not the first to argue the point that Matthew is not to be taken for a guide concerning the place and time of Christ's famed words to Peter, but Cullmann argued it in a far more sustained manner than anyone before him.[2] According to Cullmann the place and time were the night of the Last Supper, possibly the Cenacle itself. According to Matthew, the place was "the neighborhood of Caesarea Philippi" (16:13), an expression which does not exclude the immediate vicinity of that place. It is not even contradicted by "on the road to the villages around Caesarea Philippi," the specification given by Mark (8:27), and certainly not by Luke's failure to specify the place where "Jesus was praying in seclusion" (9.18). The area of Caesarea Philippi was full of secluded places conducive to prayer in solitude. What in particular militates against seeing these three specifications as hardly reconcilable is the unanimity with which, as will be seen, the three Synoptics specify the time, exactly a week before the Transfiguration.

The disagreement between a scholar, however distinguished, of our times and an evangelist, whose writing remarkably weathered two hundred years of criticism, is important to consider for two reasons. One is that Christ's portentous words promising the keys of the kingdom of heaven to Peter are no less independent of their proper context than are other words if they are to reveal their real portent. The second is that regardless of the intrinsic merits of Cullmann's disagreement with Matthew, his study will certainly be remembered by future exegetes as a telling change in the fashions of biblical criticism. Today, unlike a hundred or only fifty years ago, no reputable biblical critic, who is not merely an aged warhorse of outmoded rationalism, would hesitate to endorse with Cullmann the authenticity of the words:

> Blest are you Simon son of John!
> No mere man has revealed this to you,
>   but my heavenly father.
> I for my part declare to you,
> You are 'Rock'
> and on this rock I will build my church,
> and the gates of death shall not prevail against it.
> I will entrust to you the keys of the kingdom of heaven.
> Whatever you declare bound on earth,
>   shall be bound in heaven
> Whatever you declare loosed on earth
>   shall be loosed in heaven (Mt 16:17–19).

This declaration and promise followed Christ's eliciting

the view of the twelve concerning his real status. In reply, the twelve reported such views as their master's being another John the Baptist, or Jeremiah, or Eliah, or one of the prophets. "And you," he turned to them, "who do you say that I am?" "You are the Messiah," Simon Peter answered, "the son of the living God" (Mt 16:15–16). Today the authenticity of all this is no longer an issue that first needs airing at length before further questions may be considered.[3] It no longer would do to claim that the notion of church (*ekklesia*) was foreign to Christ or that he could not have the consciousness of being the Son of the living God. It is also widely realized nowadays that the unmistakably Semitic and particularly Aramaic character of Christ's declaration could only be directed at Peter himself and that it could not be the product of times post-dating the destruction of Jerusalem which led to the scattering of Judeo-Christian communities.

No evidence of grammar will, of course, ever overpower the stubborn resolve which claims that by rock or foundation Christ could in no way mean Peter but only Peter's faith. Cullmann, it is well to recall,[4] had no sympathy for that Protestant resolve which in fact defies its own logic. Once in the grip of that logic, one soon becomes so uneasy about faith connected with any well defined individual as to embrace a faith independent of any human instrumentality, be it that of the preaching of the Bible and even its very words. It is that logic which does not recoil from taking keys, always very specific items made for very specific purposes, for an ultimately unspecified faith known only to the "Spirit," perhaps because the latter is taken for a reality *wholly* inaccessible to the human mind's specifications.

As with any other solution, the one proposed by Cullmann should be weighed not only by what it contributes but also by what it takes away. The gist of the contribution which Cullmann intended to obtain by his drastic reassignment of the place and time of Christ's words to Peter is that a smooth and logical context would thereby be provided for them. A curious contention and hardly in tune with a pattern in the Gospels where from almost the very start of Christ's public mission (and in fact from the infancy narratives on)[5] heart-warming sections often and suddenly turn into heart-rending forewarnings and forebodings. Not paying proper attention to that pattern, Cullmann found too abrupt Matthew's turning the subject from Christ's promises to Peter to His eventual crucifixion which in turn prompted Peter's heated protest and Christ's sharp rebuke of him.

Cullmann saw a smoother sequence from exalted promises to debasing humiliations in the words and events centering on the Last Supper. In particular, he saw a more spontaneous connection between Christ's messianic self-revelation before the high priest and His immediate facing the cross. In the same context a similar spontaneous transition is found from Peter's readiness to stand by Christ to his reluctance to accept the suffering that would have become his share had he admitted his discipleship to the high priest's maidservant. The same broader context also contains Christ's promise to Peter that he would not only repent but would eventually function as source of strength for his brethren. It is into that broader context that Cullmann wanted to reassign Peter's confession of Christ's divine sonship because there several parallels would suggest its sequence, a twofold declaration on Christ's part. In the first, Peter was declared to be the rock and the holder of the keys of the kingdom of heaven. The second contained Christ's prediction of his crucifixion to be immediately followed by Peter's protestations. Such a sequence would, according to Cullmann,[6] perfectly fit the inner logic of the events planned by Jesus for the night preceding his crucifixion.

Yet those events hardly suggest a hiatus into which the words spoken according to Matthew (who receives plenty of support from Mark and Luke) to Peter at Caesarea Philippi could be accommodated.[7] To relocate those words within the broader context of the Last Supper is not a matter of finding the few minutes which it takes them to be uttered. What is needed is an obvious and suitable juncture in the sequence of events stretching from the preparation of the Last Supper to Christ's condemnation by the Sanhedrin or to his appearance before Pilate. While during those fateful hours Christ's command over the sequence of events was time and again manifest,[8] Peter's utterances during the same period were hardly such as to invite Christ to ask the question: "What do people say the Son of Man is?" In fact, Peter repeatedly tried to coax his master into actions which did not at all fit His own plans. For Christ it was enough to wash the feet of the apostles, but Peter wanted to have his head washed as well. Again, Christ did not want to be defended by the sword which Peter had drawn. By putting back the severed ear of the high priest's servant, Christ in fact undid what Peter had done. All this was in line with Jesus' mastery in preparing with his words and deeds specific actions and responses on the part of his apostles instead of letting them set his pace. It was only in reference to the power of darkness symbolized by the night of the impending trial, hardly a situation created or wanted by Peter, that Christ spoke during that very night of Peter's role as a future source of strength for his brethren. This, too, was much more understandable if it was a reminder of an enormous status already conferred on Peter. The absence of any initiative on Peter's part preceding his confession at Caesarea Philippi should, indeed, seem an argument in favor of that locality as the stage set by Christ himself.

Whatever occasions there may have been for Christ during the night preceding his crucifixion to prompt the famed dialogue between him and Peter, a dialogue which included the conferring on Peter the keys of the kingdom, that occasion could not be the time when Christ was dragged into Caiaphas' house and later to Pilate's residence. Nor could that occasion be Christ's self-revelation as the Messiah before the Sanhedrin. As Christ was solemnly questioned there, he was hemmed in by a large gathering. Communication between him and Peter was restricted to a mere look as registered by Luke with graphic terseness.[9] It is in fact most unlikely that Peter could have heard from across the courtyard Christ's statement about himself as the Son of the living God so that he would have been prompted to add his own confession of faith in his master's divine sonship. And even if he had been able to do so, Christ was certainly not in a position at that time to reward Peter's confession by entering into a most momentous dialogue with him. Neither the recital by the Synoptics of the Last Supper, nor the one by John suggests a logical juncture at which one could readily attach the extension to all the apostles of the power of binding and loosing, a power first given to Peter individually.

It is no less difficult to conjure up for that night either a situation or a scenery as suitable as the neighborhood of Caesarea Philippi with its graphic contrast between a huge foundation of rock and a mere stone, as a scandalous trap into which Peter could turn for Christ.[10] Different, of course, would have been the case for the morning and afternoon preceding that night. Unlike previously, when Jesus walked at daybreak from the Mount of Olives to the Temple to teach there and returned to the Mount of Olives in the evening, on that Thursday he did not go to the city until darkness had set in. During daytime no object was more conspicuous to the eyes of anyone staying on the Mount of Olives than the rocky elevation on which the Temple stood. There were also on any path on that mount plenty of small rocks and stones for the annoyance of anyone walking there. But during most of that day, which may have been propitious for Cullmann's tying the famed dialogue between Jesus and Peter to the Last Supper, Peter was absent from the scene. Early that day Jesus sent Peter and John into the city to find the owner of the room where they were to prepare the Passover Supper.[11] With Peter being absent there could be no dialogue between him and Jesus, whatever the appropriateness of the scenery. There were, of course, plenty of small rocks on the path which Christ and the twelve followed on their way from the Cenacle through the Kedron Valley back to the Mount of Olives. Those stones could indeed be occasions for stumbling in the dark, but the rocky elevation on which the Temple stood was not an object to point at during the night in order to make an all-important point. Certainly there seemed to be no occasion during that day and night for a reference to keys. No keys were mentioned, for instance, in connection with access to the Upper Room.

Quite different was the visible background in connection with the dialogue between Christ and Peter as assigned by Matthew to the neighborhood of Caesarea Philippi. Far more importantly, it was a background or circumstance as much foreseen and foreordained by Christ as were all his comings and goings during his public ministry. That Christ directed his steps toward Caesarea Philippi with an eye on Peter may be surmised from the fact that Peter was very much a part of the miraculous catch of a fish with the tax coin in its mouth. The miracle, which meant to convey not only Christ's absolute superiority over the Temple, that is, the Old Covenant, but also Peter's special relationship to Christ, took place shortly after Christ and his disciples had returned to Capernaum from the neighborhood of Caesarea Philippi.[12] It was a fitting crowning of Christ's making Peter the foundation of the new Temple or the Church of which He was the ultimate foundation. The two fully possessed in their own respective ways the same function of being the foundation which, and this cannot be emphasized enough, is quite of the same nature as the function of being the exclusive holder of keys that alone give access to the kingdom of heaven. Here too, as will be seen, the Scriptures assign to Peter a role which they assign to Christ as well.

The intrinsically most important argument on behalf of Caesarea Philippi as the place where Christ established Peter in his primacy is the response which Christ gave there, according to Matthew, to Peter's declaration of his divine sonship. Such a declaration, transcending all human insight, could not be left without an appropriate comment on Christ's part. Clearly, what is to be explained is not so much what Matthew's narration contains as what is absent in the recital of Mark and Luke. In fact, their silence on Christ's words to Peter prompted a modern Protestant commentator to characterize their recital as a body without a head, a mere torso.[13]

Compared with Cullmann's taking lightly these considerations and circumstances, his attitude toward the external evidence is a rank slighting. He did not even hint at the geographic and historic backdrop at Caesarea Philippi for Peter's confession and for Christ's reply to it.[14] Not only was that backdrop extraordinary but it also provided Christ with the kind of contrast on which his divine pedagogy relied time and again.[15] Caesarea Philippi, neither a large city nor on the main roads, was a brand new Roman place with all the splendors of Hellenistic culture: stadium, amphitheater, palaces, forums, baths, to say nothing of its magnificent setting. As such it must have been a byword among poor Galileans. Located at one of the three main sources of the Jordan, Caesarea Philippi also had an ample source of fresh running water, the greatest treasure in a dry land like Galilee. As Jesus and his small troupe approached the city, in all likelihood from the south, they first encountered several sharp rises of the terrain one of which provided the first stretches of the Jordan with charming cataracts, long ago an inspiration for David.[16] The last and most spectacular of those rises was a broad rocky wall with an almost vertical fall of about 200 feet. It could appear as the outcropping of the vast rock foundation of the snow-capped peaks of Hermon to the north. That wall of rock could not be missed by anyone in the vicinity of Caesarea Philippi which, as a pagan town, was off limits for Jesus and his disciples. They did not have to enter it to see the chief decor of the city, a resplendent temple of Jupiter, crowning that wall of rock. Nor did they have to enter the town to come within a stone's throw of a famed sanctuary of Pan cut into that wall right next to the source of the Jordan.

The scene unfolding before the eyes of those simple Galileans presented the starkest contrast between the humble conditions of their Jewish piety and a pagan civilization in its novel splendor. Such a contrast was a most appropriate stage for Christ's eliciting Peter's confession and for His own reply to it. For on the road to Caesarea Philippi nothing could be more natural for them than to make a comment or two on the emperor in Rome holding all power over their land. But their master suddenly wanted to know of the people's views about him and not of their views about the great of the world to whom in another context he made a pointed reference, and again for the sake of contrast (Mt 20:25). The greatest of those great was of course the emperor, a successor to Caesar Augustus who founded the Empire and was venerated, together with Jupiter, in that temple. Pagan cultural lore had by then sufficiently penetrated even the backwater areas of Palestine and certainly the half-paganized land of Zebulon and Nephthali where most of the twelve hailed from. A chief tenet of that lore was that the emperor in Rome was the son of Jupiter, the ruler of the gods of Olympus. When under a sudden inspiration, Peter declared Christ to be the Son of the true and living God, he could hardly fail to think of the very different pagan consensus.

No less could Peter's mind be free of such associations as he heard himself being declared by Christ the rock foundation on which the new Temple, the Church, was to be built by Him. Peter must have been struck by the vicinity of that wall of rock and Jupiter's temple on the top of it. On hearing of the superiority of that Church over the power (gates or jaws) of the netherworld, he could not fail to notice a dark hole gaping in the wall, the sanctuary of Pan. Few pagan ceremonies were so hellish as the ones connected with the cult of Pan, a name which aptly gave rise to the word panic. Pan's sanctuary there, together with Jupiter's temple, were perfect symbols of the dominion of the sinful netherworld which was to be overcome by the kingdom of heaven. That sinful world, Plutarch is the witness, had, indeed, a premonition that pagan worship would come to an end if Pan were ever to fall silent.[17] The promise of the keys of the kingdom of heaven, a symbol of the vastest conceivable power, could hardly have had a more appropriate background and a background more appealing for Galileans than the one available in Caesarea Philippi. In its newly–built splendor that town nestled on the edge of that biblical land beyond which stretched all the worldly powers still to be exposed to the power of God's kingdom.

Had Cullmann not ignored completely the background, rich in geographical and historical pointers, provided by Caesarea Philippi, he would perhaps have paid proper attention to the keys promised to Peter as representing power properly so-called, even in purely biblical terms. The less than two pages Cullmann devotes to the subject of keys in a book of over 200 pages on Peter in the New Testament, and in particular to Mt 16:16–19, are a classic in lopsided proportionality.[18] By pondering at some length the meaning of keys as power, Cullmann, who was as fleeting on this point as possible, might have perhaps perceived that the petrine ministry had to be much more than the hand-wringing of one unsure of his authority and power over all the rest. He might have also perceived that if the apostolic church, still vibrating with the fresh memory of her divine Founder, needed that petrine power, the same had to be even more true of the Church the more she moved in time from the moment when the risen Christ conversed with the twelve about the kingdom of God. Instead, Cullmann emphasized the limits set for a professional exegete who, according to him, had no right to see the Bible in the light of the still-living Church. Hoping that in this way he could cut off inferences from the primacy of Peter to that of the popes, he failed to see that the same move would logically cut the exegete off from the New Testament which only the Church can guarantee as a scripture worth reading with unique attention.

The point at issue here is not so much the radical separation which Cullmann set up between the apostolic and the post-apostolic church. In fact, Cullmann deserves gratitude for spelling out unequivocally the strict logic of the Reformation at a time when that logic began to vanish in the minds of so many ecumenists on both sides. The point is rather the freedom with which a scholar is allowed to speculate and still retain scholarly reputation. For if Cullmann's very speculative transfer of the "key" words from Caesarea Philippi to the Cenacle should be considered a scholarly procedure, the same credit should not be denied to a brief guess as to what Peter may very well have seen and thought when those words were spoken to him at Caesarea Philippi.

The Keys of the New Temple

In addition to the very plausible conjecture that Peter's designation as the rock had for its background that huge wall of rock outside Caesarea Philippi, another conjecture should seem not much less appropriate. Anyone standing just outside the town on a road leading to its main gate may quite possibly have caught a glimpse of the keys operating it. To speak of the keys of the kingdom of heaven in front of a city gate symbolizing the powers of a world which Christ often and emphatically denounced, was a pedagogy that almost imposed itself. The keys of a city gate were but a superior class among keys of all sorts, all of them parts of daily life in the Palestine of Peter's time. By then doors and keys had for long been inseparable utilities and a source of many a metaphor in Jewish parlance. Jesus himself spoke of the entrance to the kingdom of God as something narrow (Lk 13:22), an adjective which conjures up something as specific as the difference between rich and poor, or a wide gate and a needle's eye. He specified the gate to the sheepfold as the place which the enemies of the kingdom, thieves and wolves, avoid. He made that place so specific as to declare his own actual person, the most specific being ever, to be the door itself. As to a metaphoric reference to keys by Jesus, the twelve were soon to hear it while guests with him at a dinner arranged by a pharisee who invited other pharisees and lawyers as well. It was a dinner party which heard Jesus rebuke the pharisees as hidden tombs and say further harsh things about them, and which also heard a lawyer object: "Teacher, in speaking this way you insult us too." Far from being taken aback, the master likewise took on the lawyers by stating among other things: "Woe to you lawyers! You have taken away the key of knowledge. You yourselves have not gained access, yet you have stopped those who wished to enter" (Lk 11:52). Such were, indeed, powerful words about a specific power symbolized by an always specific key.

Most if not all the pharisees and lawyers present acted also as rabbis. As they completed their training for that office, they received from their teachers and the rabbinate a key which symbolized their authority to teach God's message. Some rabbis had that key sewn in their robes; others carried it on their girdle as a blunt reminder of the mission and authority they assumed.[19] It was that key which symbolized their power "to loose and to bind," that is, to declare this or that action as not contrary or contrary to divine dispensation embodied in the Law of Moses. Not that the rabbis, then as now, had been in agreement on all points. In fact disputes among them were so numerous in Jesus' time as to let the expression "to loose and to bind" become a standard reference to the endless disagreements that raged a little earlier between the two main rabbinical authorities, Shamma and Hillel. What the one loosed, the saying went, the other bound, and vice versa.[20] Josephus Flavius did not hint at anything novel in referring to the power of binding and loosing as part of the arbitrary usurping by the pharisees of the power of the pious queen, Alexandra: "They banished and reduced whom they pleased; they bound and loosed [men] at their pleasure; and to say all at once, they had the enjoyment of royal authority, whilst the expenses and the difficulties of it belonged to Alexandra."[21]

It was not, however, casuistry and abuse that represented the most expressive aspect of the rabbinical lore and practice about the power of keys.[22] Rabbinical tradition was particularly rich in stories and reflections about Eliah who was considered the greatest figure, next to Moses, of the Covenant. One such reflection, often recorded in Talmudic literature, was about the keys given by God to Eliah. The first was the key or power over rainfall, the second was the power over death. But when Eliah begged the Lord for a third key, or power over human conception, he had to return the two other keys.[23] Only God could have the three keys or powers simultaneously. A dramatic story about keys, harking back to early rabbinical lore, related to the destruction of the Temple by Nebuchadnezzar. On seeing the fire engulfing the cedar linings and roof of the Temple the priests, who held the keys of the Temple in their hands, threw them upward and cried out: "Ruler of the World, watch over your house. Here are the keys you have handed over to us. We have not been reliable stewards, worthy of the King's work and of his table."[24]

It is, of course, a mere conjecture that any of these details had come to Peter's mind as he heard his master denounce the abuse of the power of keys in the hands of lawyers, scribes, and pharisees. It should be enough to register the historical reality of a wide awareness among Jews of those times of the broad meaning of keys. Of all the ramifications and nuances of that reality Christ was fully aware. That reality was part of the fullness of reality to which he gave meaning and of the fullness of time in which he came. Fullness was the hallmark of his knowledge, although he did not study the Scriptures (Mk 6:2). Indeed, whatever has since been learned about any aspect of the historical reality of the times that saw the Word become flesh provided countless further proofs of the unlimited bearing and applicability of all his words, not the least of which was his utterance about the keys of the kingdom.

The time of that utterance and of his passing by Caesarea Philippi may have very well coincided with Yom Kippur, the great expiatory day of the Jewish liturgical year.

Such a view was first proposed in 1947 by the Swedish biblical scholar, A. Risenfeld, and subsequently elaborated by others.[25] It rests on more than one hint, explicit and implicit, in the narrative of which Peter's confession of Christ and the keys promised to him are a part. An immediate sequel to the event at Caesarea Philippi is, in all three Synoptics, the transfiguration of Jesus. So immediate is that sequel and so important in the eyes of all three as to be given an otherwise very rare specification of the number of days which elapsed between the two events. Matthew and Mark speak of "six days later" (17:1 and 9:2 respectively), whereas Luke of "about eight days" (9:28), both expressions being Hebrew ways of denoting a week. One week separates Yom Kippur from Yom Sukkot or the feast of the Tabernacles in mid-September. Quite possibly, the actual celebration of that feast, which included the construction of booths from branches and foliage, made Peter propose the erecting of three booths, one for Christ, one for Moses, one for Elijah. If, indeed, the event at Caesarea Philippi coincided with Yom Kippur, then the rites of that holiday may reasonably be expected to contain valuable information for a full understanding of the words which Christ and Peter uttered at Caesarea Philippi. The better-known part of the rites of Yom Kippur was the placing by the high priest of the people's sin on the scapegoat which then was chased into the desert. The real climax of the rite was, however, the high priest's entry into the Holy of Holies to pronounce there the sacred tetragrammaton YHVH (Yahveh). In what took place at Caesarea Philippi it is not impossible to notice symbolic allusions to the act of the high priest, allusions which indicate the replacement of the Old Covenant with a new dispensation.

The first to be noted is the utterance by Peter of the true name, that is, the true nature of Jesus, Son of the living God, just as Yahveh, or He Who Is, was by far the deepest insight comprehensible by human mind into the nature of the living God. The second is Jesus' declaring Simon, son of Jonah, to be Rock (Peter), or the most fundamental and therefore highest office in the Church to be built on it. Since the Church or the New Covenant is a restructuring of the Temple, the Old Covenant, from its very foundations on, the restructuring of Simon, son of Jonah, as foundation (rock) may have had its archetype in the praises accorded in the Book of Sirach to the high priest, Simon, son of Jonah (Jochanan), of Maccabean times:

> The greatest among his brethren, the glory of his people,
> was Simon the priest, son of Jochanan,
> in whose times the house of God was renovated,
> in whose days the temple was reinforced (50:1).

The designation by Christ of Simon, son of Jonah, as *Kaipha* (the aramaic form of the Hebrew *kepha* or rock) could just as readily evoke the name of another high priest, the one actually serving, Kaiapha, who on that very day pronounced the holy name in the Holy of Holies. As a high priest, Kaiapha alone had the symbolic key, that is, the power of access to that place, especially connected with the presence of God. That the vault in the Temple floor in which the keys of the Temple were kept was called *kipha*, may add a coincidental touch to explicit parallels between Peter's names and the names of two high priests who served in the Temple at critical junctures.

Connection with the rite enacted in the Temple will appear even closer if one recalls that Matthew, just before relating the event at Caesarea Philippi, reported Christ's warning about the necessity of being on guard against the yeast of Pharisees and Sadducees (16:6). The right of the latter to celebrate Yom Kippur was strongly contested by the Pharisees of Jesus' times. Therefore, more than one indication suggests that the exchange of declarations between Christ and Peter at Caesarea Philippi meant not only the establishment of the new people of God at Caesarea Philippi "in the Galilee of nations" (Mt 4:15) indicating its universality, but also the simultaneous implicit abolition of the Temple as the appropriate place for the supreme functioning of the high priest. The special presence of God will henceforth be in the community of the faithful, a structure of living stones but nonetheless very tangible and built on such specific foundation as a particular human individuum can be. That his role is symbolized by tools so specific as keys, which always serve most specific purpose, should seem therefore quite logical.

To the Semitic mind, far more sensitive to symbolism and analogies than is the modern mind bent on logical rigor and factual evidence, there had to be ample food for thought in a series of parallels detectable between the celebration of Yom Kippur in Jerusalem and the foundation of the Church at Caesarea Philippi. One such parallel is between the rock of Moriah, which Abraham's sacrifice of Isaac predestined to be the site of the Temple, and Peter, the living rock-foundation of the New Temple built of living stones into the Body of Christ. Another such parallel is the high priest's uttering the name through which God revealed his very nature and Peter's pronouncing that name of Jesus which only the Father could reveal about Jesus' true nature. A third parallel is between the Temple as built, attacked, destroyed, rebuilt (and to be destroyed once and for all) and the Church which is to withstand even the gates or power of hell. Still another parallel is between the placing of the people's sins by the high priest on the scapegoat and the power of binding and loosing given to Peter and later to the twelve together. Since only sin could hinder one from entering the kingdom of heaven and from staying alive within it, the power of binding and loosing had to include the power of absolution from sins, or else the keys which gave Peter supreme control over the kingdom would be meaningless.

Any of the three roles couched in three images (rock, keys, binding and loosing) would have sufficed to establish Peter's ministry as that very factor that ultimately and alone assures the cohesiveness and endurance, or indefectibility, of the living edifice which is the Church. Assurance of that cohesiveness is the objective of a single and universal foundation as specific as a human being, Peter, can be. The same objective is aimed at in the specification of access to the kingdom of heaven in terms of a set of keys, which are not keys if not very specific, deposited in the hands of a specific individual. The power to bind and loose as conferred again on the same specific person would have again been sufficient to make the matter of spiritual cohesiveness and endurance of a visible society a most specific and fundamental affair. Even in that latter regard the very fact of Christ's conferring that power first on Peter alone and only subsequently on the twelve as a college which includes Peter, would have secured a special and pivotal role for him and his ministry. By setting up that ministry through three synonymous utterances, in the same breath and in a most expressive setting and time, Christ could have only one purpose: the buttressing of that ministry against the forces of subjectivism that have never ceased fragmenting mankind, intellectually as well as socially. Since the onset of so-called modern, that is, very modish times, those forces have become particularly threatening. They now provide, almost daily, ever-fresh illustrations of what the history of the Church has always shown: fragmentation is in store for all groups and trends that try to implement the reality of the ideal of the Church without making use of its petrine foundation, without recognizing the role of Peter's keys, and without acknowledging the specific role assured to him in the process of binding and loosing.

Key Acts in the Acts of the Apostles

The church of the apostles was fully aware of the fact that it could not do without Peter's keys if the kingdom of heaven was to grow by leaps and bounds. While those keys are never mentioned in the Acts of the Apostles, their use is in full evidence. The first major opening of the gates of that kingdom on the first Pentecost was an act in which Peter played an obviously leading role. It was to him that special divine guidance came in the form of a vision (10:9–16) when those gates were to open for the Gentiles without their being subjected to Mosaic rites legislated by key-carrying rabbis. Only awareness on the part of the apostolic church explains why it was left to Peter to exclude from that kingdom Ananias and his wife (5:9–10) whose sudden death symbolized the supreme rule of the power of death outside that kingdom. Simon Magus, who wanted to have unlawful access to the treasures of that kingdom, was reprimanded by Peter in a tone no less authoritative (8:20–21). Peter played a prominent role in perhaps the most crucial opening ever of the gates of that kingdom, the admission there of the newly converted Paul.

Paul's often misinterpreted protest of Peter's vacillation in a purely practical matter, the observance of ritual laws in the midst of Christians coming from Judaism, is in fact a proof of Paul's awareness of the importance of any use, however nonessential, of the petrine keys. Those keys were between the lines as Peter in his second letter provided a divinely inspired key to the reading of Paul's letters, a key all too often ignored to their utmost peril by those opposing to Peter's keys the Bible: "Consider that our Lord's patience is directed toward salvation. Paul, our beloved brother, wrote you this in the spirit of wisdom that is his, dealing with these matters as he does in all his letters. There are certain passages in them hard to understand. The ignorant and the unstable distort them (just as they do the rest of Scripture) to their own ruin" (2 Pt 3:15–16). Few passages ever inspired so much distortion as Paul's statement on Christ as the foundation of the Church, his celebration of faith as foundation of Christian existence, and last but not least, his standing up to Peter. This last detail, it is well to recall, was reported by Paul only after pointing out that when he first went up as a Christian to Jerusalem he saw Peter in whose exclusive company he chose to stay for an entire fortnight (Gal 1:18 and 2:11).

Peter had for many years a close first-hand knowledge of Paul's thinking when by offering that often ignored key to Paul's letters he displayed a shepherd's concern for the flock's welfare.[26] He was the kind of shepherd whose assurance of his office was so firm as to be exercised with that humility which is the sign of true strength. On the one hand, he could rebuke "the bold and arrogant men who despise authority" (2 Pt 2:10) and he was not afraid to call a spade a spade. Such sentences of his as "Constantly on the lookout for a woman, theirs is a never-ending search for sin. They lure the weaker types. Their hearts are trained in greed. An accursed lot they are!" (2 Pt 2:14), are an ever timely indictment of the times and certainly of these times. On the other hand, he counseled the elders against exercising their role of shepherds by lording it over the flock (1 Pt 5:3). Such a counsel could only come from a chief of shepherds who in the same breath was not reluctant to refer to Christ as the chief shepherd.

Clearly, Peter was neither equating his role as chief

shepherd with that of Christ, nor was he belittling it, let alone voiding it with specious references to faith alone. Not for a moment did he see a contradiction between Christ's calling himself the gate, the sheepfold, and the door, and his having been given the keys of that sheepfold which is the kingdom of heaven on earth. That kingdom, however, was not heaven itself. About the onset of heaven it was he, Peter, who gave a wise warning, so necessary to balance Paul's feverish longing for an impending finale, that "in the Lord's eyes, one day is as a thousand years and a thousand years are as a day" (2 Pt 3:8). Once, however, the end of time was at hand, all offices, however exalted, would cease. Such was in particular true of the office of keys in its apocalyptic perspective. There Christ is the holder of the key of David "who opens and no one can close, who closes and no one can open" (Ap 3:7). There an angel is given the key to the shaft of the abyss out of which, when opened, "smoke poured like smoke from an enormous furnace (Ap 9:1). Later, an angel appeared holding a key to the abyss and a huge chain in his hand so that he may chain Satan for a thousand years" (Ap 20:1–2).

Whatever the true meaning of the millennium on earth at the end of the ordinary course of history, the great choice which historical times are to provide is not a choice between the nondescript heaven resembling a nirvana and an equally nebulous hell. Nor were the true heaven and true hell in any sense similar to that other denial or specificity, the reveling in syncretism which characterized the pagan olympus as well as the pagan hades, a syncretism which made meaningless the keys held by sundry gods and goddesses that supposedly controlled the access to both of those realms. The choice was rather between a most specific heaven centered on the most specific beatific vision of a triune God, the most inconceivable specific dogma among all dogmas, and a hell centered on a most specific pain, the strictly eternal barring of man from the most specific purpose given to his very nature. Clearly, in historical times, that are always most specific, the holding high of that choice had to be most specific in its various manifestations. This was even more appropriate because the choice was inseparable from the exercise of a most specific power. It was symbolized by objects, keys, that are either very specific, or are not useful tools at all.

CHAPTER 3
AWARENESS OF THE KEYS

The Age-old Question

In these times, when enthusiasm for the Bible is very much alive, it is well to recall the relative youth of the New Testament with respect to the New Covenant, the Church. The latter had been in vigorous existence for almost two decades before a single piece of the New Testament was composed. In fact, the third generation of Christians was already on its way into the Church when St. John put in writing his apocalyptic visions, the last, chronologically too, of the canonical writings which form the New Testament. As to the formal listing of those writings, or the New Testament canon, its first extant major form, known as the Muratorian fragment, was not drawn up for another three generations or so, that is, around 200 A.D. Well before that, short phrases began to appear in early Christian writings such as in the letter of Clement of Rome and in the letters of St. Ignatius of Antioch, which readily pass for implicit quotations from what later became known as the books of the New Testament. Acquaintance with the plan of salvation given by Christ and living it genuinely invited in the history of early Christianity an insistence on the intensive study of "apostolic" writings. A proof of this is Tatian's *Diatessaron*, a meticulous fusion of the four Gospels into one narrative, which dates from the closing decades of the second century. It includes Christ's promise of the keys to Peter in its entire context. Such would hardly have been the case had those words of Christ been a late addition to the original narrative.

In a study devoted to those words a reference to the earliest extant context, in which they appeared, would not be pedantry even if no other lessons were to be on hand. The *Diatessaron* postdates the year 170, the death in Rome of Justin Martyr who had Tatian as disciple. Soon after his master's death Tatian's orthodox period came to an end. On his return to his native land, Syria, Tatian cast his lot with Gnosticism, then entering its prime decades, and composed the *Diatessaron* perhaps as a scriptural weapon against the "visible" church short on gnosis, that is, "spiritual" enlightenment. Had he heard of suspicions about the authenticity of Mt 16:16–19, he would have had more than one reason against including it in the *Diatessaron*.[1] As a devotee of the Gnostic sect known as Encratities who held matter evil, forbade marriage, abstained from meat, and venerated the demiurgos, Tatian could not feel sympathy for the ecclesial authority conveyed by keys entrusted to a flesh and blood person. Gnostics, old and new, have always professed to have their own keys to truth: so many interpretations of some written words in terms of secretive illuminations of the mind. Around 180 or so, the church of Rome not only was a mighty opponent of Gnosticism in all its variants, but also had for some time claimed authority over individual and local interpretations. This claim was manifested by a series of actions taken by the bishops of Rome which amply witnessed their consciousness of Rome's special status over other churches.

Explicit outside witnesses to that consciousness were soon to make momentous appearances. Within a generation or two St. Irenaeus in Lyon declared the obligation of all churches to cohere with the church which is in Rome,[2] and St. Cyprian, as will be seen, acknowledged the force of an appeal, however unjust in his eyes, "to the chair of Peter" (ad cathedram Petri). The real thrust of such phrases failed to be blunted by that historical criticism which is attentive to everything except to development from the implicit to the explicit, from the circumstantial to the essential, from the generic to the specific, which alone qualifies for that development which is continuity in history. St. Cyprian's main concern was related, as will be seen, to the disciplinary question of absolution from sin, one of the two main issues which in due course directed attention to the significance of the keys given by Christ to Peter. The other such main concern, the concern of Irenaeus, was more doctrinal in character. Final recourse to a specific external living authority was, Irenaeus rightly sensed, indispensable for the survival of orthodoxy to which Gnosticism posed a gigantic threat.

As far as public arguments went, Gnosticism rested its case with the written word, which even in the case of revelation did not cease to be words invariably suggestive of more than one nuance. A word, any word in fact, can always be a means of endless refusal to concede a point. In the hands of a clever dialectician any word can be an effective basis for showing that the reasoning of his opponent, who agrees to debate on the basis of written words as the form of *ultimate* appeal, can never be conclusive. The reason for this is what Whitehead so felicitously called "the Fallacy of the Perfect Dictionary."[3] With the exception of words denoting strictly quantitative entities, words have meanings whose contours admit margins of indefiniteness and also partially overlap with the meaning of other words. Hence the lexicographers can forever improve their definitions of most words. Words are therefore so many slippery fish. Without a proper net on hand, words cannot be retained for conveying meaning with no possibility for further exceptions to be taken to a given proposition. Such a net cannot be construed of further words if arguing in a circle is to be avoided. A merely natural discourse has no safeguard against being drawn into this merry-go-round of which learned academies, prestigious universities, and scholarly journals are all too often the professional platforms.

A discourse which claims to have supernatural origin and content is rightly expected to have a built-in protection against such a sad fate. The protection, or the net referred to above, has to be the living word in the form of an authoritative decision on the meaning to be taken for the basis of any further discussion and inference. The Gnostic is not, of course, troubled by the intrinsic uncertainty hanging around words, and certainly around written words which have no intrinsic defense against being taken in more than one sense. It is enough for him that, in the absence of a logically conclusive refutation of his position, he is free to hold his interpretation of it or any interpretation whatsoever. For the principal aim of the Gnostic, old and new, is to secure the principle of subjective interpretation and of individual authority.

This is not a tendencious injection of latter-day points into the intellectual problems of early Christians. Ignatius of Antioch, for whom St. John the Apostle was still a personal acquaintance, is a witness that the *docetae* of his time, an early variant of Gnostics, posed to the orthodox precisely the problem of arguing in a circle. His letter to the Philadelphians contains the problem as clearly stated as possible, although without containing the only answer which provides the escape hatch from that circularity:

> Do nothing in the spirit of factiousness, but in accordance with the teaching of Christ. For I heard certain

persons saying "If I find not this doctrine of faith in the archives, in the gospel, I believe it not." And when I said to them "It is written," they answered me "That is the question." But as for me, my archives are Jesus Christ, the invisible archives are his Cross, his Death, his Resurrection, and faith through him; wherein I desire to be justified through your prayers.[4]

Such a passage is rich in that instructiveness which through the logic it embodies has a validity that never becomes dated. Indeed, in these modern times that witnessed the triumph of historical research in establishing original texts beyond reasonable doubt, agreement on what was meant by what was said is not much stronger than before. Worse, the Gnostic of St. Ignatius' day could come up with the rejoinder: If those archives are invisible how could their contents be visibly demonstrable? To be sure, immediately before ascribing the problem posed by the factious, of which the fragmenting of the Gnostics into innumerable factions was a prime example, St. Ignatius specified "the return to the unity of God and to the community of the bishop."[5] Yet while he said all the right things, including the "invisible archives," St. Ignatius did not yet put them in the sequence which does not become an arguing in a circle only if the first thing in that sequence is the very bishop which is chronologically the last.

The whole development of the idea of the Catholic Church during the first six centuries is a progressive awareness of the logic of that sequence, or the apostolic succession. Those six centuries, coming to a peak with Gregory the Great and in fact earlier, with Leo the Great, if not even already with Pope Damasus I (366–384), saw the progressive formulation of what is called Roman Catholicism. According to very important Protestant scholars, such as Harnack and others, who can hardly be suspected of "Romanism," the visible Church had already in the early second century an awareness of herself which was distinctly that of Roman Catholicism,[6] an awareness of the apostolic succession of bishops among whem the bishop of Rome wields the power of primacy. References to the keys of Peter are not the most conspicuous aspect of that development insofar as they are relatively few, though invariably telling. Their story is not only the story of the growth of that awareness but also of its background which must be taken into account lest certain patristic statements on those keys remain in a vacuum. There the only thing to turn to is that self which keeps protecting its own interpretations by answering every demonstration with the words, "That is the question." Once its premises are granted, such a tactic is immune to a cut-off point unless the never ending fragmentation invariably invited by it is such a point, an ominous evocation indeed of the point where all is vanishing.

Spirituals and Spirituals Again

The first of these backgrounds to be recalled is Montanism which had Tertullian for its most illustrious victim.[7] He brought into the Church a brilliant legal mind and a gripping mastery of both Latin and Greek penmanship when in his mid-thirties, around 195, he asked for baptism and became a priest shortly afterwards. Twenty years later he was exalting the role of prophecy. In doing so he not only slighted any and all priesthood but also made light of the submission, enjoined by St. Paul, of all gifts of prophecy to the common good of the body. He kept nothing of the reverence which no less a prophetic spirit than Hermas showed toward priests in particular and authority in general. In the second decade of the third century the rise of Montanus and of his two associates, Prisca and Maximilla, was already history. No longer did crowds throng to a plain near Pepuza in Phrygia where those three promised the heavenly Jerusalem soon to appear in the clouds.

Frenzy, when not at high pitch, could appear prophetic inspiration not necessarily leading to uncontrollable convulsions and hysterical utterances. Such inspiration could but greatly appeal to a temperament like that of Tertullian (known by his contemporaries as *vir ardens* or burning soul) in whom an incisive legal mind was joined with a passionate commitment to the cause in which he believed. Once in the hold of Montanist prophetism the mind in question could not help carrying its logic to its very limits. Hence the most logical thing for Tertullian, the Montanist, to do was to discredit ecclesial authority, the ever gravest obstacle to the supreme rights of "prophetic" inspiration.

Most revealingly, Tertullian took on the authority of the bishop of Rome in tacit acknowledgment of the pivotal status of his authority in the Church. In doing so Tertullian was most careful not to omit references to the keys given to Peter. As a good lawyer Tertullian knew that it would be self-defeating for him to deny everything to Pope Callistus, the target of his diatribe. He allowed the Pope "the duty of maintaining the discipline" and "the headship of ministry, though not the headship of empire." Such was a clever way of reducing the pope to the level of an administrator however exalted. Intrinsic authority the pope could not have, let alone the "vast power of the forgiveness of sins," and certainly not on the basis of Christ's words to Peter. Clearly, Callistus and his predecessors must have referred to those words or else Tertullian would not have stated:

> Because the Lord said to Peter: "Upon this rock I will build my Church," . . . "To thee have I given the keys

of the Kingdom of heaven," or "Whatsoever thou shalt bind or loose on earth shall be bound or loosed in heaven," you therefore assume that the power of binding and loosing has descended to you or to any church related to Peter.[8]

For Tertullian such an inference was arrogance incarnate: "Who and what are you to show mercy, who conduct yourself neither as prophet nor as apostle and are destitute of the virtue that is necessary for one who is merciful?"[9] In the eyes of a Montanist, Callistus' alleged lack of virtue settled matters. But Tertullian could not deny the lawyer in him, who would settle only with conclusive arguments. He insisted that Christ's words were addressed to Peter's person alone and rephrased Christ's words with the needed emphasis: "On thee, He said, will I build my Church and unto thee will I give the keys, that is, not unto the Church."[10] If such was the case, not only the successors of Peter were excluded but all bishops, nay, the entire Christian community insofar as it was a *Church*. Conversely, all those had the power of the keys conferred on them who were as spiritual as Peter was: "As this power was conferred upon Peter personally, so it belongs to spiritual men, whether apostle or prophet." Hence Tertullian had no choice but to say: "The Church indeed will forgive sins but only the Church of the Spirit, through the voice of a spiritual man, not the Church which is merely a collection of bishops."[11]

But the force of that logic threatened even the spirituals if it was true what Tertullian added in the same breath: "For justice and judgment belong to the Lord, not to a servant; to God alone, not to a priest."[12] The spirituals were certainly not priests, but if they claimed to be servants (had a Christian any other right than to be a servant?), then their privileged position, too, was threatened. Tertullian could not, of course, be logical to the extent of providing a criterion to distinguish true spiritual persons from Montanus, Prisca, Maximilla, and their kindred. Only those could do this who saw matters as did the anonymous author of an antimontanist tract written shortly before Tertullian became Christian. The description there of Montanus and of the two women as ones "whom the devil stirred up and filled with the spirit of lies" should seem far less important than the remark that "their manner was contrary to the constant custom of the Church handed down by tradition from the beginning."[13]

Of that tradition few were so spirited and incisive defenders as Tertullian was in his Catholic days. Then he kept insisting that in confronting heretics the most important thing was to deny the very supposition on the basis of which they wanted to argue their case. Such was the gist of Tertullian's method in his *De praescriptione haereticorum* or "ruling out of heretics." The word *praescription* stands for that move which in Roman legal practice aimed at dismissing the opponent out of court right at the outset. The heretics, Tertullian stated, had no right to argue against Catholics who had been legitimate heirs to the full apostolic tradition. Tertullian's reasoning tellingly contains a reference to the keys given to Peter. To the claim of heretics that for the full grasp of truth ample time was needed so that the Spirit might reveal its richness to whomever it chose, Tertullian replied: "Was anything withheld from Peter, who was called the rock on which the church should be built, who also obtained the keys of the kingdom of heaven with the power of loosing and binding in heaven and on earth?"[14]

In the context of Tertullian's reasoning this meant the subsequent transmission of the power of keys to the Church, and with such a fullness as to invest the bishops with intrinsic authority. Hence any effort from the ranks to set up rival bishops was tantamount to schism, and was indeed the "mother of schisms." The Catholic unity pivoted in the bishops had its contrast in the intrinsically critical attitude of schismatics toward their own presiding officers. In Tertullian's inimitable phrase, "schism is their very unity."[15]

The beginnings of Tertullian's Catholic period coincide with the last years of the two decades which Clement of Alexandria spent in that city as head of a catechetical school. What he said about the keys of Peter reflect, as was also the case with Tertullian, the inner working of basic presuppositions or, in a broader sense, the main proclivities of an individual's bent of mind. Unlike Tertullian, Clement always remained in union with the Catholic Church but invariably spoke of her in particular and of the work of salvation in general in terms of a special perspective. It was the perspective of gnosis or of the spiritual man's allegorical and mystical insight into the tenets of faith. To be sure, gnosis was the growing old "in the study of doctrines."[16] Clement never failed to acknowledge the overriding importance of that tradition which distinguished the community of the faithful from heretics. He emphatically noted the existence of apostolic teaching for three generations before the rise of those who "in the times of Hadrian [117–138] first invented heresies." He celebrated the true Church "which is really ancient." He rejoiced in the Church's "oneness" which has "nothing like or equal to itself" and "surpasses all things else" and which assures the Church a "pre-eminence and is the principle of her constitution."[17]

About the specific factor that assured that oneness, Clement's gnosis offered little tangible because like all gnosis it was irresistibly drawn to abstraction and to spiritual contemplation, if not to a plain cavorting in allegories and metaphors. Of course, by saying that "the Scripture and voice of the Lord, such is our criterion and the discovery of the things [of gnosis]"[18] he was not entirely lost in abstractions. Yet, while the Scriptures were certainly tangible, Clement's reference to the voice of the Lord contained no specifications, although the very context demanded specifics as to what gave access, a key, to the proper understanding of the Scriptures, to say nothing of the voice of the Lord. For right there and then Clement summed up the predicament of heretics, whose fondness for the Scriptures he could hardly ignore, as the ones who have only a false or counterfeit key:

> Not having the key of entrance, but a false and (as the common phrase expresses it) counterfeit key, they do not enter as we enter in, by drawing aside the curtain, that is, the tradition of the Lord, but by making an opening in the side, piercing clandestinely through the wall of the Church, and stepping over the truth, they constitute themselves the mystagogues of the souls of the impious.[19]

What was the true key? What were the walls of the Church? When would one be guilty of stepping over the truth of tradition? For the Catholic answer stressing loyalty to the bishops (an answer voiced repeatedly and prominently long before Clement and an answer soon to be connected with the keys of Peter), one would look in vain in Clement's profuse works, one of which was most aptly called a "spread-out carpet" (*Stromata*). As a teacher he was a *paidagogos* (the title of another long work of his) in the Greek sense which stood for inner enlightenment through *logoi* or notions rather than for that concrete loyalty to tangible truth which has been the touchstone of the Christian message ever since the Logos had become flesh. The irony was even keener because the Christian in Clement was certainly stronger than the Greek. Otherwise, he would not have coined that priceless dictum that heretics "glory in being a school rather than a Church,"[20] a prophetic indictment of latter-day advocates of theological faculties as the supreme interpreters of revelation.

Not a few moderns, at times even with the martyr-like heroism of Origen, a continuator of Clement's school, have their theological reasonings prefigured in Origen's failure to strike a proper balance between the spirituality of gnosis and the concreteness of Christian truth. In times like ours, when adepts of a so-called transcendental Thomism are found to transcend long-held dogmas and traditions, and in particular those about sin and hell, a look at Origen's dicta on the keys of Peter may have more than a mere historical interest. The keys given to Peter represented, according to Origen, so many virtues. There were as many keys as there were virtues and whoever was made spiritual through virtues possessed so many keys to heaven:

> Let us see in what sense it is said to Peter, and to every Peter, "I will give unto thee the keys of the kingdom of heaven." In the first place I think that the saying, "I will give unto thee the keys of the kingdom of heaven," is spoken in consistency with the words, "The gates of Hades shall not prevail against it." For he is worthy to receive from the same Word the keys of the kingdom of heaven, who is fortified against the gates of Hades so that they do not prevail against him, receiving, as it were, for a prize, the keys of the kingdom of heaven, because the gates of Hades had no power against him that he might open for himself the gates that were closed to those who had been conquered by the gates of Hades. And he enters in, as a temperate man, through the opened gate—the gate of temperance—by the key which opens temperance; and as a righteous man, by another gate—the gate of righteousness; and so with the rest of the virtues. For I

think that for every virtue of knowledge (gnosis) certain mysteries of wisdom corresponding to the species of the virtue are opened up to him who has lived according to virtue; the Savior giving to those who are not mastered by the gates of Hades as many keys as there are virtues which open gates equal in number which correspond to each virtue according to the revelation of the mysteries.[21]

That virtues could open the gates of heaven from which only sin bars anyone was true enough. In that sense virtues could justly be called keys. Whether such was the meaning of Christ's words to Peter was another matter. And it was still another and most serious matter whether Peter, and bishops in general, had no longer the keys once their lives were sinful. Although Origen knew of another meaning of keys standing for authority not for virtues, it was of little interest to him. The logic of spiritualism coupled with a mistaken theology was claiming its rights which simply destroyed the rights of hierarchy:

> When those who maintain the function of the episcopate make use of this word as Peter, and, having received the keys of the kingdom of heaven from the Savior, teach that things bound by them, that is, condemned are also bound in heaven, and that those which have obtained remission from them are also loosed in heaven, we must say that they speak wholesomely if they have the way of life on account of which it was said to that Peter "Thou art Peter" . . . But if he is tightly bound with the cords of his sins, to no purpose does he bind and loose. And perhaps you can say that in the heavens which are in the wise man—that is the virtues—the bad man is bound; and again in these the virtuous man is loosed, and has received an indemnity for the sins which he committed before his virtue.[22]

If such was the case, no case could be made for a hierarchy, nor for an authentic interpretation of the Scripture itself. For Origen could claim only as long as he was free of sin that he was right in depicting as "puffed up men [those] who have fallen into the ruin of the devil"[23] and as such claim to themselves the right of absolving other sinners. Ultimately, the same force of logic undermined Origen's exaltation of virtues as well. Origen, an admirer of Plato and of the Stoics, who alike saw in the periodic reconstruction of all within a Great Year the ultimate framework of existence, tried to graft this vision on the Christian outlook on heaven and hell. But if hell was not eternal neither could the kingdom opened by virtues be eternal. Thus logic demanded the abolition of a strict distinction between virtue and sin, or keys and their counterfeit kind.

Not that Origen had carried his logic to such disastrous ends. In fact, he was ready for a martyr's crown, hardly an attitude if his deepest convictions had been more Greek than Christian. He was in fact so convinced a Christian in the traditional sense as to visit Rome around 210 because it was the most ancient Church and the bishop of Rome was the first on the list of bishops to whom Origen sent letters pleading his own case against his own bishop in Alexandria! As always, Christian convictions were one thing, the logic of the bent of mind of a theologian, however Christian, another. Theologians with the verve of Origen often seem to their contemporaries to be far ahead of their times. Not only can they be far behind, but their opponents can turn out to be the voice of the future, that is, of true survival. An illustration of this is the next phase in the history of patristic references to the keys of the kingdom.

A Champion versus a Savior

The unity of the Church and of the episcopal authority within it had few more passionate champions than St. Cyprian, bishop of Carthage from 248 until September 14, 258, the day of his martyrdom. Had he not gone into hiding at the very start of his episcopate, he would have in all likelihood been among the first and chief victims of Decius who in the fall of 249 unleashed one of the most violent persecutions. In that case there would not have arisen in the church of Carthage an opposition party that wanted to replace Cyprian with another bishop, nor would Cyprian's *De unitate ecclesiae* have been written. The source of dispute was the attitude toward the *lapsi*, or Christians who fell away as the persecution raged, but afterwards truly repented. Could they be re-admitted into the Church? In his hiding Cyprian was unwilling to show mercy and certainly not until that time when the persecution had blown itself out and the church of Carthage could be convened by its rightful bishop. This seemed to not a few in Carthage a denial of spiritual rights, a denial even more unjustifiable as it came from one who did not seem to have the courage to face martyrdom. Would it not therefore be more spiritual to let the community's martyrs, that is, those tortured but not executed, decide which of the *lapsi* were truly repentant so as to be re-admitted into the Church?

Such was the essence of the confrontation between a "spiritualist" notion of the Church and a notion which was "authoritarian" in the most profound sense. According to Cyprian, every bishop governed his flock with that authority which Christ gave to the apostles, and in particular to Peter himself. In more than one letter written by Cyprian before he composed his *De unitate* the reference to Christ's words to Peter appear in that "authoritarian" sense. This is especially the case in his 33rd letter, a draft of his *De unitate*, where in support of the divinely constituted authority of each bishop he quoted in full Christ's words to Peter:

> Our Lord, whose precepts we must fear and implement, states in the gospel where He lays down the dignity of bishops and the constitution of the Church in speaking to Peter: "I tell you that you are Peter and on this rock I will build my church and the gates of hell will not subdue it, and I will give you the keys of the kingdom of heaven and what you bind on earth shall be bound in heaven and whatever you loose on earth will be loosed in heaven." Therefore through tenures and successions the ordination of bishops and the very reason of the church reaches the present so that the church be *established* (constituted) on the bishops and all actions of the church be ruled by those very prelates.[24]

Such is also the scriptural support of Cyprian's argumentation in *De unitate* where he begins with the never-ceasing efforts of the devil to sway Christians. Since idolatry had noticeably lost its appeal under the spread of Christianity, the devil's new strategy aims at undermining the unity of Christians. No greater safeguard can be found on behalf of that unity than attention to Christ's words to Peter. Cyprian then quotes again the passage containing the reference to the keys and adds that although the Church begins through the Church built on Peter, all bishops share the power of Peter. The unity of bishops in turn derives from the very fact that all bishops integrally share that power: "Episcopatus unus est, cuius a singulis in solidum pars tenetur."[25] If such is the case, only bishops can transmit that power. Those who, like the spiritualists, set up their own bishops are wrong because

Awareness of the Keys 69

"without anyone giving the episcopacy to them they assume the name of bishop."[26]

Like any theological work written with a view on a special situation, and on a highly disputatious situation at that, the *De unitate* too is restricted to a very specific aspect of a very broad problem. The immediate objective, the upholding of the right of the lawful bishop against a faction within the local church, is presented with vigor and sweep. The broader aspect, the question of the unity of bishops, is not broached there. The logic of a sharp focusing on a particular question could therefore force Cyprian to dispute the existence of a "bishop of bishops."[27] The ecclesial experience engaged him, however, in procedures which clearly suggested the contrary. For the same ecclesial experience, from which Cyprian derived his passionate reminders of the need of all bishops to cohere, was the sole justification for Cyprian's continual convening of the bishops of Northern Africa of which Carthage was a metropolis. Moreover, he knew all too well that the bishop of Rome invited far greater attention than the bishop of Carthage in convening a synod of bishops.

Indeed, even without convening such synods, recourses to the bishops of Rome had been made with far reaching consequences and touched off just as far reaching rulings on their part. Cyprian also knew that no provincial synods, not even the synod of Carthage which in May 251 heard Cyprian read the *De unitate*, could settle matters. Shortly after that synod another spiritualist group appealed to Rome against Cyprian. As one would expect, Cyprian was indignant but his indignation could not hide his awareness of the preponderance of the Roman See. The emissaries of the faction, he complained to Pope Stephen, "dare to sail even to the chair of Peter and carry letters from schismatics and seculars to the principal Church, the source of sacerdotal unity."[28] Such was an all too clear admission that the unity of the Church not only had its source in the Church first founded on Peter but that source lived on in the particular church of Rome presided over by the successors of Peter. In writing with such clarity of the primacy of the church of Rome only a month after the public reading of his *De unitate*, Cyprian could naturally intend for its genuine text the so-called "conflated" version. There it is stated that although Christ "gave all apostles the same authority, he established only one chair ... What Peter was were also the others, but Peter was given the primacy so that [as a result] one church and one chair is in evidence."[29]

During the rest of Cyprian's office there were further appeals to Rome, not always from Carthage, in which he became involved. All those incidents showed the fragility of a unity which was to come merely from a cohesion of good will with no particular bishop being the reference point and arbiter. On the one hand, Cyprian was not too reluctant to play such a reference point. In assuming the role of arbiter in a dispute between two bishops in Spain, Cyprian not only contradicted the theory of a "non-conflated" *De unitate* which stood for the settling of all local matters on the local level but also contradicted plain geography. Was Spain, as Cyprian lamely hinted, farther from Rome than from Carthage?[30] No less inconsistently, on seeing that the bishop of such a great see as Arles refused, four years after the synod of Carthage, to accept its policy on the *lapsi*, Cyprian urged Rome to bring that bishop to heel. Tellingly, he did not appeal to the bishops around Arles, and much less did he do what his "non-conflated" theory implied, namely, appeal to the faithful, the *plebs* of Arles, to depose their bishop and elect another one.

Cyprian had an even more serious problem for his "non-conflated" ecclesiology. The problem arose in his own

African backyard and carried the dubious African heritage of spiritualism—which had already ruined a Tertullian and brought discredit to Origen, the theologian—to its full logic. When the lives of some African bishops turned out to be unworthy of their office, Cyprian and others felt that personal sinfulness made void sacerdotal powers. He took the view that heretical and schismatic prelates and presbyters did not administer validly the sacrament of baptism, that very opening of the kingdom of heaven. Cyprian, like some of his fellow-African bishops and some bishops elsewhere and beforehand, declared the baptism administered by heretics to be invalid. After all, was not heresy a sin, and was not sin *the* barrier to the kingdom of God? Was not the conferring of the gifts of the Holy Spirit the very opposite of sin?

Cyprian's declaration, "All heretics and schismatics fail to give the Holy Spirit,"[31] was adopted by the synod of Carthage in the Fall of 255. Not all the bishops in Africa agreed, however. The dissenters could refer to the ancient custom according to which heretics were not rebaptized. Their reliance on tradition was in full accord with the tie that connected every bishop to the Apostles, and with the immediate thrust of Cyprian's *De unitate* but not with its narrow logic. The latter got the upper hand as Cyprian made another synod of bishops agree with his views which he pregnantly expressed by setting up the theological reasoning against apostolic tradition: "What matters is not a ruling about custom but a demonstration by reason."[32] The same logic blinded Cyprian to the extent of trying to bring even Pope Stephen around. The latter refused to receive the emissaries of Cyprian who at that time began to insinuate to friends that Peter never held primacy nor claimed it ever to himself. But what revealed in full the ecclesial disaster lurking behind Cyprian's theory of the episcopate was contained in his letter to Stephen: "We neither do violence to any, nor lay down a law, since each bishop has, in the government of his church, free control of his will and owes an account of his conduct to the Lord only."[33]

Contained in this claim was the potential destruction of the unity of the Church so dear to Cyprian. He could have spared himself a theological debacle had he ever considered that the keys were given only to Peter. Not far away were the times of their being considered with fair frequency. Not that Stephen referred to the keys in making his famed endorsement of the validity of baptism administered by heretics. He did not argue about his or other bishops' will; he merely laid down the law as to what opens and closes the kingdom of heaven. He turned the keys in those doors with a decision which, though at first considerably resented, was adhered to universally in the long run and most memorably so. Only specialists remember today that Firmilian who thought to speak in the name of the future in registering his and many other bishops' indignation against Stephen: "Even I in that respect rightly took exception to Stephen's so great and obvious stupidity, namely, that he was boasting in such a way about the place of his episcopate and claimed to hold succession to Peter on whom were placed the foundations of the Church . . . Stephen who preaches to possess Peter's chair through succession [to that chair]."[34]

No turning of Peter's keys ever was so momentous in the history of the Church. It made possible in the long run that ecumenical movement which today rightly recognizes the overriding importance of the validity of baptism in all Christian denominations. The savior of the future Church was Stephen because already the whole past was with the see he held. In analyzing the situation of the Church as it existed two generations before Stephen, Harnack and other leading Protestant historians of Christian dogma and church constitution plainly acknowledged, as was already noted, the Catholic, or Roman, character of Christianity already in its early stage. As to the present, or Stephen's days, the most telling judgment on the overriding importance of his see was passed by none other than Emperor Decius. That most resolute enemy of Christians "would have preferred to hear that a rival claim to his empire had been elected in Rome than that a bishop had been elected there." We owe this report on Decius to none other than Cyprian.[35] Clearly he had no excuse. Nor do those who ascribe the ascendency of the bishop of Rome either to imperial favor, or to the power vacuum created by the fall of the empire. Constantine was half a century away, and the fall of imperial Rome one and a half centuries still in the future.

Peter's Keys from Nicea to Augustine

To a superficial observer an emperor, Constantine, looms large at the start of the dozen or so centuries that stretch from the exit of the Church from the catacombs to the ecclesial cataclysm triggered by Luther. The Council of Nicea proved itself to be far more important, though at the same time more subject to superficial criticism. Legion are the scornful remarks about the debates during that council about a mere iota, the sole visible difference between *homoousion* (of the same substance) and *homoiousion* (of similar substance). No two long words with subtly, though drastically, different meanings could, indeed, give a more similar visual appearance. Were the bases and the tops of the letters composing both words to be traced on paper, the result would be very similar to the profiles of two almost identical Yale keys. Whatever their almost complete visual identity and the almost complete identity of locks two such keys would operate, either of the two would be totally useless except for the proper lock and door. Of those two long words, both very specific, only one could serve as a key to truth and to operate a most special door, the door of the kingdom of heaven, the kingdom of truth. Orthodoxy, or truthful doctrine, has always been and will forever remain a very specific affair, because truth is very specific, and certainly the truth of salvation given in Christ.

No wonder that the greatest defenders of orthodoxy at Nicea and later have always been staunch supporters of the chair of the one who succeeded Peter in his office and held therefore his keys. The support which Athanasius sought in Rome and found there is too well known a story to be reviewed here, though a story that cannot be pondered often enough. In the fight for that orthodoxy, which had to be won against Arius or else Christianity would have been soon reduced to a Judaizing sect, there were some minor figures which deserve special attention in this story on Peter's keys. One of them is St. Hilary of Poitiers, a stalwart in the fight against semi-Arians, who had his eye on the homoousion of Nicea as he commented on the famed passage in Matthew:

> A worthy reward followed Peter's confession because he saw God's Son in man. Blessed is he who was praised for his seeing and perceiving beyond the range of human eyes. Since he did not gaze at flesh and blood but saw, through revelation, the Son of the heavenly Father, he was found worthy to recognize first what was God in Christ. Oh, blessed foundation of the Church [who became the rock] through being designated by a new name, and through the construction of that rock which destroys the infernal laws, the gates of hell and all barriers of death! Oh blessed janitor of heaven to whose judgments are entrusted the keys of eternal portals, and whose ruling on earth is a foregone authority in heaven, so that whatever is bound or

loosened on earth, obtains the same validity in heaven![36]

Another "minor" figure, St. Optatus, bishop of Milevis in Numidia, not far from Carthage, will quickly grow in stature if his fight against Donatists is recalled as a prelude to Augustine's campaign a generation later. Augustine but further articulated two points emphasized by St. Optatus. One is that Peter was first given the keys which later on were communicated to the other apostles.[37] The other is the primordial importance of the succession of the bishops of Rome in deciding where was the true Church.

The need to insist on the Church's power to forgive sins against Donatists and all their kindred "spiritualists" made almost inevitable the insistence that all apostles and all their successors had the power of keys, as a power tied even in Matthew to the power of loosing and binding given to the twelve as well. Such a stretching of the meaning of the passage in Matthew could have led to anarchy in the Church if pivotal importance had not been attributed at the same time to the Roman succession. Only a deliberate oversight of this latter point can prompt one to rehash an old superficiality and make anti-Roman hay out of Augustine's ignorance of Greek (and Aramaic), which left him undecided whether Christ founded the Church on Peter or on his faith.[38] Only ill-will can turn into a champion of a "spiritualist" invisible church that Augustine who repeatedly greeted Rome's decision as a *rescriptum* or in Roman legal terminology a decision against which there was no further appeal. *Rescriptum* is the crucial word in the context which gave rise to the now hallowed paraphrase, "Roma locuta, causa finita," the high point of the sermon which Augustine preached on September 23, 417, to the clergy and people of Hippo. The sermon was occasioned by his receiving Pope Innocent's reply, or *re-*

scriptum, to the deliberations sent to the "apostolic see" by two councils, one in Carthage, the other in Milevis, on Pelagian heresy.[39]

Augustine would not have been his real self had he not coined a most felicitous phrase vibrating with both deep spirituality and full Roman orthodoxy even in reference to the keys of Peter which he at times was wont to interpret allegorically. He did so in speaking of that "miserable people" who later became known as Cathars: "For while in Peter they refuse to recognize the Rock and will not believe that to the Church were committed the keys of the Kingdom of Heaven, they have let those keys fall from their own hands."[40] For Augustine the twelve were no more conceivable without their head, Peter, than the Church was conceivable without the chief apostolic see, Rome. As to the former, his interpretation of the tax money (didrachma) miraculously caught by Peter is a classic for its directness: "When the Savior commanded that which was due to be paid for himself and for Peter, he seemed to have paid for all because even as all sources of magisterium were in the Savior, so also after the Savior they were all contained in Peter, for he appointed Peter head of all so that he may be the shepherd of the Lord's flock."[41]

Peter's headship was for Augustine the handy assurance of apostolicity: "If the order of the succession of bishops is to be considered, with what great certainty of truth and security can we number them from Peter! For thus the Lord addressed Peter, who represented the whole: 'Upon this rock I will build my Church and the gates of hell shall not prevail against it.' " Augustine's listing by name 34 bishops of Rome forming the link from Peter to Anastasius (398–401), noteworthy in itself, is especially instructive in two respects. First, he stated the orthodoxy of them all, "as no Dontanist can be found among them. Second, he also considered the case if one or another among them had been a traitor:

> This would not be a stumbling block for the Church and innocent Christians to whom the provident Lord said of bad prelates: "What they say, do; what they do, don't." They say and don't do, so that secure might be the loyal hope which, being anchored not in man but in the Lord, is never dissipated by the tempest of the sacrilege of schism, unlike those are dissipated who read in the sacred books about churches to whom the apostles had written and who have [recognized] no bishops in them. Is anything more perverse and more insane than to say, "Peace with you" to those reading those letters and separate [at the same time] from the [union of] peace of those churches to whom those letters were written?[42]

In asking this powerfully pointed question Augustine must have first of all thought of the longest of those letters, written to the Romans, a favorite with him. Its being abused a thousand years later as a chief tool of disunity would have been a most perverse policy for Augustine. As one who believed in the Gospels only because the "authority of the Church vouched for them,"[43] Augustine was very consistent in decrying schism as "the most sacrilegious of all sins because there could be no just cause whatever for rending the unity of the Church."[44] Thus when Augustine spoke of the keys of Peter as keys given to the whole Church, he could only have in mind a Church structured in the apostolic succession of bishops, with the successors of Peter as their pivotal line of descent, and not an invisible church of "faith." Whatever Augustine's emphasis on the spiritual reality of the Church, the root offense against the Spirit animating the Church was in his eyes an act quite material or visible. It amounted to the kind of declaration of independence whereby one cut oneself off the only one root which the Church, planted as a palm tree by the living waters, could have. Augustine unmistakably identified that root with Rome as the see of Peter.

True, that see existed only for the sake of the universal Church, which entirely received the keys, but the universal Church had Rome as her only root because the keys were primordially given to Peter: "Who would not consider detestable the fact that they [the Luciferians] cut themselves off from the root? . . . For not without reason does Peter among all the apostles represent the very person of the Church, since to that Church were given the keys of the Kingdom of Heaven when they were given to Peter. Thus when it is said to him, to all is said: And I give you the keys of the Kingdom of Heaven . . ."[45] Celebrate as Augustine could in inimitable ways the universal Church, the genuineness or orthodoxy of that Church was in his eyes inseparable from adherence to Peter and his successors.

Augustine's "Romanism" owed much to that both tangible and intangible impact which had been made on him by St. Ambrose in Milan. By then Ambrose memorably argued against the Jovinians, another brand of those ever-reappearing spirituals who, in their fervor, do away not only with the power of the Church to forgive sins but also with the need to forgive sin at all. The Novatians' stance was in Ambrose's eyes a rejection of Christ's willingness to save and heal all, of that very Christ who said even to Peter: "Unless I wash your feet, you will have no share in me." Such was Ambrose's introductory thought to his often quoted declaration: "What share can have in you, O Lord, those who do not receive the keys of the kingdom, denying as they do that they have the obligation to forgive sins? This they [the Novatians] rightly state about themselves. But they have not the inheritance of Peter who do not have Peter's seat which they pick apart by wicked divisiveness; yet they wrongly deny that even in the Church sins can be forgiven, for it was said to Peter: 'I will give you the keys of the kingdom of heaven.' " Ambrose then turned the table on the Novatians seeking support from St. Paul, by quoting to them his words to the Corinthians: "If you forgive a man anything so do I. Any forgiving I have done has been for your sakes and before Christ" (2 Cor 2:10). "Why do then the Novatians read Paul, if they consider him to have erred so grievously as to vindicate to himself his Lord's right?"[46] Rejection of Peter was a rejection of Paul as well, a logic casting its shadow far into the future when a Newman, still Anglican, realized that missiles aimed at Rome were to hit first Canterbury,[47] and even more so Wittenberg and Geneva.

In arguing against the Novatians, Ambrose had on hand a theme which of necessity invited a reference to Peter's keys. Some of Ambrose's most telling endorsements of the petrine office occurred, however, in an incidental way, in telling evidence of the naturalness of his conviction about Peter's and of his successors' primacy. Two such cases occur in Ambrose's commentary on Paul's Second Letter to the Corinthians. In speaking of Paul's reference to the Corinthians as virgins espoused to Christ (11:2), Ambrose clarified some preconceptions about virginity, celibacy, and the married state, and recalled the fact that most of the apostles were married and memorably Peter. The latter's stature was, however, such as to discredit any slighting of him on account of his married status: "Is it then appropriate to accuse the apostle Peter who, since he was the first among the apostles, is so much more the first among all others?"[48] No less than the foregoing statement of Ambrose, this question of his too should seem to have a perennial relevance, especially at a time when not a few among "all others" act and speak as if they were the first in the Church.

A chapter later (12:11), in reflecting on the factions among the Corinthians, Ambrose reminded them that John the Baptist obtained no power over Jesus by baptizing him. To this corrective to the Corinthians' infatuation with the order in which various persons baptized them, Ambrose added the almost incidental remark which has the incisiveness of an entire treatise: "Andrew preceded Peter in following Christ and yet not Andrew but Peter received the primacy."[49] Just as unplanned should seem the comment, soon a famed dictum, which the passage "and the persecutors fell down backward" (Ps 40:15) prompted Ambrose to make. It would have been clearly enough for Ambrose's purpose to recall that Judas and other persecutors of Jesus drew back and fell to the ground in the Garden of Gethsemani. But Ambrose went on:

> The persecutor falls to the ground and into hell. Christ [falls] on the risen, Christ falls on the rock, Christ falls on the Church. Hear how Christ falls on the Church! In the background was Peter who followed him as he was led by the Jews to the house of Caiaphas, the head of the Synagogue. Peter is the one to whom he said: "You are Peter and on this rock I shall build my Church." *Where Peter is, there is the Church; where the Church is, there is no death, but eternal life* [Ubi ergo Petrus, ibi Ecclesia; ubi Ecclesia, ibi nulla mors, sed vita aeterna]. And therefore he added: "And the gates of hell do not prevail over it, and I give you the keys of the kingdom of heaven." Blessed [is that] Peter, over whom the gates of hell do not prevail, and before whom the door of heaven does not shut itself; on the contrary he destroyed the vestibules of hell, opened the celestial ones. Being placed on earth, he opened the heaven, closed the hell" (Italics added).[50]

There was in all this not a hint that what performed those stupendous deeds was Peter's faith and not Peter himself.

Another late-fourth-century stalwart of orthodoxy was Jerome, a short-tempered scholar who could readily pick a fight with any and all. Disagreement arose even between Jerome and Augustine, though not concerning the manner in which the keys of the kingdom were possessed by the entire Church. The manner, Jerome argued, implied a capital provision aimed at forestalling the possibility of dissensions resulting in schisms, all too possible when the same keys were at the disposal of so many: "Although all the apostles received the keys of the kingdom of heaven, yet among the twelve only Peter singly was chosen so that with the head being established occasion for schism be removed."[51] Few saw indeed so keenly as Jerome did in the closing decades of the fourth century the threat posed to the universal Church by Arianism, returning on the coattails of semi-Arian bishops. For Jerome the situation resembled the return of the Deluge itself. The sole refuge against it Jerome saw in a recourse to the see of Peter, to whose occupant, Damasus I (366–384), Jerome wrote: "As I follow no leader save Christ, so I communicate with none but your blessedness, that is, with the chair of Peter. For this, I know, is the rock on which the church is built. This is the house where alone the paschal lamb can be rightly eaten. This is the ark of Noah, and he who is not found in it shall perish when the flood prevails."[52]

In his turn Damasus was fully aware of the foundations of his office which he was not reluctant to vindicate with a reference to the fact that "Peter alone, prior to all the apostles, received the keys."[53] Half a century earlier the same awareness was at play in the crucial role which Pope St. Julius I played in vindicating St. Athanasius, the stalwart of orthodoxy in the East against bishops who could be either naively misled or oppressively misleading. For all his interventions in the dispute raging around St. Athanasius, interventions which included the calling of a synod in Rome, and then another in Sardica (Sophia) so that all the Oriental bishops might attend, Julius had this to say: "Because Christ said to Peter, 'You are Peter and I give you the keys of the kingdom of heaven,' the Roman church has, on account of a privilege uniquely granted to it, the power of opening and closing the gates of the kingdom of heaven to whom it wishes."[54]

The Witness of the East

A graphic illustration of fourth-century awareness of the keys as deposited in the hands of Peter and of his successors is a plea in the form of a letter which allegedly Clement, bishop of Rome, wrote to James, the apostle and the "bishop of bishops" in Jerusalem.[55] The author of the letter was in all likelihood a Syrian and member of a community of Christian Jews eager to maintain their practice of observing the Mosaic Law without imposing it on Christians of non-Jewish background. The fact that the years of Clement's office postdated by decades James' death is expressive of the kind of inaccuracy which often gives away a dissimulation of true authorship. The plea is noteworthy inasmuch as it seeks support on behalf of that observance in the authority of Peter (who preferred a less drastic policy than Paul) as the one who handed down his authority to Clement. That Clement was not an immediate successor of Peter did not distract from the stress in that plea on the continuity of Peter's authority in the church of Rome. The plea is presented with a graphic touch worth recalling in some detail. First comes the notification of James about the death of Peter who "in recompense for his faith . . . was appointed the foundation of the Church and for that reason was given by the Lord's divine mouth the surname Peter.'' Then comes the description of the gathering of the church in Rome, at the command of Peter, who addresses his flock:

> Listen my brethren and associates in the ministry. As I have been instructed by him who sent me, my Lord and teacher Jesus Christ, that the day of my death is imminent, I ordain this Clement as your bishop to whom alone I hand over the chair of teaching and preaching because he was my companion in everything from start to end. Therefore I hand over to him the power of binding and loosing which the Lord handed to me so that whatever he would decree on earth, would be decreed in heaven.

While there is no reference in that context of the transference of Peter's keys to Clement, later on, as Peter's teaching and pastoral policies become the subject of the letter, it is stated:

> He [Peter] preached that all must serve the holy immaculate Church whose keys he said the bishops to be. For they have the power of closing the heaven and to open its doors because they have become the keys of heaven.

Awareness of Peter's primacy received another graphic expression in another "apocryphal" writing from the East. In the so-called Gospel of the Twelve Apostles (*Evangelium duodecim apostolorum*), a Coptic work also from the middle of the fourth century[56] as is the letter ascribed to Clement, the event at Caesarea Philippi is described in a form the elements of which are taken from an Eastern ordination rite, a telling proof of the consciousness of the origin of episcopal office in the dignity conferred by Christ on the twelve:

> Peter, thou art the beginning of the calling of the brethren. Come to me on this rock, that I may bless thee and make thee known before all the world . . . Incline thy head to me, O Peter! The right hand of my Father is laid upon thee, wherefore I ordain thee archbishop . . . Let the four beasts [of Apocalypse] praise me and my Father today and sing the "Thrice holy," for today my chosen Peter shall be ordained archbishop . . . Ye thesauries of heaven and ye dwelling places of my kingdom, rejoice today, for your keys shall be given to my chosen. Ye dominions and power of heaven, rejoice, for we shall give to my chosen Peter fatherhood over tens of thousands forever. O all thou earth, rejoice today, for I have given to one who is compassionate the power to bind and loose. O Paradise, rejoice today, and shed forth a sweet odor, for I will put an incorruptible robe upon Peter forever. O Hell, be sorrowful today with thy powers, for I have pledged to my chosen Peter a covenant forever; for I will build my Church and the gates of Hell shall not prevail against . . . [this is followed by a recount of Peter's declaring Jesus to be the Son of the living God and Jesus' declaring Peter to be the blessed:] "Now go hence that I may give thy tongue the power of my tongue to loose and to bind." Then He laid his hand upon his head and all the heavenly hosts sang the Trisagion, so that the stones which were on the mount cried out with: "Worthy, worthy, worthy is the father, the Archbishop Peter." When Peter had received this great honor, his countenance shone; he shone before the apostles like the sun, like Moses of old time.

The significance of this passage, which should give pause to latter-day "doctors of the Church" contemptuous of the imposition of hands as indispensable sacramental sign, derives partly from its provenance. It was written by a run-of-the-mill author for popular consumption expecting a response from "the people" rather than from the learned.

Not that the learned failed to give their votes which came from the East no less than from the West. Prior to Chalcedon (451), where some ambitious elements from Constantinople made their first notable move to establish there a see equal to Rome, Peter's primacy received eloquent testimonies with references to his keys and in most unexpected contexts. In rejecting the objections of the followers of such heretics as Marcion and Bardesan, who wanted to be known after their leaders and who wanted Ephrem to call himself a Kephan, Ephrem replied: "Am I of Kephas? If the sheep [of Christ] had to refuse the name of Kephas, though he is the head of the apostles who received the power of keys and is taken for the shepherd of the flock, what a harsh condemnation is deserved by anyone who is not ashamed at all to let his sheep be named after him?"[57]

Unanimous was the voice of the three Cappadocians. In vindicating the power of bishops to impose penitential discipline, St. Gregory of Nyssa warned the recalcitrant: "Consider that if absolved you will be released, and if bound you will be tied with invisible fetters, because through Peter Christ conferred [on his Church] the keys of heavenly honors."[58] By tying Peter's obtaining the keys to his becoming "a rock not to be broken," St. Gregory Nazienzen clearly saw the keys too as having the same endurance.[59] St. Basil tried to stir the fear of God in some hardened souls precisely with a pointed reference to Peter's keys: "What a hardened heart would not be induced to fear God's judgment if even that great exactor of so great a judgment as Peter, who was preferred before all the disciples, who alone received a greater testimony and blessing than the rest, to whom were entrusted the keys of the kingdom of heaven, also has to hear: 'If I do not wash you, you will have no part in me'."[60]

In discussing the case of Ananias as an example of bad faith, that is, of heretical faith, St. Epiphanius, bishop of Constantia in Cyprus, emphasized submission to Peter as the source of correct faith: "In every way was the faith confirmed in him who received the keys of heaven, who looses on earth and binds in heaven. For in him are found all the subtle matters of faith."[61] As one would expect, the biblical story of Simon Magus was enlarged in the *Catechesis* of St. Cyril of Jerusalem with the apocryphal story in which Peter's word makes Simon Magus descend precipitously from the higher regions to the ground. No less naturally St. Cyril saw Peter's act in the light of his prerogatives: "The word of Peter was needed because Peter, the ground (rock) is also the one who carries around the keys of heavenly regions."[62]

The East's most eloquent and sustained witness on behalf of Peter's and of his successors' primacy was, of course, St. John Chrysostom.[63] For him, Peter was the "mouth of the apostles," the "conductor of the apostolic choir," the "fisherman of the world who fished for the whole world," nay, the "ruler of the entire world." The contrast Chrysostom drew between Jeremiah and Peter is just as telling about the universality of Peter's office. Jeremiah was made into a column of brass so that he might prove stronger than an entire nation, but Peter was made into a firm foundation so that it may extend all over the world and be stronger than all the worldly powers. Peter, according to Chrysostom, was appointed by Christ "to the see of the world because he entrusted him with the care of the whole world." To the question, why James was made the bishop of Jerusalem, Chrysostom had no hesitation in replying: "Christ made Peter not the teacher of that see but of the world." As to Christ's questioning Peter whether he loved him, Chrysostom's reply is no less to the point: "The master asked those questions so that he might teach us how much at heart he has the headship over these sheep."

Unlike some latter-day Catholic theologians and exegetes taken aback by Peter's denial of Christ, Chrysostom is far from being troubled. According to him, Christ allowed Peter to fall so that He might have an even more dramatic background to strengthen the other apostles' confidence in the one who was given the keys, by promising His prayers so that Peter would in fact strengthen the twelve and their successors. Such was the answer Chrysostom offered to his powerfully phrased question:

> He who built the Church upon his [Peter's] confession and so fortified it that ten thousand dangers and deaths should not prevail against it; he who gave him the keys of heaven and made him lord (possessor) of so much authority, and who needed no prayer for this (for he said not 'I have prayed' but with authority 'I will build' and 'I will give'), how did he need prayer that he might save the soul of one man [Peter]? The answer is to give confidence to the disciples, whose faith was weak.[64]

And just as learning humility and drawing confidence were the divinely intended lessons of Peter's fall for the apostles, much the same was the gist of divine pedagogy in respect to Peter, according to Chrysostom. In commenting on the post-Resurrection scene where Christ rebuked Peter who did not want John to join them, Chrysostom wrote: "He [Christ] moderates him [Peter] that he might not in the future have the same fault, when he should receive the government of the world, but that remembering his fault he might know himself." Concerning the outbreak of jealousy among the twelve as to which of them was the greatest, Chrysostom traced that incident to their realization of the prominence given by Christ to Peter. While the twelve could tolerate the pre-eminence of three—Peter, James, and John—they could not bear the even greater prominence given to Peter. And, according to Chrysostom, part of Jesus' answer to their indignation was his choosing Peter for the miraculous catch of the fish with the tax coin in its mouth, and that the tax was to be paid only on behalf of himself and Peter.

Chrysostom certainly did not notice anything derogatory to Peter's prominence in his handling the election of Matthias, the replacement of Judas. On the contrary, he saw in it the humility of a leader truly assured in his prominence. In order to cut off the possible charge of favoritism, Peter entrusted the outcome to lottery, although he had the power of constituting an apostle. On reflecting on Chrysostom's interpretation Erasmus noted that in Chrysostom's view Peter "habet jus constituendi par omnibus [apostolis]," that is, Peter had a constitutional power equal to that of all the twelve taken together.[65] Thus, according to Chrysostom, Peter did not have to call the council of Jerusalem; he alone could have settled all its business. Unlike many modern exegetes, Chrysostom did not overlook that Peter spoke last at the council as the one who had the last word. In commenting on Paul's assertion of his right to take along a sister-woman, Chrysostom called attention to the order in which Paul referred to the similar procedures of the apostles, the brethren of the Lord, and Cephas. "He [Paul] puts the leader last, for in that position he places his most powerful point. For it was not so wonderful to list the others . . . as it was to name the primate entrusted with the keys of heaven."[66]

Had Chrysostom been severed from communion with Rome for seventeen or perhaps twenty-six years as some claim, one would expect Chrysostom to sing the praises of Antioch, the first see of Peter and the see also of St.

Meletius and St. Flavian who for a while were the bone of contention between East and Rome. Chrysostom certainly praised Antioch, but all his praises were only a prelude for even greater praise for the see of Rome, the ultimate see of Peter:

> God has had great account of this city of Antioch, as he has shown in deed, especially in that he ordered Peter, the ruler of the whole world, to whom he entrusted the keys of heaven, to whom he committed the office of bringing all in to pass a long time here . . . But though we received him as teacher, we did not retain him to the end, but we gave him up to Royal Rome. Nay, but we did retain him till the end, for we do not retain the body of Peter but we retain the faith of Peter as though it were Peter himself; and while we retain the faith of Peter, we have Peter himself.[67]

Of course, that faith, the faith of Peter, had to include all the things that Peter had to believe in, among them the power of keys entrusted to him. Had Chrysostom not had that faith he would not have written a grateful letter to Pope Innocent for the efforts made on his behalf in those terrible years that saw the greatest doctor of the Eastern church and the greatest ever to occupy the see of Constantinople, the second Rome for some, run for dear life, threatened as he was by the evil that befell the Eastern churches: caesaropapism. Its threat to the church in the West was foiled largely because of the papacy's proximity there.

The continual threat of heresies presented, of course, a problem of its own which found in the see of Rome a powerful antidote, often sought and acknowledged by the churches in the periphery. Pope Innocent's solicitude for the churches of North Africa ravaged by Pelagius' heresy received, as was seen, the gratitude of Augustine, the greatest divine of the Western church. Augustine was also the one who saw no difficulty in either of the two acts of Innocent's successor, Pope Zosimus, to whom the Pelagians presented their case anew and purportedly with new evidence. Before this happened and before Zosimus learned of the rejection of that purported evidence by another synod of Carthage, Zosimus had made a declaration of the authority of the see of Rome "whose judgment no one should dare to dispute because so great an authority is attributed to the apostolic see by the tradition of the fathers." They, as Zosimus continued, knew fully both the fulness of powers given to Peter and his successors and its transmission in full to Rome where culminate "all human and divine laws and discipline."[68] Augustine's remark about the momentary hesitation of Pope Zosimus, who gave a hearing to a new plea of the Pelagians, that Zosimus should have rather looked up Innocent's rescriptum, was a recognition of Rome's authority.

Leo the Great and the Roman Centuries

Half a century later when Leo the Great began to preach on the anniversary of his election as bishop of Rome, and returned to a thematic reflection on the sharing by the popes of the office of Peter, he added to the subject only finesse but nothing substantive that had not been stated long before, either by acts or by words. The scores of bishops who gathered from all over Italy to hear those sermons could find nothing new in Leo's assertions that "the whole Church finds Peter in Peter's see,"[69] that the "honor of leadership, that is the honor of episcopate must be referred to the true head Christ,"[70] and that "the solidity of the faith of Peter, chief of the apostles, is perpetual in the Church."[71] But Leo certainly articulated with penetrating finesse the ontological nature of Peter's surviving in his office:

> He was ordained before the rest in such a way that from his being called the rock, from his being pronounced the foundation, from his being constituted the doorkeeper of the kingdom of heaven, from his being set as the umpire to bind and to loose, whose judgments shall retain validity in heaven—from all these mystical titles we might know the nature of his association with Christ. And still to this day he more fully and effectually performs what is entrusted to him and carries out every part of his duty and charge in him and with him, through whom he has been glorified. And so if anything is rightly done and rightly decreed by us, if anything is won from the mercy of God by our daily supplications, it is of his work and merits whose power lives and whose authority prevails in his See.[72]

Had Leo ever so slightly felt that he was claiming to himself something that was not entirely his, he would not have liberally spoken of Peter's keys as shared also by all bishops. But what they all shared Peter possessed in an eminent degree: "To Peter that power [of the keys and of binding and loosing] is confided singularly because the figure of Peter is set before all rectors of the Church." Indeed, that figure is not only one but also unique for God could have worked in many different ways: "Of all the world only one Peter is chosen who is put at the head of all the preaching to the totality of nations, of all the apostles and of all fathers of the Church, so that although in the people of God there are many priests and many shepherds, nevertheless Peter rightly rules all whom principally Christ rules as well."[73] Such was that "only Peter," so Leo declared in his fifth anniversary sermon, "who never ceased to preside over this see and who indefectibly obtains a consortium with the eternal priest."[74]

Consortium or sharing represented in Leo's reflections on the primacy of Peter and of his successors that aspect which is the touchstone of the Catholic doctrine about it and the touchstone of all doctrine which is Catholic. It was on that ground that Leo explained how Christ and Peter both could be rock. In fact Leo was so aware of the pivotal character of that aspect as to let Christ say: "Although I am the unshakable rock, the cornerstone, the foundation other than which no one can lay . . . you Peter are also a rock because you share in my strength, so that whatever power is appropriate to me will be common to you and me through sharing."[75] The same idea of sharing was stated shortly afterwards by St. Maximus, bishop of Turin, who in his fourth homily on Peter declared: "Rightly deserves a share in Christ's name [rock] he who also merited the sharing of [Christ's] work [to be the rock]."[76] Only that perspective of sharing made possible and justified what is possibly the most incisive and startling utterance on the keys of Peter, an utterance of St. Maximus: "Clavis coeli lingua est Petri," or "Peter's tongue is the key of heaven."[77]

This notion of sharing was a direct derivative from the realism which belief in the Incarnation must include if it is to keep its real object. The words spoken by the Incarnate God were expressive of an unflinching and sweeping realism which joined with no hesitation the material and the spiritual, the natural and the supernatural. The one who claimed that only the spirit gives life claimed in the same breath that eternal life could only be secured by his real body to be eaten as real food. No wonder that the realist aspect of Neoplatonism, the doctrine of participation, was found by the fathers and especially by Augustine as a useful means for interpreting revelation. The same was even more true of Aristotelian realism resting on the doctrine of the analogy of being, or the various degrees to which various things embody the same reality.

That both sacramental realism and the exercise of hierarchical power, and in particular of papal power, flourish together should not therefore be surprising. This is not to suggest that whatever is a high point for easy historical classifications is also an unmitigated blessing. The brevity of the High Middle Ages and the long crisis into which ecclesiastical reality turned afterwards is a case in point. The peril which indiscriminate use, if not overuse, presents to everything, however good, spared neither the medieval sacramental practice nor the papal power as practiced in the Middle Ages. The latter, contrary to some recent claim, did not have its first protagonists in early Franciscan theologians. Whatever their contribution to the notion of the primacy of the Roman see and of its infallibility, it was for them a natural contribution. Their spiritual father, the saint of Assisi, started both his rules with a call for obedience to the Roman pontiff. And whatever the evangelical and lay spirituality inspired by Francis, who declined priestly ordination and urged his sons and daughters to confess their sins to one another, he reminded all of them that only a confession made to a priest made them the beneficiary of the power of absolution.[78] Or as Paul Sabatier, a Protestant and one of the great students of the life of St. Francis, acknowledged: "Those who would set him up as a kind of precursor of Protestantism would be completely wrong . . . If I have deserved the reproach, I regret it."[79]

Precisely because Francis not only held high but also practised to the hilt the virtues of evangelical simplicity, the latter never was taken by him as a pretext to denounce popes and prelates whose lives were a far cry from it. No less importantly, Francis fully practised even the most difficult aspect of his preaching which under no circumstance allowed the repudiation of a superior who happened to command something contrary to the spiritual good. He raised no complaint and much less did he incite secession, when he, Francis, faced expulsion from the order, following the takeover by the talented and worldly Fra Elias who decided to subdue those wanting to live in truly evangelical poverty. Augustine's warning that no cause could justify schism was now echoed instinctively by another genuine stalwart of the gospel: "Should a superior command something contrary to their spiritual good, though the friars should not obey him, let them never separate themselves from him, and let them love him in proportion to his persecution of them."[80]

By Francis' time the power of the keys had come into so frequent use as to lead to plenty of abuses as well. Not that its use, as some contended, had mostly been rank abuse. At any rate, the supreme spiritual authority of the bearer of Peter's keys was reflected lucidly in Christian consciousness throughout the so-called Dark Ages. In the eighth century Venerable Bede registered one such instance as he discussed the case of some of St. Columba's spiritual sons, who long after his death wanted to retain his custom of fixing the date of Easter. Around 663 or so, the matter was brought before King Alchfrid by bishop Colman who made much of St. Columba's holiness. The opposite or Roman custom of fixing the Easter date was argued before the king by Bishop Wilfrid who brought his speech to a close by quoting Christ's words to Peter: "To thee I will give the keys of the kingdom of heaven." To the king's question, whether St. Columba had received similar authority from

Christ, Bishop Colman could only say no, to which the king replied:

> Agree ye both in this without any controversy, that these words were principally spoken unto Peter, and that unto him the keys of the kingdom of heaven were given? When both had answered, yea, the king concluded and said: Then I say unto you that I will not gainsay such a doorkeeper as this is; but as far as I know and am able, I will covet in all points to obey his ordinances, lest perhaps when I come to the doors of the kingdom of heaven, I find none to open unto me, having his displeasure, which is so clearly proved to bear the keys thereof.[81]

Almost half a millennium later, when the Dark Ages were to turn convincingly into the High Middle Ages, the office of the bearer of Peter's keys loomed just as large in Christian consciousness. Then as now great orators heavily relied on what was truly agreed upon by their audience, immediate and wider. Such an orator was Bernard of Clairvaux, who with his words could launch a crusade, as he uttered the great oratorical question ending on a famed hyperbolic phrase: "Who is more powerful than the one who was obeyed by the earth as it returned the dead; . . . who with the breath of his mouth struck down Simon Magus in the air; who received so singularly the keys of the kingdom of heaven that Peter's sentence should precede the sentence of heaven?"[82] In addition to being a great orator, Bernard was also a great saint, fully aware of the spiritual demands to be faced by the bearer of such power. Not only his former confrère, Pope Eugenius, but many around the latter had to become familiar with the contents of Bernard's essay in which Eugenius was given a powerful portrait of the lofty idea of a pope: "Who art thou? A great priest. A great priest—the chief pontiff. Thou art the prince of the bishops, thou art the heir of the Apostles, thou art Abel in primacy, Noah in government, Abraham in the patriarchate; in order thou art Melchisedech, in dignity Aaron, in authority Moses, in judgeship Samuel, in power Peter, in unction Christ. To thee the keys have been delivered, the sheep entrusted."[83]

Twilight with a Dark Finale

Something of that lofty and at the same time deeply spiritual vision shines through the dire warnings of which the papacy was the target during its Babylonian captivity. The future of the papacy was never in doubt for Dante, whatever his antagonism to some contemporary popes. He was full of reverence for St. Peter and his keys, as shown by many passages in the *Divina commedia*, where even the purely secular city of Rome is seen endowed with a special strength for renewal, whatever its occasional degrading into "a nest of depravity."[84] It did not occur to St. Bridget of Sweden to question the need for popes, cardinals, bishops, and priests after she identified them, in turn, as the doors, the hinges, and the floor of a "ruinous church" where

> the doors are hanging crooked, the hinges on which the doors should turn are rusty, or they have been twisted so that they do not fit any longer, the floor inside the church is full of deep holes, into which one can fall and be drowned, the roof is tightened with pitch and burns with a sulphurous flame, smoke is issuing from the burning roof, a mist rises from the pitfalls in the floor, the walls are blackened with soot, so that you cannot see any longer what color they once had.

No touch of revolt can be sensed in her utterly disconcerting interpretation of the floor, the bishops and priests,

> whose avarice is bottomless, and from whose lives in arrogance and luxury a stench arises which almost stifles the angels in heaven and the friends of God on earth.[85]

Even during that dark period of the Church, the Babylonian captivity of the papacy in Avignon, popes were not lacking who dared to see the situation for what it was, and to decry it, as Benedict XII did in no uncertain terms:

> The worship for which the clergy was established, is neglected; holders of benefices and canonicates, having loosed the reins of reason and modesty, have flung themselves into fields of license, pursuing their untamable passions. But, still more dangerous and disastrous, a great number of ecclesiastics, having shamefully cast off the yoke of continence to which they had subjected themselves, have followed, even as the horse and mule devoid of intelligence, their animal instincts, rather than the rule of reason, and they wallow in the slough of lust, and they keep concubines under the wing of her who should be the mother and guardian of good morals, that is, of the Church of God, that they have changed into a disorderly place, without stopping to consider the incalculable harm they are doing to their own selves.[86]

Whatever his spiritual independence, Benedict XII was not really a free agent. In view of the captivity which Avignon meant for the papacy, the efforts of some earlier popes such as Innocent III and Boniface VIII to let papal supremacy in temporal matters be recognized, may not seem a reckless grab for power. Barbarossa was still fresh in memory. The future could hold much worse in store and did, in fact, under

Henry VIII and Napoleon. Those great popes of the 13th century undoubtedly found subtle support in the artistic cliché, by then very old, which almost invariably puts two keys in Peter's hands. That artistic symbolism became a shadow cast far into future times. Paul VI must have felt something of its presence, as he emphatically noted to the Roman nobility gathered before him that the Church wanted to use henceforth only one key, the key of spiritual power.[87] It was a symbolic reply not only to those still hoping for the return of old political advantages through alignment with the Church, but also to those non-Catholic Christians who had a lingering doubt as to whether Vatican II had really turned a new leaf. The doubts in question were not strong. For the most part Protestants now widely concede that the Reformation had no small support in the vast entanglement of the Church in temporal goods and power, which were coveted by princes, nobles, and burghers, to say nothing of soldiers of fortune. It was not an emissary of Leo IX, of Clement VII, or of Paul III to rebels in the North but a former Catholic priest, turned rebel to the quite logical degree of claiming to himself the spiritual liberty and authority which Luther reserved to himself, Thomas Münzer of Anabaptist fame, who reminded Luther and his associates as early as 1524:

> That you appeared before the empire at Worms at all was thanks to the German nobles whom you had cajoled and honeyed, for they fully expected that by your preaching you would obtain for them Bohemian gifts of monasteries and foundations, which you now promise to the princes.[88]

By Luther's time the transfer of a property had for long been sealed by the remittance of the keys to its gates. No such orderliness could, of course, be observed in the expropriation of monasteries and other ecclesiastical properties, the largest in European history until the Jacobins and Bolsheviks came along, which Luther triggered by his message. The force of his words was enough to let many a monastery be abandoned by its occupants with no concern whatever for its keys. They felt that owing to the liberation by Luther of Christ's words they themselves could loosen the binding force of their solemn vows. But the keys to many monasteries had to be grabbed by force and by that secular force which in the Germany of Luther's time rested largely with the princes. For the survival of Lutheranism the support of no prince was more crucial than that of Landgrave Philip of Hesse, one of the most lustful characters in an age rich in lurid stories.

Lurid is also the only word, both theologically and morally, to characterize Luther's acceding to the landgrave's request that his lustful attention to a maiden of only sixteen be given ecclesiastical approval although he had been married for over two decades. In this ecumenical age, when tactful dialogues between Lutherans and Catholics count in the eyes of many Catholic theologians much more than the official and solemn declarations of their Church, the recall of such a story may count for a rude re-opening of a long-covered cancerous excrescence. But the story,[89] in which Luther played the principal role for over two years (1539–41) and which witnessed him ready for equivocations, dissimulations, and plain lies — all in the name of *the* "Word," is indispensable for an understanding of the next phase in the story of the words whereby the *Word* gave Peter the keys of the kingdom. The unsavory dialectic, which made itself manifest in Luther's handling of a most unsavory case, was a perfect illustration of the twofold logic of the Reformation. One was mere expediency in practical matters, the very charge which the Reformers constantly made against Rome. Their expediency implied among other things an unabashed reliance on the secular arm. Luther and his "general staff" (including Melanchton) could only tremble on learning of the landgrave's threat that if his taking that maiden was to remain equivalent to a mere concubinage and not a real marriage, he would side with the emperor and enforce all the legal sanctions against marriages attempted by monks and priests. The other aspect of that twofold logic consisted in a continual recourse to purely personal convictions (identified, of course, with the promptings of the Holy Spirit) as to what was God's revealed word, often believed to be objectified by its merely being printed.

Already in his dispute with Thomas Münzer on the question of the baptism of infants, Luther had to fall back on his own authority. This he did as if he had been a new pope. Infant baptism could only be justified if there was authoritative ecclesiastical tradition, a traditional power of keys to the kingdom, a power already rejected by Luther. In his handling the course of events, which led to his approving the landgrave's bigamy, his unabashed subjectivism forced Luther to uphold the righteousness of a plain lie which only the farthest stretch of imagination can equate with the Holy Spirit. He did so at the gathering of his "general staff" in Eisenach in the middle of June 1540, a gathering that desperately sought a solution to a problem despairingly impossible to resolve if both gospel and landgrave were to be satisfied. On the first day of that conference Luther declared: "What harm could it do if a man told a good, lusty lie in a worthy cause and for the sake of the Christian Church?" Two days later, on June 17, he added: "To lie in case of necessity, or for convenience, or in excuse, would not offend God, who was ready to take such lies on himself."[90] Such a lie could now serve as a key to be used not only to keep open the flow of the landgrave's good will, but also to open the kingdom of God for liars with an implicit justification of Judas whom Luther must have had in mind.

The lie in question was to tell the public that the landgrave was merely to take a concubine, hardly a major offence in a lustful age. This might have been enough for Luther to dodge the force of Christian logic, but hardly the logic of a practically pagan landgrave who in turn was caught in the most creditable logic of a maiden whom nothing less could satisfy than a real marriage. Thus Luther and his staff had to declare, and they did indeed, bigamy as an act pleasing to God. Now they really needed the landgrave's protection because the laws of the Holy Roman Empire, old laws promulgated again in 1532 in witness of the lawlessness unleashed by the Reform, had decapitation as punishment for bigamy.

This story has been recounted here for two reasons, both standing for an inner logic. One of them is often witnessed in the lives of those who most vehemently decry the papacy's abuses and are found in the end guilty of abuses of even worse kinds. In this respect Calvin's career is no less telling. The one, whose *Institutes* provided a badly needed conceptual structure for Reformed ideology, had to modify a phrase which in the first edition of the *Institutes* read as follows: "It is criminal to put heretics to death. To make an end of them by fire and sword is opposed to every principle of humanity."[91] Obvious should seem the reasons for that retractation. During the first five years of Calvin's rule in Geneva, heretics (that is, all those breaking the various disciplinary laws of a theocratic regime) fared very badly indeed. Thirteen of them were hanged, ten decapitated, and thirty-five burned at the stake. The latter was the kind of supreme cruelty about which such an unsympathetic observer of the pre-Reformation (and post-Reformation) Catholic Church as Stefan Zweig wrote: "To its honor it [the pre-Reformation Catholic Church] had for more than a thousand years hesitated to burn anyone alive simply because he insisted upon interpreting Christian dogmas in his own way."[92]

Zweig's remark was, of course, made in connection with Calvin's decisive instrumentality in the burning of not an ordinary heretic but of Michael Servetus, a heretic with European reputation. It was not from the side of counter-reforming Rome but from Reformed circles that came the first outcries against the supreme authority which Calvin claimed and assured to himself as a spiritual dictator.[93] And dictator he was, attentive to the slightest contestation of his supremacy. In the minute books of the Town Council of Geneva there are entries which record prison sentences for the "offense" of referring to Calvin not as Maitre Calvin but as mere Monsieur Calvin. The picture painted even by Calvinist historians[94] of Calvin's Geneva makes it appear that a most oppressive espionage system was set up there by Calvin, or at least with his full connivance, in the interest of "orthodoxy" and that he did his very best to justify it on theological grounds. No surprise. He could even justify the extra agony inflicted on heretics by unskilled executioners with the words: "It cannot have happened without the peculiar will of God that the condemned persons were forced to endure such a prolongation of their torments."[95] No less revealing should seem the torment of those burghers of Geneva who feared for their lives lest spies listening through the keyholes of their houses overhear their family conversations reduced to a mere whisper. That an administration guided by Calvin, who most radically rejected the traditional meaning of the keys given to Peter, had to spy through keyholes may seem logical; but it is sad. For whether one thinks of Luther's official approval of bigamy or of Calvin's systematic imposition of spiritual dictatorship in the name of the newly won Christian freedom, the rank abuse of power should seem less saddening than its coolly reasoned approval.

The other logic in question has nothing to do with personal probity to which the Reformers were especially committed by the inner logic of having made so emphatic claims to spiritual reform. Nothing would be more mistaken than to see in Luther only the hapless condoner of bigamy and in Calvin the spiritual tyrant, or in Reformation a mere onrush of weaklings unable to resist the pressure of opportunities. Long before Luther and Calvin came to the scene, the logic of Protestantism had been at work and in a way which meant to be distinctly spiritual. It animated some Franciscan spiritualists[96] and soon produced its theology which quickly ushered in the philosophy germane to it. Exaggerated longing for spiritual reality called for that intellectual exaggeration, nominalism, which in turn rapidly saw the real vanish in its bottomless bucket. Luther was a nominalist without even realizing it. Nor did Calvin care to take stock for himself of the philosophy in terms of which he was theologizing. Only much later did it dawn on Calvinists and Lutherans alike that they had been reading the Bible with a set of nominalist glasses which had nothing to do with it. By then, in the wake of what Kant had wrought, it was too late to make a consistent claim to that reality, the sacramental reality of the power of the keys, without which Christian community, let alone the Church, is unable to function. It was also part of that logic that its most thematic expression should have first come in a book by Luther which he rewrote twice in proof of the importance he attached to its subject. Very logically he entitled it *On the Keys*. It is indeed the key, both with its logic and its tone, to that breaking up of Christian unity compared with which the schism between West and East should seem a very minor matter. Luther's *On the Keys* signaled a dark finale for the twilight of Roman centuries. It also opened a new phase insofar as it anticipated all that had to be said within Protestantism on the keys which Christ gave to Peter.

CHAPTER 4
PETER'S KEYS IN PROTESTANT KEY

Two Reformers, One Inconsistency

As a young Augustinian monk, Martin Luther showed an early dislike for theology and a fondness for biblical studies. It was as a teacher of the Scriptures that he obtained a chair at the University of Wittenberg, succeeding there Staupitz, his superior, mentor, and future protector. Whatever his professional status, Luther always remained a turbulent mind, rebelling against mental discipline, be it called for by systematic theology or by a systematic study of the Bible. Rhapsodic is the most benevolent thing one can say of his handling of both disciplines. Actually, his handling of both was all too often sheer manhandling. He was not reluctant to insert repeatedly the word *alone* in rendering Paul's Letter to the Romans. As a result justification by faith became a matter of faith *alone*, and wrath and sin *alone* were the fruits of the Law.[1] His bible translation was a monument of style also in the sense that, as theological, intellectual, and political history proved it all too often, style carried far more weight than disciplined thought and sound scholarship. The rank liberties which Luther took with the text of the Bible were so many proofs of his despised Italians' dictum, *traduttore, traditore*. They also witnessed the true mentality of Luther's famed tract, *The Liberty of Christians*, in which a rhapsodic prose distracts from continually recurring inconsistencies.

Less rhapsodic though equally inconsistent is the much less remembered handling by Luther, the biblical theologian, of the main scriptural passages relating to keys. In his commentary on Isaiah he took the keys placed on the shoulder of Eliakim for the complete power he was to wield in the house of David. Similarly, he took Rv 3:7 as an application of Isaiah's passage to Christ, who himself stated that all power in heaven and on earth were given to him:

> It was customary for his [Jewish] people to carry keys around the neck and on the shoulder. "I will give him the keys" [Rv 3:7] means he will be the treasurer, the overseer of provisions and money, who will receive and disburse, and *without whose authority* no one will receive or expend *anything*. This is what it means to close and to open (Italics added).[2]

Such interpretation did full justice both to the text and to the entire tradition of biblical scholarship. There was nothing original in it, nor did it require qualifications suitable for a chair of biblical theology. Luther, the biblical theologian, did not display the elementary qualification, required from a mere beginner let alone from a scholar, of remembering his own words, when it came to his interpreting the keys of the kingdom given to Peter. In what he said of that passage in Matthew 16:19 there was no trace whatever of his understanding of the keys placed on the shoulders of Eliakim. In fact, in his long treatise *On the Keys* (1530) he not once considered the passage in itself. Of course, the power of keys was synonymous with the power of binding and loosing to which Luther continually returned in that treatise. But precisely because the two powers were synonymous, they were not identical; one had to contain a nuance which was lacking in the other. Furthermore, while the power of binding and loosing was given to Peter and to the twelve as well, the power of keys was given to Peter alone, a point which Luther passed over in silence. Luther, who a dozen years earlier in his commentary on Paul's Letter to the Romans, clearly spelled out his doctrine of justification by faith *alone*, could not, when it came to Peter's keys, repeat his own words about the keys given to Eliakim. Those very words implied power deposited in a person, whereas for Luther the keys given to Peter had to become the trusting faith of any Christian.

Almost at the outset of his *On the Keys*, Luther made matters clear as far as faith, as he took it, was concerned. First, he identified "the key which binds" with "the divine threat with which God threatens the hardened sinner with hell" and the "key which looses" with "the divine promise with which he [Christ] promises the humble sinner the kingdom of heaven." Then he noted, which was not entirely untrue, that threat and promise could be "comprehended by faith alone." On such premises, which did not include man's ability to make a reasoned judgment on threats and promises, he could simply declare: "The keys of Christ demand no work on our part but faith only."[3] It was not so simple a matter to reconcile with Christ's words that complete wreck to which Luther reduced the visible Church in 1520 in his three most memorable treatises: *Christian Liberty, Address to the German Nobility* and *Babylonian Captivity*. In fact the summary of his *On the Keys*, when taken out of its context, sounded so traditionally Catholic that it might have been written by a dramatizing Jesuit of Tridentine times. Yet it was not a Jesuit but Luther who made a first by describing Peter's tongue as Christ's "key-case":

> Christ says very clearly in Mt 16:19 that he will give the keys to Peter. He does not say he has two kinds of keys, but he gives to Peter the keys he himself has and no others. It is as if he were saying: "Why are you staring heavenward in search of my keys? Do you not understand I gave them to Peter? They are indeed the keys of heaven, but they are not found in heaven. I left them on earth. Don't look for them in heaven or anywhere else except in Peter's mouth where I have placed them. Peter's mouth is my mouth, and his tongue is my key-case. His office is my office, his binding and loosing are my binding and loosing. His keys are my keys, and I have no others, nor do I know of any others. What they bind, that is bound; what they loose is free, just as if there were no other to bind or to loose in heaven or on earth. If there are any other keys in heaven, on earth, or in hell, they do not concern me. I know nothing of them. Whatever they might bind or loose is not my affair. Therefore, don't concern yourself about it either, and don't be led astray. I pay attention only to what my Peter binds and looses. I rely on that, and you should do likewise. In so doing you are already bound and loosed as far as I am concerned. For Peter binds and looses in heaven and nobody else. This is the right way of thinking and speaking of the keys."

What Luther added in the next breath was the kind of Catholicism in which the visible Church turns into a mere Christendom:

> Here we have the true significance of the keys. They

are an office, a power, a command given by God through Christ to all of Christendom for the retaining and remitting of the sins of men.[4]

The wreck to which Luther had already reduced the visible Church was a wreck not only of the superstructure but also of the very foundations. The Luther of *sola fide* could have in mind only an office without an officer, a power without a potentate, a command without a commander. It was no accident that at this crucial juncture Luther spoke of Christendom and not of Church. For Luther, 1530 or so was the time of studied vagueness of which the Augsburg confession was the chief embodiment. Christendom was yet too Catholic and the life of Christians still too heavily immersed in the reality of a visible Church to make safe the doctrine of a church of the spirit. With the exception of small spiritualist churches springing up here and there, obeying in full the logic of the Reformation, Christians by and large would have revolted at the idea of throwing overnight the visible Church into the dustbin of history.

Luther himself was such a Christian. His devotion to Mary was genuine and he had a frantic longing for Christ's real presence in the Eucharist. Yet the spiritualist in him made him at times dismiss the necessity even of baptism.[5] Luther's inherited fondness for Catholic faith was clearly incompatible with the logic of his spiritualist theology. Both exacted their due as time went on. The traditional Catholic element, which, to mention only one thing, saw the erection of Lutheran churches dedicated to St. Peter, kept within Lutheranism a longing for Peter's chair insofar as it secured unity and protected sacramental reality. The logic of Luther's spiritualism worked in the opposite direction. It opened wider and wider the doors to the supremacy of private judgment. This in turn could but invite subjectivism, which is the hallmark of modern rationalism, naturalism, and secularism, and is also the very source of the ongoing fragmentation of Protestants—mergers, ecumenism, and World Council of Churches notwithstanding.

Only those familiar with the unabashedly pagan humanism of a Goethe can appraise the true significance of the admission by prominent 20th-century Lutherans that the freedom advocated in Luther's *Liberty of Christians* is only a short remove from Goethe's ideal of humanity.[6] Only those mindful of the wilful subjectivism of German idealism would be impressed by Harnack's admission that the naturalism if not plain paganism of Kant and Fichte are beckoning in the *Liberty of Christians*.[7] It should not be difficult to guess the feelings of Luther were he allowed to return to a largely de-christianized Saxony. Nor would it be more difficult to conjure up a downcast Calvin were he to see present-day Geneva which under him had its theocratic days. Not that the same did not happen in Roman Catholic lands. But while there the de-christianization does not claim "Christian" origins, in Protestant parts the connection has become a cultural perspective against which conservative Lutherans and Calvinists can protest with little if any consistency. Their predicament is ultimately a piece of that inconsistency with which both Luther and Calvin read the passage on keys in Isaiah and in Matthew respectively. As to Calvin, he was all traditional common sense in his commentaries on Isaiah when it came to the keys of Eliakim:

> We need not spend much time, as some do, in drawing from it an allegorical meaning; for it is taken from an ordinary custom of men. The keys of the house are delivered to those who are appointed to be stewards, that they may have the *full* power of opening and shutting according to their *own pleasure* . . . By the keys, therefore, he [Isaiah] means here the government of the king's house, because the principal charge of it would

be delivered to Eliakim at the proper time (Italics added).[8]

This meaning of the keys, exuding common-sense attention to the obvious, Calvin wanted to keep in the second half of his comments. Intention was one thing, the inner logic of his theology another. He could not read Isaiah without "reforming" Matthew. Calvin lost no time in insisting that because of the plain obvious meaning of what Isaiah meant by keys, Eliakim was not to be regarded a type of Christ in the book of Revelations, for the "prophet does not here describe any hidden mystery but borrows a comparison from the ordinary practice of men as if the keys were delivered to one who has been appointed to be steward, as has been already said." The logic of Calvin's theology clearly made him jump a step as if he had a "hidden mystery" up his sleeve, although he played his cards with subtle shifts from the obvious to the hidden, if not plainly contrived. In turning in the next breath to Matthew 16:19, Calvin first reasserted the obviousness of the metaphor: "It is idle and foolish to spend much time in endeavoring to find a hidden reason, when the matter is plain and needs no ingenuity." Yet it took some ingenuity to state as Calvin did that "for this very reason Christ calls 'the office of the teaching the word' (Mt 16:19) 'the keys of the kingdom of heaven.' "[9]

Whatever this very last remark of Calvin, hardly an obvious meaning of Mt 16:19, it should have been obvious to him that everything he asserted about Eliakim in terms of the metaphor of the keys he should have asserted about Peter. Elementary consistency demanded that what could be plainly and obviously seen in Isaiah's words about Eliakim, should also be seen in Christ's words to Peter, as the words of both were the use of the same metaphor and addressed to a single person and not to an office. All that Calvin should

112 THE KEYS OF THE KINGDOM

now have done, in order to remain consistent with the Scriptures, would have been to shift his very words from plural to singular and replace 'royal house' with 'house of the King of Kings.'

> The keys of the kingdom of heaven are delivered to him who is appointed to be steward, that he may have the full power of opening and shutting according to his own pleasure . . . By the keys therefore he [Christ] means here the government of the house of the King of Kings [Rv 3:7] because the principal charge of it would be delivered to Peter at the proper time.

Had Calvin written this, Calvinist reformation and the Reformation itself might have become a powerful stimulus for true reform within an undivided Christendom, and not a dogged distraction from the obvious meaning of key scriptural passages. As to the latter, Calvin's remark in the same context on Matthew 16:19 is worth recalling as it determined countless subsequent comments on that passage. They reveal an unwillingness to take the passage in itself and to take its scene as it was. To introduce as Calvin did, "ministers" to that scene was dictated not by the Bible but by the logic of Calvinist theology. The reason formerly attributed to Christ quickly transformed into Calvin's reason: "The reason is that ministers, by the preaching of the word, open the entrance into heaven and lead to Christ, who alone is the way."[10] The appearance of the word *alone* in this context was part of that consistency which could not have remained true to itself had it passed consistently from Eliakim to Peter. That word *alone* had to be inserted right there and then, for the *soli Deo* of Calvin was a piece with Luther's *sola fides*. In neither was there room for that sole power of God which, if truly infinite, can make a creature share in his very powers.

Calvin's systematic commentary on Matthew 16:19 was to proceed along the same lines except that there he spelled out in detail the logic of inconsistency. As one would expect, he introduced at the outset the "ministers of the word," or the "ministers of the gospel."[11] No less unexpectedly he underplayed the force of the metaphor of keys insofar as it stood for power in the hands of the one holding them. He did this both with respect to the office itself and to its holder. The public office or apostleship, of which Christ begins now to speak in saying, "And I will give thee the keys," became in Calvin's version the public preaching of the gospel. The office was that of ordinary teachers of the Church, an upgrading of the office of "temporary teachers" which the twelve were, according to Calvin, until then. It was therefore inconsistent on Calvin's part to claim that in giving the keys to Peter, Christ did not confer on Peter anything that he had not received already when he was chosen to be one of the twelve. But this inconsistency was needed so that Peter's profession of faith might become in Calvin's hands the type of any profession of faith with the same rewards. The reward was anything but functioning as a foundation. The difference between *Petrus* and *petra* was for Calvin a proof that by "on this rock" Christ meant "something *totally different* from the person of Peter" (Italics added).[12] It followed therefore logically that a higher ranking either of Peter or of his successors was a mere rank and not an extra power implicit in their office:

> And even granting that something more was bestowed on Peter than on the rest, that he might hold a distinguished place among the Apostles, it is a foolish infer-

ence of the Papists, that he received the primacy, and became the universal head of the whole Church. Rank is a different thing from power, and to be elevated to the highest place of honor among a few persons [the twelve] is a different thing from embracing the whole world under his dominion. And in fact, Christ laid no heavier burden on him than he was able to bear. He is ordered to be the porter of the kingdom of heaven; he is ordered to dispense the grace of God by *binding* and *loosing*, that is, as far as the power of a mortal man reaches. All that was given to him, therefore, must be limited to the measure of grace which he received for the edification of the Church; and so that vast dominion, which the Papists claim for him falls to the ground.[13]

All this was a wasting of words because according to Calvin mortal man could have no sacramental powers. As to his designation of Peter as "porter of the kingdom of heaven," it should seem to be "prophetic" in view of the lowly status connected with the office of a porter in the present-day usage of the word. No one today would think of a porter as undisputed head of the house whose keys he holds. His office would conjure up to no one today an immovable post given in perpetuum. Indeed, in Calvin's eyes any minister was removable and automatically unqualified by unworthy conduct. As to the Church of Rome of his times, which then too had its goodly share of virtuous Christians and of saints, Calvin could see "no mark of a Church there." He made this all too clear in his *Institutes* which antedated his biblical commentaries that have just been reviewed. Typically, among the *Institutes*' thousands of references to Scripture one would look in vain for a reference to the keys placed on the shoulder of Eliakim, keys whose true meaning Calvin recognized though not without trying to take the sting out of it.

Clearly, Calvin's were efforts to make the keys given to Peter appear as not really being keys with an obvious meaning. Worse, those efforts had set a pattern. But when the obvious is resisted clarity ceases to be transparent, even if it is the clarity of the gospel. This point was made by one, St. Francis de Sales, who observed at close range what had been said in Geneva in the decades immediately after Calvin:

> Our Lord, after having said to St. Peter that he would build on him his Church, continues, so that we may know more clearly what he wanted to say, in these terms: "And I give you the keys of the kingdom of heaven." One could not speak more clearly, for he had said: "Blessed are you Simon Bar Jonah, because flesh etc., And I say to you that you are Peter and I give you etc." This "I give you" refers to the same to whom he said "And I say to you," that is, to Peter. But the [Calvinist] ministers do their utmost to muddy the clear fountain of the gospel so that St. Peter himself would not find there his keys and we might not taste there the waters of holy obedience one owes to the vicar of our Lord; and therefore they prefer to say that St. Peter received that promise from our Lord in the name of the entire Church without having received any special privilege in his own person. But if this is not to violate the [sense of the] Scriptures, nothing will ever violate it. If it is allowed to proceed in such a way in finding the meaning of so clear words, there will remain nothing in the Scriptures that might not be twisted in any sense whatsoever.[14]

Calvin must have felt something of the possibility that his interpretation of the keys of Peter might turn into a boomerang, as in fact it did when Castellio pointed a heavy finger at him as one who claimed to himself infallible authority. This is perhaps why the *Institutes'* long disputes of Roman claims invariably shift from theological arguments into denunciations of Roman depravity. This tactic proved itself to be the most effective boomerang whereby the *Institutes* can hit its author, keen as he was on logic. For one, Calvin emphatically urged that unholy comportment inside the "Reformed" church can in no way be a justification for anyone wishing to part with it on that ground. Tellingly, that unwittingly so Roman a passage in the *Institutes*[15] is introductory to Calvin's discussion there of the meaning of the keys. For another, Calvin's seeing, together with Luther, the papacy as the Beast of the Apocalypse and the pope as the Antichrist, was most unbiblical. In the Bible the denial of the divinity of Christ is the mark by which the Antichrist should be recognized. The papacy has been the most effective antagonist of that vice which in fact has become the hallmark of liberal and modernist tendencies of which Protestant churches in vain tried to dissociate themselves. To speak only of most recent years, the Roman church had the strength to deny the status of Catholic theologian to a Hans Küng precisely because of his ambivalence on the divinity of Christ. At the same time Protestant churches kept in their bosom the blatantly antitrinitarian James Pyke and the no less unorthodox spokesmen of the "myth of the Word Incarnate."

The Key to True Reform

The truth of the foregoing remarks may seem to stand or fall with a truth, which, being the truth about a particular phase of history, would hardly ever invite consensus. About the respective measure of vice and virtue in the Church of

Renaissance and Reformation times few remarks are so appropriate as a dictum of Chesterton: "Human history is so rich and complicated that you can make out a case for any course of improvement or retrogression."[16] Yet no small improvements should seem to have taken place from Innocent VIII and Alexander VI if, in Luther's very words, no one could assail the reputation of Leo X who had just declared him a "true heretic" in June 1520.[17] Only two years later it should have passed for another great improvement that, contrary to all expectations, Florenz Boeyens, a Cardinal of most austere life, was elected successor to Leo X. In that election the improvement may have come about through a direct intervention of God, at least in the eyes of those longing for reform and they were not a few in number outside Luther's camp. The Dutch-born cardinal-archbishop of Tortosa was not even present at the conclave which elected him. Nor was his name considered until, after a deadlock of nine ballotings, it was almost incidentally brought up by Cardinal Giulio di Medici on January 8, 1522. The move, perhaps a mere tactic, had a domino effect in the conclave whose two-thirds majority was no less surprised than its minority outraged. Majority and minority could now only wait for the consent of the future Adrian VI. The outcome was unexpected by all and unwelcome by many. Among the latter were Luther and his "spirituals" to whom even Pope Adrian's German nationality was no saving grace.[18]

Spiritualism was one thing, spirituality another. Christian spirituality starts with the recognition of one's sinfulness, coupled with the readiness to forgive others not seven but seventy times seven. God's forgiving our wrongdoings is predicated on the unconditional readiness to forgive those who have wronged us. Few popes were less guilty of wrongdoing than was Adrian and no pope asked more humbly and more publicly for forgiveness than he. Adrian's instruction, which his legate Francesco Chieregati was to read before the Imperial Diet gathered in Nuremberg in the fall of 1522, is spirituality itself:

> You are also to say that we frankly acknowledge that God permits this persecution of his Church on account of the sins of men and especially of prelates and clergy; ... We know well that for many years things deserving abhorrence have gathered around the Holy See; sacred things have been misused, ordinances transgressed, so that in everything there has been a change for the worse. Thus it is not surprising that the malady has crept from the head to the members, from the popes to the hierarchy. We all, prelates and clergy, have gone astray from the right way, and for long there is none that has done good; no, not one. To God, therefore, we must give all the glory and humble ourselves before him; each one of us must consider how he has fallen and be more ready to judge himself than to be judged by God in the day of his Wrath ... Therefore in our name, give promises that we shall use all diligence to reform before all things the Roman Curia, whence, perhaps, all these evils have had their origin; thus healing will begin at the source of sickness ... We desire to wield our power not as seeking dominion or means for enriching our kindred, but in order to restore to Christ's bride, the Church, her former beauty, to give help to the oppressed, to uplift men of virtue and learning, above all, to do all that beseems a good shepherd and a successor of blessed Peter.[19]

This meant also that spirituality was not to become spiritualism. The latter was self-seeking with a heavy reliance on the kind of dialectic which turns dialogue into filibuster. Its perennial modernity could be opposed only by the timelessness of the only access to revealed truth which

Adrian conveyed in St. Ambrose's words: "Away with the arguments by which men try to arrive at belief; we believe in the Fisherman not in dialecticians."[20]

Contrary to Adrian's hopes, by 1523 Luther and his spirituals were inextricably caught in their dialectic. Not that the pope had no forebodings of the worst. A month after his instructions were read by his legate before the imperial diet, he wrote to Erasmus, whom he tried to enlist in the cause of reform, that he accepted the tiara

> only because we see so many thousands of souls, redeemed by the blood of Christ . . . souls belonging, after the flesh, to peoples of our own race — led away on the direct path of destruction through the hope of an evangelical freedom which, in very truth, is a bondage to the devil.[21]

A bondage certainly it was to its own logic. No sooner had Luther and his spirituals learnt of the pope's instruction than there appeared the most distasteful anti-papal pamphlet ever written. In that pamphlet, entitled "Pope-Ass," pope and papacy were literally turned into an ass with crudely obscene connotations. Luther was so pleased with it that in 1545 the picture of the "pope-ass" was selected by him for inclusion in his collection of "Illustrations of the Papacy." As to the pope's instructions, he despised them with the words: "The pope is a *magister noster* of Louvain; in that university such asses are crowned; out of his mouth Satan speaks."[22] In March 1523 he urged the heads of all religious orders in Germany to break their vows, marry, and divide among themselves their orders' property. By then he had been for almost ten years *against* reform in religious orders. Originally an observant Augustinian, around 1514 he defected to the non-observants, a move which quickly earned him the name "apostate" among the reform-minded.[23]

This is not to suggest that Luther was a profligate, or that his often quoted hyperbolic phrases about vigorous sinning coupled with even more vigorous faith should be taken for so many categorical incitements to sin.[24] Not a saint either, he was a baffling mixture of vice and virtue. The gamut of his comportment freely swung back and forth between raging hatred and quiet domesticity. He did not yield to the countless opportunities to make himself rich from the proprietary spoils of the Reformation. A hard working man, he was always mindful of his duties as a teacher and minister. Unlike Calvin, who notoriously shied away from ministering to victims of the plague, Luther could rise heroically to the occasion. When in mid-1528 the plague took hold of Wittenberg and many, including the university itself, fled the city, he stayed behind to attend the sick and the dying. Whatever his continual denunciations of acts of devotion, devout he was to the core. But in his entire spiritual physiognomy one virtue, that of humble submission, was conspicuously missing, although it had been the mainstay of Christian righteousness ever since the Sermon on the Mount. There, loving submission even to one's enemies was held high and the readiness to go an extra mile with the one unjustly imposing a mile-long service was declared to be the road to perfection. Humble submission to authority was an ever recurring theme in the canonical letters written by the apostles and in all the great classics of Christian spirituality. It certainly was a major theme in the *Imitation of Christ*, a product of German spiritual soil and already a hundred years old when Luther came to the scene. Without that virtue, no other virtue could be safe and no project or course of action sure of heavenly provenance. In the unanimous view of all masters of spirituality it was the par excellence antidote to evil, individual and corporate. Luther, the Augustinian friar and a great admirer of the bishop of Hippo, could hardly be ignorant of the importance laid by St. Augustine on the virtue of obedience which makes sense only if there is ecclesial authority properly so–called.[25]

As a matter of fact, awareness of humble submission as the indispensable tool in coping with any and all problems within the Church was all too vivid among the best in the Christendom of Luther's times. A most instructive case in point was the vast letter on the unity of the Church which Reginald Pole addressed to his cousin, Henry VIII, in late 1536. By then Pole had been repeatedly the target of the efforts of Henry who wanted his cousin's talent and royal blood (a Tudor and a Plantagenet with almost as much claim to the throne as Henry could muster) to serve English caesaropapism. Pole had enough strength to decline the archbishopric of York when Henry offered it to him on the death of Cardinal Wolsey in late 1530. He had at that time not enough perspicacity to size up a festering situation, although he could not fail to notice the rebuffed king's momentary urge to kill him.[26] He did not refuse the king's financial help which in 1532 made it possible for him to remove himself to the continent. It was there that he heard in the summer of 1536 the news of the beheading of John Fisher and Thomas More which sent shockwaves of indignation through the entire Christendom though not through Wittenberg. Pole himself was shaken as never before: "Then I judged that those words of Isaiah pertained to me no less than they did to the prophet himself: 'Lift up thy voice like a trumpet' "(58:1).[27]

Pole's voice was the voice of Christian humility which tempers indignation however justified. Whatever the firmness with which he spelled out the evil of the king's position, the sincerity of his love and respect for the king could not be doubted. As far as arguments went, Pole's immediate targets were the advisers of Henry on the primacy of the pope, one of them being Richard Sampson, bishop of Chichester. Pole's staunch and lengthy defense of the traditional meaning of Matthew 16:16–19 need not be reviewed here in detail. Mention should, however, be made of his pointed reminder to the king that if he wanted to know about the meaning of apostolic succession and of the list of the popes of the first four centuries, he could find it in St. Augustine.[28] No less important should seem Pole's reference to the Council of Florence where East joined West less than a hundred years earlier in recognizing the primacy of Peter and of his successors.[29] As to the meaning of the keys given to Peter, Pole emphasized three points. One was the global character of the powers symbolized by the keys:

> Christ said: "And I will give to thee the keys of the kingdom of heaven. And whatsoever thou shalt loose on earth, it shall be loosed also in heaven" (Mt 16:19). What was the need for promising such great things to Peter in that passage, if not to give Peter the principal position of being the head of the Church? Justly, indeed can Peter speak like Moses whom God appointed leader of the people of Israel and as head of the Synagogue: "Lord why hast thou laid the weight of all this people upon me? I am not able alone to bear all this people" (Nm 11:11–14). For thus Peter could speak when he heard he had been made the rock upon which the weight of the Church would rest, the rock that should support the Church: "Lord, why hast thou laid the weight of all this people upon me?" For Peter's multitude was different by far. This multitude did not embrace one people but all nations. It embraced the inheritance of Christ concerning which it is said: "Ask of me, and I will give thee the Gentiles for thy inheri-

tance, and the utmost parts of the earth for thy possession" (Ps 2:8).[30]

Another point was the unfailing access for the holder of that power to divine assistance:

> When therefore, Peter understood such a burden would be laid upon him—for he certainly knew if he had only a brief moment for thinking about it—could he restrain himself from crying out with great tremor: "Lord, why hast thou laid the weight of all this people upon me?" (Nm 11:11). But Christ anticipated all these thoughts of Peter . . . He immediately continued his words without interruption and added: "And the gates of hell shall not prevail against it." This was just as though Christ had said: "When I say I will build my Church upon you, do not fear lest you cannot sustain such a position against enemies. For I have broken gates of brass, and burst iron bars . . . I have crushed the power of your enemies, visible or invisible . . . I will open heaven to you. I will give you the power to open it for others. I will give you the keys of heaven so you might then perpetually summon assistance against every kind of enemy. I will renew a covenant of friendship. I will bring peace. It will be such a peace that whatsoever you loose upon earth it shall also be loosed in heaven. Whatsoever you bind upon earth it shall be bound in heaven."[31]

The third point was the undiminished measure of Peter's power, the sharing in it by the twelve notwithstanding:

> Here we can understand the magnitude of the power given to Peter! How clear these words are in this passage, how much they point in every respect to the person of Peter when it is said: "I will give to thee the

> keys of the kingdom of heaven"! This is so evident that if nothing else had been presented, this very great authority conferred upon Peter in that passage saying: "Thou art Peter, and upon this rock I will build my Church" would alone have shown most clearly the magnitude of the position entrusted to Peter. It would have shown most clearly that he had been made head of the Church. Sampson's presenting the fact that the same power of remitting and loosing sins was afterward given to all the apostles, in no way at all diminishes Peter's dignity. Though these words were declared to all the apostles as well as to Peter, they were declared to Peter in a superior way than they were to the other apostles. This great power conferred upon the apostles, moreover, did not diminish the dignity of Peter any more than the dignity conferred upon Moses by God was lessened when God took this same spirit from Moses to whom he had given it, and imparted it to the seventy ancients.[32]

And in recalling Moses' rebuke of Joshua, a young man who felt Moses' position threatened by the seventy, Pole remarked with gentle sarcasm: "Who except the young man fears this?" — a remark that cut to size Johnny-come-lately self-made popes. Pole had cut them to size long before he came to the doctrinal points about the keys also in respect to the key to true reform. Concerning the question constantly raised by the Reformers about unworthy prelates, Pole asked Sampson to consider what Peter would say if he returned to earth?

> He would see a Church in which the people are governed by the bishops and the bishops by the archbishops, a Church where all the authority of these rulers is subordinated to that of one man who acts in the place of Christ ... Would Peter judge that this

order should now be taken away on account of the more or less disorderly life of one man? Who can think Peter would do this? Who except some impious person would attribute this to his most holy character? Especially since all men know that he who holds the position of supreme head in the Church, whether he be good or bad, does not receive the honor bestowed. The honor is conferred not on a man but on the person of Christ through man.[33]

Then Pole quoted from Peter's first letter the injunction to obey unjust rulers because "this is thankworthy, if for conscience towards God, a man endure sorrows, suffering wrongfully. For what glory is it, if committing and being buffeted for it, you endure? But if doing well you suffer patiently: this is thankworthy before God" (1 Pt 2:19–20). From this Pole drew for Sampson's consideration the inference that Peter who urged obedience to unjust pagan rulers would hardly require less with respect to such rulers who are also Christian, let alone with respect to a ruler over matters spiritual. With that, Pole turned to the king:

> Do your followers say this man is the Roman pontiff? Surely, when they have gathered together all the shameful things in his life, for the satisfaction of their own wanton desires, these men can say nothing more insulting about an evil pontiff than that he was a ruler professing the religion of Christ, that he harshly threatened those who did anything contrary to religion, even though he himself took no part in religious observance. What then? Shall we obey such a man? What does Peter say? Indeed, Peter does not speak of such a case. But if this ruler were a stranger to religion, if he even opposed religion, nevertheless Peter thinks he should be obeyed. All the more, therefore, should we conclude that it would be Peter's opinion that that man

should be obeyed. This is so even though he professed religion and was most severe in his judgment of those who were heretics and were withdrawn from religion. If we can thus truly conclude, so would Peter also reply to this question . . . You, however, select a few of the worst pontiffs and place all their vices before our eyes. Thus you would lead all away from obedience to the pontiffs. But other Christians well know how very good some pontiffs have been! . . . By your deceptions you place before our eyes the vices of a few. As though there never were any pontiffs, as though authority had never been given to one of them, you would take away all authority from the vicar of Christ. Would you remove the apostolate itself by mentioning only the name of Judas and relating only his crime and treachery toward the Lord, while you passed over in silence the names and virtues of the other apostles? By this one act you show that you rival Judas himself in the magnitude of your crime. Just as Judas handed over Christ the Lord to the leaders of the priests, you are now betraying the vicar of Christ and with him, all priests. You do this when you hand him over to the rulers and kings. By this one crime you betray the universal Church.[34]

And so was betrayed Christian spirituality. Pole had the courage to remind Henry that his own habits were not at all better than the habits of the worst popes. Not that Pole rested his case with good pontiffs. Had he done so he would have cast doubt on the spiritual merit of obedience:

But what if he were a good pontiff? Would this be a sufficient reason why we should venerate him? Are we not accustomed to venerate the person of Christ in the pontiff rather than the uprightness of any man? If no Christian can say that he bestows honor upon the uprightness of a man and not upon the person of Christ alone, of what concern is it to me whether that man is good or bad in whom only the person of Christ is honored? . . . If an image of Christ is to be venerated, does it matter whether that image is beheld portrayed in gold or wood? Will you honor an image made from gold or ivory? Will you bestow insults and confer less honor upon an image fashioned from wood as if from something cheap and rotten? How does the wickedness of pontiffs pertain to me, since I know it cannot impede me unless I so desire? For all their power is for edification; none of their power is a hindrance to anyone's soul. But what if the wickedness of one man who is pontiff is truly not a hindrance to Christians but instead a benefit? What if it displays even more the glory of Christ? For what great and remarkable thing would we do by bestowing honor upon a good pontiff? As if even the pagans themselves do not do this! By the very fact that we seem not to be deterred, however, by human vices; by the very fact that we nonetheless venerate the image of Christ in him who sits on the tribunal of Christ and maintains the unity and harmony of the Church; by this very fact we show ourselves truly Christians. In this way the glory of Christ is especially demonstrated.[35]

Last but not least, refusal to accept unworthy pontiffs was a sign of lack of faith in Christ's power; a sign of inability to hear the voice of the great architect of the Church:

Simon Bar-Jona was the name of a man; what he himself had received from his father according to the flesh still remained in his weak nature. But when Christ said he would establish him over the Church, he changed this name. He added immediately: "And I say to thee: thou art Peter; and upon this rock I will build my Church" (Mt 16:18). Indeed Sampson, if you can hear the voice of the architect, you need not fear any weakness. If you fear that he cannot do this, he is the same who made all things out of nothing. His word is his deed. You heard him say that Simon Bar-Jona was Peter. Reflect now that it has been done. Simon is Peter. From a weak foundation comes a stable effect. And upon this rock the Church has been founded. There should be no further fear that the winds or the rushing floods will destroy the edifice. The edifice is now founded not on sand or Simon; it is founded upon Peter. If you will still doubt concerning this, consider the very great power of the architect. You behold him who created everything by a word! What terrifies you now? Is the hand of the Lord shortened? Can he not preserve such a fragile work, can he not make it permanent since he created all out of nothing all that will endure forever?[36]

Faith indeed was the ultimate foundation of loyalty to Christ's words and work. And if such a faith was to be genuine, it had to be tested like gold in a furnace. Roman Pontiffs could be so wrong as to mistake at times their most loyal sons for their worst enemies. To this possibility not even the most spiritual popes were an exception. Long before his accession to Peter's chair in 1555 Paul IV was a foremost champion of reform and spirituality. A founder in 1522 of the Theatine Order, the future Paul IV was a cardinal colleague of Pole in the commission charged with the reform draft of what later became the framework of the Council of Trent. Pole was made papal legate to England and Archbishop of Canterbury by that same pope who, on account of Pole's distrust of Spain, lost trust in the loyalty of Pole who with Mary Tudor's help reconciled England with Rome. While Mary kept to herself the pope's order that Pole return to Rome, she had to inform him of the papal decree which put an end to Pole's office as papal legate.

The news broke Pole's health (he was in the grave within half a year) but his loyalty remained unbroken because his faith was riveted on objective truth and not on subjective assurance, an assurance which set the tone of all that the Reformers and their successors said about faith. It brought about, already in Luther's Wittenberg and in Calvin's Geneva, the worst Babylonian captivity in store for Christians, the captivity to private interpretation. Worse, it could not be their own interpretation but an interpretation imposed on them by Reformers unable to agree among themselves on more than one crucial doctrinal point. The air of superiority was in evidence even in those few among them who were ready to allow "for the sake of peace and general unity of Christians" the continuation of the papacy as a purely human institution, provided the "pope would allow the gospel."[37] It was a concession restricted to the part of Christendom still under the pope and a concession not to be considered by the vast majority of the Reformers. Nor would they perceive that by rejecting hierarchical authority they could not impose in its place the gospel but only their private interpretation of it, never a key to objective meaning.

The Key to the Keys

An ever fresh instructiveness would have been retained by Pole's book even if it contained only the inner theological logic which is at work whenever the obvious meaning of a key scriptural passage is accepted or resisted. What makes Pole's book even more valuable is the broaching there of the more philosophical point of obviousness or rather the attitude to it. Since no sceptic is ever sceptical about his own scepticism, and no determinist is reluctant to make up his mind freely, it would be most surprising to find a Protestant who would protest even his own Protestantism. Protestantism is no less dogmatic than Roman Catholicism and in fact even more so if dogmatism is taken for a rigid concentration on a narrow aspect of a multifaceted message. It shows something of Pole's penetrating mind that he began his vast, perhaps too vast, *Defense of the Unity of the Church* with this very point. A thoroughly loyal adherent to Peter's chair and to a millennium-and-a-half-old Catholic Church, he was anything but a narrowminded adherent. His departure from the second session of the Council of Trent has often been taken, somewhat maliciously, for proof that he was much too broadminded with respect to the Lutheran doctrine of justification by faith alone. Pole certainly had a deep grasp of the role of faith not only as it stood for an objective creed but also as a subjective act. No less vivid was his loyalty to the idea and fact of Christian monarchy of which his beloved England was a case. But he was not blindly loyal. In fact, he was most clearsighted concerning the central intellectual issue with respect to Henry. Pole would have already come very close to the heart of the matter had he merely noted that arguing from the Scriptures is rather fruitless with anyone, who like Henry places "so little value on the general agreement of the Church."[38] In fact in the absence of any general agreement which, if it stands for meaning and not merely for the same jargon, is also epistemological, any discussion about any text, be it *Beowulf* or *The Thousand and One Nights*, can at most establish what was actually written. The truly important question of what was meant by what was written demands for its resolution, if it is to be broadly accepted, such an epistemological consensus. In the absence of it, disputes and even dialogues inevitably deteriorate into futile reassertions of already worn-out statements. In Pole's phrasing of Henry's position, this was equivalent to Henry's hearing one single phrase from the Scriptures much more vividly than other phrases. Or as Pole confronted Henry:

> You hear only the words "Honor the king," words you interpret contrary to the authority of Peter whose honor you now dispute. You claim you are his equal in honor and power. I offer no new examples here when I say you hear the words of Christ presenting the most valuable testimony on behalf of Peter's entrusted authority: "And I will give to thee the keys of the kingdom of heaven" (Mt 16:19). You hear that the care of Christ's flock is entrusted to Peter in the words of Christ himself: "Peter lovest thou me? Feed my lambs" (Jn 21:17). Though you hear all these words, you are moved even more by those words of the apostle: "Honor the king" . . . Although you present only one point having not even the most tenuous resemblance to an argument from reason, as long as it may be distorted in accord with your own desires you grab at it, retain it, and cling to it. Yet you demand, God willing, that I should believe you are guided by the light of reason. You can say this because you and your followers claim some kind of power that surpasses reasonable proof.[39]

Had Pole argued more broadly against the Protestant position he could have still said much the same. He merely should have changed the phrase "honor the king," as the phrase alone to be heard, to the phrase "justified by faith alone." His reference to some kind of power that surpasses reasonable proof should of course have stayed as the punchline certainly valid for Luther.

As is well known, Luther perceived the inner logic of his position to the extent that ultimately it was not the Bible but the undefinable power of the "Word" which served for him as the ultimate forum of appeal. There only his presumed infallibility could, however, serve as that forum. There the supreme criterion of truth was Luther's own sense of superiority which manifested itself in utterances that put him in a class by himself among interpreters of the Scriptures. The class is that of uninhibited condescension with respect to any passage in the New Testament which is not a blaring forth of salvation by faith, a condescension which Luther was not reluctant at all to make known to the widest possible audience, namely, the readers of his famed Bible translation. Since he found in the Epistle to the Hebrews many subjects other than his favorite subject, he felt "we cannot put it on the same level with the apostolic epistles." Had Luther been possessed of genuine humility toward all words that come from the mouth of God, that is, inspired by the Holy Spirit, he would not have been constrained to write in the same preface to the Letter to the Hebrews that "we should not be deterred if wood, straw, or hay are perhaps mixed with them [precious notions], but accept this fine teaching with all honor."[40] The fine teaching was about Christ's priesthood, a priesthood seen through Luther's own opinion about it. The latter set the tone also, and not surprisingly, of his preface to the letter of James. Refusing its authorship to the apostle James, Luther wrote: "But this James does nothing more than drive to the law and to its works. Besides, he throws things together so chaotically that it seems to me he must have been some good, pious man, who took a few sayings from the disciples of the apostles and thus tossed them off on paper . . . In a word he wanted to guard against those who relied on faith without works, but was unequal to the task."[41] Such comments, unique in the history of Christian exegesis, are clearly revealing of an overbearing measure of one's sense of exclusive adequacy to the task. That exclusivity was a piece with the exclusive importance Luther accorded to his favorite theme.

Protestants often said much if not all this about the Roman Catholic position as a narrow-minded focusing on certain passages of the gospel. A decision about the merit of their turning the tables on Roman Catholics, or rather about the prospect of finding a genuine common ground between Protestants and Catholics on precisely the crucial topics, is influenced by modern developments both harmful and helpful. Among the former is a shying away from plain statements. Not that one would wish the return to times when vain efforts were made to reply in kind to Luther's unsurpassable vulgarity. Yet one wonders whether the new resolve to avoid expressions far less offensive than say "Lutheran cloaca"[42] (indeed, whether the most praiseworthy resolve to speak only words of genuine charity about separated Christians) should issue in a fear to call a spade a spade, let alone to recall indisputable facts. It is almost impossible to find a book written by Catholic theologians during the past 30 years or so in which one would find the plain statement contained in the largest book on the keys, written by a Catholic theologian in 1660. There the plain fact is stated that the meaning given by the Reformers to the keys in no way implies power to remit sins but is merely a declaration that the sins of those listening to the preaching of the word are forgiven.[43]

Whatever the ever stronger orientation in modern Lutheranism and Calvinism toward an appreciation of the sacraments (including that of ordination) and toward ecclesial authority deposited in concrete individuals, clear reminders of the erstwhile Protestant position may be helpful in keeping the air clear as erstwhile positions never entirely lose their influence. Unfortunately, there is little premium on a theological clean-air policy in an age bent on fighting air pollution. A sign of that lack of appreciation is, for instance, the low degree of awareness about lessons of history. Possibly this is a result of the ever more voluble American voice on the theological scene, a voice reflecting the American mind which does not include historical consciousness among its best qualities.

A case in point is the lack of broad awareness of the relevance which dialogues now long past may have for present-day ecumenical dialogues. Almost exactly 300 years ago such a dialogue took place between two prominent French bishops, Bossuet and Choiseul-Praslin, the latter being in charge of drawing up the declaration of the French clergy on the standing of the pope in the Church. Although sharing Choiseul-Praslin's view that the pope was not infallible, Bossuet resisted his colleague who wanted a declaration denying even the indefectibility of the see of Rome. To Bossuet this seemed to contradict the plain words of Christ to Peter. In the ensuing private debate, which Bossuet later recalled with some animus, Choiseul-Praslin warned that any strict indefectibility accorded to the see of Rome was equivalent "to the infallibility of its occupant in speaking *ex cathedra*, the very thing claimed by the ultramontanes."[44] This warning of impeccable logic drove Bossuet toward falling back to ever more tenuous specifications of the Roman see's indefectibility. Tenuous should indeed seem the indefectibility accorded by Bossuet to the see of Rome which he saw falling into error, though never in a contumacious and hardheaded manner, only to be led back to the truth by the sister churches. Clearly, then, if Peter's see, which received Christ's promises, was not indefectible, the sister churches, who could not claim such promises, had to be indefectible and infallible,—a classic case of reduction ad absurdum which greatly delighted Bossuet's now completely forgotten colleague in the episcopacy.

Keeping such historical dialogues in the focus of awareness, the harm of shortsightedness in many new ecumenical position-papers could greatly be lessened. Even more effectively could ecumenical encounters be made harmless if sustained attention were to be given to epistemological stances underlying classic theological positions. This is not to suggest that one should expect even remotely as much from mere philosophical debates as from trends in ecclesial reality and experience such as the growing sacramental realism within Protestantism. However, when it comes to conceptual clarification, epistemology determines both the establishment of the meaning of crucial passages and even more so the formation of a consensus about them. Here helpful prospects are buttressed by two factors. One is the forceful reminder served by Karl Barth about the epistemological impossibility of the Reformed position. Of course, he said nothing new with that. The same was done with the same kind of transparent implicitness by Harnack, but the latter's undisguised rationalism could create the impression that it was not the Reformation as such that was the source of that impossibility. No such doubts could be entertained about the neo-orthodox Barth. While with his sustained insistence "on the impossibility of the word of God on the lips of a man"[45] (even though that man is an ordained minister) Barth certainly brought into focus an epistemological impossibility, his primary concern was not philosophical, not even theological, but mystical.

Undoubtedly, there is something deeply mystical in that *soli Deo gloria* which makes one face with magnanimity one's own predestination even to hell and which also lets one feel assured that one is delivered from hell through that faith which annihilates him in relation to God. But the irrationality of this *credo quia absurdum*, which Barth implies in the words, "with God everything is possible,"[46] will not cease being an epistemological impossibility with which the 20th-century Protestant may not wish to settle as easily as his 16th-century counterpart. Neo-orthodoxy, not yet two generations old, has already seen its halcyon days. This century of ours, unlike the 16th century, is heir not only to three centuries of ever faster scientific progress, but the very witness of an explosive advance by which science sheds rational light on a truly cosmic scale. Irrational as some of the fashionable philosophical interpretations of science may be, the startling feats of 20th-century science impose a continual recognition of the full rationality of existence.[47] In such a milieu, the Protestant celebration of epistemological impossibility may turn into a longing for the possibility of objective meaning, be it the Trojan horse of that analogy of being which for the neo-orthodox Barth had rightly to appear the invention of the Antichrist himself.[48]

The other beneficial factor relates to a growing consensus about the sense of Mt 16:16–19 as far as Peter himself is concerned. The once popular dismissal of Christ's words to Peter as a 2nd-century Romanist interpolation has today little if any appeal in Protestant realms that are also scholarly. In fact, scholarly respectability is more increasingly limited there to the position that Christ not only said those very words to Peter but that he meant Peter and not his faith. Such is a most valuable advance which was espoused, most importantly, by Karl Barth too.[49] The chief document of that advance is Kittel's *Dictionary of the New Testament*.[50] It has carried to thousands of reference shelves all over the world the portrayal which Cullmann gave of Peter's standing in the New Testament in a now classic monograph over a quarter of a century ago.[51]

Cullmann has in fact tolerated no slighting of the power symbolized by the keys. It is not at all likely, so he strictured the view of a fellow Protestant, Zahn,[52] that the power of keys meant only the allocation of private apartments within the kingdom of heaven and not the control of its very entrance. The keys were in Cullmann's eyes a logical sequence in Christ's statement on the Church as an edifice to be built and on the gates of hell as the symbol of the Church's chief opponent. Nor did Cullmann refrain, unlike Luther and Calvin, from admitting that the meaning of the keys as full power in the case of Eliakim was just as valid in Peter's case:

> Just as in Isaiah 22:22 the Lord puts the keys of the house of David on the shoulders of his servant Eliakim, so does Jesus hand over to Peter the keys of the house of the kingdom of heaven and by the same stroke establishes him as his superintendent. There is a connection between the house of the Church, the construction of which has just been mentioned and of which Peter is the foundation, and the celestial house of which he receives the keys. The connection between these two images is the notion of God's people.[53]

Cullmann, who put this function of Peter in that infinite perspective which Christ's real resurrection alone makes real, struck another no less valuable and realist chord. He ascribed to Peter, as the holder of the keys, a real instrumentality in the process by which the faithful share in the resurrection of Christ: "What is customarily called the power of keys makes of him in a way the human instrument of resurrection. He is destined to lead the people of God into the kingdom of resurrection. Such will be his task on earth after the resurrection of Jesus." Christ's stricture of the pharisees, who closed the kingdom of God (Mt 23:13), was for Cullmann a further hint that the function of admitting into the kingdom of heaven would belong to "Peter, the chosen rock and not to them."[54] Cullmann saw the same allusion lurking behind Christ's subsequent words about the pharisees who turn their proselytes into sons of hell, twice worse than they themselves (Mt 23:15). "It is significant," concluded Cullmann, "that these words follow in Matthew the ones on the closing of the kingdom of heaven; we are therefore entitled to establish in Mt 16:19 a connection between the keys of the kingdom of heaven and the apostolic mission."[55] It should not, therefore, be surprising that such a scholarly bow before the traditional sense as being the obvious sense of Christ's words is followed by an unqualified statement on Cullmann's part that Peter's special position among the twelve was in no way lessened by the fact that the twelve too received the power of binding and loosing.[56]

Caught in Worn Tracks

It would have been too much to expect that Cullmann's widely hailed book would shunt from well-worn tracks some theological trains of thought. For more than four hundred years *faith*, instead of *Peter* and *keys*, was written with a resolve which even today treats the reader to a series of non-sequiturs. A case in point is the chapter, "The Keys of Heaven," in *Christian Hope and Second Coming* by P. S. Minear, one of the few modern Protestant writers taking up a patently sensitive topic for edification. To be sure, the keys in the New Testament have an eschatological perspective which is not entirely the perspective of historic times to be lived through by the Church prior to the onset of the end of time. Not to keep in focus this distinction could only serve the purpose of distracting from the endurance through time of ministry in general and of Peter's ministry in particular. This seems, indeed, to be Minear's aim who, not unexpectedly, made much of Christ's calling Peter not only Rock but also Satan. According to him two other passages "warn us against too narrow a view of the promise whereby the keys would be given to Peter." One is Mt 18:15–19 in which "the power to bind or to loose was promised not only to Peter but also to any congregation where Christ is present in the loving exercise of forgiveness or judgment."[57]

Minear's is hardly a rigorous exegesis; it is made even less rigorous by the double reference to loving exercise. In this age of all-too-heavy reliance on the word "love," emphatic references to it can easily distract from that fact that whatever one's loving, one can exercise a power, lovingly or not, only if one has it. The other passage is Jesus' recognition that even the Jewish tribes "had the power to enter the kingdom and to open the door for others" (Lk 11:52). For Minear this also meant that the power of the keys does not "become the exclusive property even of the Christian Church," as if to prove to what lengths one can be lead by emphasis on the *loving* exercise of power and on taking "disciples" in Mt 18:15–19 not for the twelve but for any group of believers in Christ.[58] Whatever the truth in Minear's arguments, the Catholic interpretation of Peter's keys is not at all incompatible with his claim that "the keys were not intended as means by which one religious institution could lay claim to temporal power over another." It escaped Minear that with his claim he denounced politically established Protestant churches, none of which kept a theological basis for claiming the keys in that corporate institutional sense in which the Catholic Church did and still does.

The reluctance of some Protestants to accept Cullmann's clear position seems understandable. If Peter and the twelve had been established as real channels of grace, it is very difficult to assume that this human instrumentality was to cease with their death. It is well-nigh impossible to find serious justification for "ministry" within Protestant ecclesial context if the post-apostolic church is radically deprived of apostolic instrumentality. As a result, not all Protestants are ready to follow Cullmann who clearly spelled out that radical break between the apostolic and post-apostolic Church. Cullmann should have at least been congratulated by Protestants and Catholics alike for having revealed in full his train of thought about that radical break. According to him Christ could not have in mind a long future for the Church (and therefore the prospect of an apostolic succession) because he erroneously expected his second coming to take place in the near future.[59]

That the ultimate price for discrediting apostolic succession has to be a postulating of an error on Christ's part (an error subtly destructive of his divinity as interpreted by the dogmas of Nicea and Chalcedon) did not dawn on Cullmann in full. He remained convinced that a genuinely orthodox position was left open for him. By positing that radical break at the demise of the apostolic generation Cullmann hoped to achieve more than to advance by one and a half century what Harnack and his rationalist colleagues located in the middle of the third century. That Harnack's religious sociologism and historicism allowed for no dogmatic meaning, was true enough. The ultimate reason for this was, however, Harnack's denial of Christ's resurrection, a point not noted by Cullmann. Nor did Cullmann notice that his own attributing an error to Christ put him potentially very close to Harnack's "christology." It was therefore a wholly secondary matter to insist, as Cullmann did, that there was no exegetical merit in the agnosticism of Harnack according to whom it was impossible to know what Christ said, let alone what he meant.[60]

At any rate, once that break was posited by Cullmann, agnosticism could at best be transcended on the exegetical level but not on the dogmatic level. For it was the sheer agnosticism of the absolute Barthian opposition between Word and word that alone could be accommodated within a position predicated on that break. Whatever its accordance with the inner logic of the erstwhile Protestant position, it could have but limited appeal among those Protestants who today watch with dismay the groundswell of Fundamentalists and Evangelicals relishing that very logic. The efforts (if not mere wishful thinking) to discern an "episcopal" office inherent in classical Lutheranism (and Calvinism too!)[61] are all too clear evidences of a longing for a third position, a *via media*, between the Roman Catholic position and that of the Reformers. Already Harnack noticed this as a historic phenomenon, a good reminder for some present-day ecumenical experts on the Church who cannot believe that there may be nothing new under the sun and who take this or that ecumenical report for genuine originality and historic breakthrough. But as Harnack warned:

> The Reformation [of the sixteenth century] not only destroyed the ecclesiastical constitution [Kirchenverfassung] of the Middle Ages, but also broke off all connection with the Kirchenverfassung of the second and third centuries . . . The people of Western Europe are still either Catholic or Protestant. *Tertium adhuc non datur*. It is Luther who created for them this alternative, and it is an alternative which concerns us more than all the philosophical and scientific culture of the present time, or all its technical applications. The people are, however, on the lookout for a *tertium genus Ecclesiae* under which they may find shelter for their higher life.[62]

That such a third way is, indeed, an impossibility can be surmised from the "learned ignorance," if not plain equivocation, which exudes from recent scholarly symposia aimed at establishing that *third way* with a reference to Peter's power and especially to his keys. Such efforts almost invariably give themselves away by their taciturnity on the keys. A good illustration of this is the result of discussions on Peter in the New Testament by a group of Catholic and Protestant theologians in New York in 1971.[63] The printed record of nearly 200 pages is certainly noteworthy in that not one of its chapters or paragraphs can be attributed to any of the participants, a fact reminding one of the proverbial lack of individual responsibility for common property. No less noteworthy is that only two paragraphs, covering less than two pages, are devoted to the keys, less than the space devoted to the miraculous catch of fish, for instance.[64] Each of these two paragraphs deals in turn with two possible biblical backgrounds. One is the keys given to Eliakim which calls for an acknowledgment of power, though with some vacillation:

> *If* this were the background of Matthew's "keys of the kingdom," then Peter *might* be being portrayed as a type of prime minister in the kingdom that Jesus has come to proclaim, and the power of binding and loosing would be a specification of the broader power of allowing or refusing entrance into the kingdom. What else might this broader power of the keys include? It might include one or more of the following: Baptismal discipline; post baptismal or penitential discipline; excommunication; exclusion from the eucharist; the communication or refusal of knowledge; legislative powers, and the power of governing" (Italics added).[65]

Very revealingly, this list does not include the power of defining true knowledge as if the kingdom of heaven were not that eternal life which consists, in the very words of the one calling himself truth, "in knowing you, true God and whom you have sent, Jesus Christ" (Jn 13:7). The other background is the "gates of hades" as suggested by

Cullmann.[66] Here the notion of power shrinks either to Peter's preaching whereby after Pentecost the kingdom of heaven is made known to the multitude, or to what is an equivocation about power, namely, to the "power of forgiving sin through baptism," which, as is well known, even a pagan can administer. In either case Peter is hardly needed, let alone his keys.

A more recent ecumenical book,[67] also partly on Peter, which consists of specifically individual contributions, mentions the keys only twice with some comment which in both cases make meaningless the notion of power. Understandably, a Baptist and a Calvinist were responsible. While the Lutheran contributor stated at least that in Mt 16:19 the keys were given only to Peter,[68] the Catholic contributor claimed that "historically it is most difficult to ascertain just what Jesus did intend for his Church. The New Testament already gives us a picture colored by the theology of the community in a post-resurrection situation."[69] Such a statement makes sense only if either the passage on the keys is not an accurate rendering of Christ's words and not even authentic in a broader sense or there is something intrinsically incomprehensible about keys. Is one supposed to think that since keys are ancient objects they cannot make modern minds click? That something of such a presupposition may have been at play behind the foregoing quotation is suggested by the phrase which introduces it: "For the modern mind, steeped in historical consciousness, the ancient category of 'divine institution' has become problematic."[70]

That the modern mind is very uneasy about anything divine or supernatural is true enough. But the modern mind is no less uneasy about any institution, even if it is a constitutional government properly so-called. The Constitution of the United States is indeed becoming the prey of the fleeting fashions of the actually prevailing consensus. To lay the tag "historical" on all this is justified as long as one remembers that "historical" has, under the impact of Darwinian randomness, become equivalent to the abolition of anything with clear contours and permanency. It has now become a tyrannical academic fashion to see ideas and concepts as so many animal species struggling for survival and with only as much truth content as can be assigned to transitory success.[71] Those mindful of the craving of modern theologians for fashionability, will not be surprised on seeing professors of theology soon imitate their secular counterparts in celebrating incoherence in the name of God, Revelation, Bible and Religious Experience.

To the modern mind steeped in Cartesian rationalism, Humean scepticism, Kantian apriorism, Machist sensationism, and Popperian falsificationism, everything has indeed become problematic, even the problematic character of problems. Only the inescapable requirements of daily life and common sense can open the eyes of the modern mind, even the minds of many modern theologians, to the evidence of plain daylight. Examples of this come along in the most unexpected contexts even in connection with the subject of Peter's keys. Let mention be made here of only two such contexts, both from still widely used biblical commentaries written for the benefit of the working pastor and preacher, who has to face not dreamy-eyed graduate students hungry for hollow sophistication but real men hungry for concrete truth. In the *Biblical Illustrator* the following is quoted re Mt 16:19, "And I will give unto thee the keys of the kingdom of heaven," from a sermon preached at the ordination of elders:

> When I first entered upon the work of the ministry among you, I was exceedingly ignorant of the vast im-

portance of church discipline. I thought that my great, and almost only, work was to pray and preach. I saw your souls to be so precious, and the time so short, that I devoted all my time and care and strength to labor in word and doctrine. When cases of discipline were brought before me and the elders, I regarded them with something like abhorrence. It was a duty I shrank from; and I may truly say it nearly drove me from the work of the ministry among you altogether. But it pleased God, who teaches his servants in another way than man teaches, to bless some of the cases of discipline to the manifest and undeniable conversion of the souls of those under our care; and from that hour a new light broke in upon my mind, and I saw that if preaching be an ordinance of Christ, so is church discipline. I now feel very deeply persuaded that both are of God; that two keys are committed to us by Christ— the one the key of doctrine, by means of which we unlock the treasures of the Bible; the other the key of discipline, by means of which we open or shut the way to the sealing ordinances of the faith. Both are Christ's gift, and neither is to be resigned without sin.[72]

Such honest admission shows that even though the modern mind cannot be a key to the meaning of keys and in fact hardly a key to the meaning of anything, ecclesial reality may still be a solid ground to fall back upon in search for that meaning. Of course, since the human mind, modern or not, needs, as does all other human reality, the healing of redemption, a genuine recognition of the meaning of the keys may serve as a clue as to what that healing may bring about for thought's tortuous ways. Here, too, let another commentary be consulted for a hint, possibly unintended. In the *Interpreter's Bible*, where the foundation established by Christ is still Peter's faith (or anyone's faith for that matter), reference is made[73] to Chesterton's famous words:

> All the empires and kingdoms have failed, because of this inherent and continual weakness, that they were founded by strong men . . . But this one thing, the historic Christian Church, was founded on a weak man, and for that reason it is indestructible. For no chain is stronger than its weakest link.[74]

To this the following comment is added:

> No, not for that reason but because the weak man has now acknowledged Christ, and because Christ makes him strong. But Chesterton has a partial truth: Christ chooses to build his Church on weak men who confess him, and who thus discover in him power beyond that of man. To this society each man brings his gift, and they become one life—the Agape, the Love.

Had Chesterton's statement been quoted in full,[75] such confusing comment would not have become necessary. But to quote him incompletely was needed for another reason. In the next page, typically enough, the following and only the following is stated about the keys promised to Peter:

> The keys of the kingdom would be committed to the chief steward in the royal household and with them goes plenary authority. In Is 22:22 the key of the house of David is promised to Eliakim. According to Paul, Jesus is the only foundation (1 Cor 3:11), and in Rv 1:18; 3:7, Jesus possesses the key of David and the keys of death and hades. But in this passage Peter is made the foundation (cf. Eph 2:20, where the Christian apostles and prophets are the foundation and Christ is the cornerstone and holds the keys.) Post-apostolic

Christianity is now beginning to ascribe to the apostles the prerogatives of Jesus.[76]

Chesterton should have been quoted again because he spoke of keys in reference to the truth of Christianity with the verve of realism and specificity which alone can bring the modern mind (even the mind of theologians and biblical scholars) back from the nebulous and vague to the real which is always specific (including the reality of the supernatural). To begin with, already the Chesterton of *Heretics* (1905) was aware of what a quarter of a century later the Roman Catholic Chesterton expressly said in connection with Peter's crucifixion upside down:

> I have often fancied his humility was rewarded by seeing in death the beautiful vision of his boyhood. He also saw the landscape as it really is: with the stars like flowers, and the clouds like hills, and all men hanging on the mercy of God.[77]

Perhaps this super-Copernican turn back to earth so that skies may be seen will be hastened by the accelerated rate at which science brings mankind face to face with the entire cosmos as a stunningly specific reality. Then the keys, including the keys of the kingdom, will be seen for what they are: exceedingly specific things made for exceedingly specific plans, such as the plan of salvation. Long before Chesterton became a Catholic he knew that since the human condition was complex, explanation of it (nay the redemption of it) had to be complex and therefore specific. He came to grips with the problem also in the particular perspective of seeing whether the accusers of Christianity were mad—precisely because their defenders were right:

> If it [Christianity] is right at all, it is a compliment to say that it's elaborately right. A stick might fit a hole or a stone a hollow by accident. But a key and a lock are both complex. And if a key fits a lock it is the right key ... I tested this idea by asking myself whether there was about any of the accusers anything morbid that might explain the accusation. I was startled to find that this key fitted a lock.[78]

Such a view of keys and of what they are for, locks, is very different from shouting "faith" and "I believe" which all too often become void of specific objects. Such an outcome is the nominalist curse which has shadowed Protestantism (and constantly threatens Catholicism) ever since its rise. A curious fact because nominalism wanted to accept only the particulars, the specific. Being an extreme, it led to the other extreme where all specifics disappear, including keys, together with the keys of the kingdom of heaven. Once Protestants discover along these lines the key to the meaning of those keys, and if they succeed in enlightening Catholic ecumenists about their findings, they will have made their greatest contribution to implementing Christ's prayer, "that they may be one." To reserve the right of any "denomination" to act out its own "tradition" (left unspecified) and to hope at the same time for that oneness, implies an oversight of its very specific nature as spelled out by Christ. Insofar as he was a "model-maker" in ecclesiology, he set for that oneness no less a specific model than his own oneness with his Father in heaven.

CHAPTER 5
THE KEYS OF AN OPEN CHURCH

Peter's Keys at Vatican II

As he was bringing to a close a long speech which opened on September 29, 1963, the crucial second session of Vatican II, Pope Paul VI offered vistas memorable for their vastness:

> In this Council from which a window opens out upon the whole world, the Church looks with especial solicitude on certain groups of men: on the poor, the needy and distressed, the starving, the suffering, the imprisoned . . . The Church also casts her eyes on men of learning, in literature, science and the arts . . . With the utmost enthusiasm she welcomes their experiments, endorses the efforts of their genius, safeguards their liberty . . . She has eyes too for workingmen, for their personal dignity and the dignity of their work . . . She turns her eyes to the rulers of nations. Often enough she has had to appeal to them with serious words of warning; today her words are full of encouragement and confidence. Take heart, you who guide the destinies of nations. Today you are in a position to supply the good things your people need: food, culture, order,

the dignity that belongs to free citizens living together in peace . . . The Catholic Church looks further still, beyond the confines of the Christian family . . . She looks beyond her own sphere, and regards those other religions which preserve the awareness and the conception of the one supreme, transcendent God, creator and sustainer . . . and she hastens to assure them of her due regard for everything they have which is true and good and human.[1]

These vast vistas were seen as if from a window, as widely opened as it could be. A window evokes a wall, a wall a house which is never built without a door that can be opened and closed. That Paul vi had no other idea in mind of the Church than such an edifice must have already been clear from the words which he shortly beforehand addressed to the representatives of non-Catholic Christians:

> The recent unity movement among separated Christian communions . . . makes two things plain: Christ's Church is one and should be one; and that this mystic and visible unity cannot be achieved except by one faith, participation in the same sacraments, and the proper unifying effect of a single ecclesiastical regimen—allowing, however, for a variety of languages, traditional rites and customs, local prerogatives, different schools of spirituality, legitimate institutions, and freedom of choice in the activities of daily life.[2]

Somewhat earlier in the same speech, Paul vi further implied the vision of a house undivided and under one supreme control as he broached the pivotal topic to be discussed during that second session, the notion of episcopal collegiality:

> We await this discussion with eager anticipation and

genuine confidence. The doctrine to which We are referring is that of the episcopate, its functions and its relation to Peter. Indeed, this doctrine ought to be gone into very thoroughly (while at the same time we hold safe the dogmatic pronouncements of the First Vatican Council concerning the Roman pontiff). For Us personally it will provide doctrinal and practical standards for the exercise of Our apostolic office. This universal office has been endowed by Christ, as you know, with the fulness and sufficiency of power. Nevertheless, it can marshal to itself added support and assistance from an ever more effective and responsible collaboration (in ways and means to be determined) of Our beloved and revered brothers in the episcopate.[3]

In line with all this the result of those discussions, the "Dogmatic Constitution on the Church," contained the notion of a Church which, however wide her windows were opened and however wide her doors swung, remained a house with keys. By naming that document not only a constitution but a dogmatic constitution, the Council hardly wished to encourage views according to which such labels should be eschewed on account of their alleged incomprehensibility to modern minds. Nothing, indeed, in that dogmatic constitution suggests a Church so open as to have no keys to its doors, and perhaps not even doors. The Church in that dogmatic constitution remains a monarchical society pivoted on the successor of Peter because, to quote its very words, "although all apostles received the power of binding and loosing, our Lord named Simon Peter *alone* the rock and keybearer of the Church and appointed him shepherd of the *whole* flock"[4] (Italics added). Accordingly, the dogmatic constitution speaks only of such episcopal collegiality which is "assembled under one head" and in which the bishops "faithfully recognize the primacy and pre-eminence of their head, and exercise their own authority for the good of their own faithful."[5] To that dogmatic constitution the collegiality of bishops is not that jovial togetherness which "collegiality" invariably conveys in secular parlance. The collegiality of bishops is rather a strict coherence of an organism to its one and only head: "The Roman pontiff, as the successor of Peter, is the perpetual head and visible source and foundation of the unity of the bishops and of the multitude of the faithful."[6] Without the approval of that head no action of the college of bishops,[6] all of whom must be solicitous not only for their own flock but also for the entire Church, is valid, not even when that college is actually gathered in a council: "A council is never ecumenical unless it is confirmed or at least accepted as such by the successor of Peter. It is the prerogative of the Roman pontiff to convoke these councils, to preside over them, and to confirm them."[7] Clearly, the keys, even to an ecumenical council, were in the hands of the successor of Peter alone.

Clear as all this could be, clarity was never the longed for aim of the so-called conciliar movement. Democratic deliberations tend to be lost in vagueness, or if not, the ensuing interpretative process will gradually turn into vague pronouncements statements which were fairly definite when first formulated. To forestall such an eventuality in the case of the doctrine of collegiality, an "explanatory and prefatory note" to it was communicated to the Council "from higher authority," that is, from Paul vi himself. The note's four points state, in a condensed form, the following:

1. The college of bishops is not an inheritor of the apostles' power in that full sense in which the pope is the inheritor of the powers entrusted to Peter.
2. While the episcopal consecration gives an ontological participation in the college of bishops, the enter-

ing of a newly-consecrated bishop into communion with the successor of Peter makes alone legitimate and organic the use of what devolves on him from that consecration.
3. Only the college of bishops, which cannot exist out its head, is the subject also of supreme and full power over the whole Church. This must be allowed of necessity if the fulness of power of the Roman pontiff is not to be jeopardized.
4. While the college of bishops is in full act only on specific occasions, such as when convened into an ecumenical council, the power deposited in the pope is always activable. "As supreme pastor of the Church the sovereign pontiff can always exercise his authority as he chooses, as is demanded by his office itself."[8]

The foregoing points indicated the presence in and especially around the Council of a perception about the Church which had little room for a real Peter with real keys in his hands. Indeed, no sooner had Paul VI made his reference to the open windows of the Council than those open windows became perceived as an open Church, nay as an open house, which had no doors, no keys, not even walls, and was an easy prey for gate-crashers with much vaunted academic credentials.

From Broken Keys to Broken Catholics

The wide open windows of Vatican II, a council, which let us not forget, was the brainchild of a pope, John XXIII, had to be the cause of great rejoicing. Joy in turn creates its own utterances, not all of which, even when hyperbolic, should be taken as a sign of malice or of plain misunderstanding. It is not at all likely that by seeing Vatican II as the crumbling of the walls around the Catholic Church George B. Caird contemplated an end to the papacy in particular and to Roman Catholicism in general.[9] But phrases, especially if catchy like "open church," have their own logic whereby they become autonomous messages, severed from their origin. Before long reporters, who hardly ever care for important qualifications, began to preach a new ecclesiology, as if Vatican II meant to transform the Church from a "closed monarchy" into an "open democracy." To this superficial thinking no small assistance was given by some council theologians (*periti*) and by some would-be such experts. Thus contrary to the official documents of Vatican II, the Church soon began to be spoken of as a mere place with no property rights and residential rules. Such a place did not suggest at all a need for keys. The rapidity and vigor by which the new perception took hold of the imagination constitute a most instructive topic for students of the psychology and sociology of religion. The revelations which such a study might hold in store were powerfully suggested by a cover story of TIME. Its issue of November 22, 1968, showed on its cover, above the saddened face of Paul VI, the two keys of Peter broken into pieces. Only five short years after he had spoken of the "open windows of the council" the Roman Catholic Church was, in the perception of many, an edifice with wide-open cracks which made the keys of Peter no more useful than any broken piece of metal would be as a key to the gate of a scrap-iron yard.

Whatever the professed claim of TIME or other secular news media about being only reporters of prevailing perceptions, their professed secularism has its own logic of wishful thinking and myopia. The wishful thinking makes the media see mainly the tide of secularism which on some fronts seems to be steadily on the rise. That it has also its ebbing fronts is hardly ever of interest to them. As to the myopia, it is evident in the systematic oversight of the survival value of the solemn pronouncements of the Catholic Church. Since the media prefer to see only broken keys, they see mostly broken Catholics, clergy and laity. While hardly ever is a word said by journalists as to what is at the basis of that process, books extolling the idea of an "open" church rarely fail to provide a hint. For whatever train of thought helps build the "open" church with no walls and doors, it also leads to a symbolic breaking of the keys. This logic makes itself evident even when the intentions are the very best and supported by the very best training. A case in point is the *Open Church* by M. Novak, pieced together from his journalistic reports about Vatican II during 1962 and 1963.[10] Not that Novak saw that logic in 1963 when his book was published. But he spelled it out unwittingly for the simple reason that throughout the book he echoed theological and philosophical views which embody that very logic.

In the late 1950s when Novak discontinued his theological training at the Gregorianum, those views were seen by many to be responsibly progressive. That estimate received its first major public challenge when Maritain, whom Paul VI embraced in the full glare of St. Peter on the conclusion of Vatican II, published his misgivings, *The Peasant from the Garonne*.[11] It was most appropriate that such a challenge should come from the foremost Roman Catholic metaphysician of this century. For at the basis of the sad process which leads from an "open" church to the closing of seminaries, novitiates, and motherhouses by the hundreds if not thousands, there lies, as in all similar processes in the past, a problem of understanding, the chief problem of metaphysics. As an avid student and admirer of *Insight* by B. Lonergan, one-time professor at the Gregorianum, Novak tied to that book the question of insight as the key to the train of thought animating the preparations and deliberations of Vatican II.[12] Among those deliberating there, fairly large was the number of those professing a philosophy similar to the one in Lonergan's now rarely consulted book.

The logic of Lonergan's *Insight* has by now largely advanced beyond the positions specified there, which were not as original as generally believed. Lonergan merely articulated in a manageable volume some basic contentions of a huge five-volume set, the history of epistemological doctrines by Joseph Maréchal, professor of philosophy in the Jesuit scholasticate in Louvain.[13] That great and laborious set was far more than a mere recital of past opinions. Maréchal could rightly look upon his work as *his* story of the history of epistemology, a story construed to serve a major lesson for Catholic philosophers. Thomism, he claimed, could be kept meaningful for modern times only by grafting Kant onto it. The lesson spread widely, especially within the Society of Jesus which sent to its scholasticate in Louvain many of its future theologians and philosophers to learn at the feet of Father Maréchal. One could only wish that Father Rahner had from the start made it clear that his true philosophical roots were in Louvain, that is, in his having been instructed by Father Maréchal about "a more open and lively contact with Kant."[14]

Strange roots and foreign soil indeed. After all, what can there be in common between two philosophies which radically differ in their very fundamentals? On the one hand, for a philosophy which wants to retain a meaningful tie with God's revealed name, He Who Is, the fundamental truth has to be the truth of things existing. Or as Chesterton once memorably put it: "There *is* an Is!"[15] The fundamental proposition of Kant's philosophy is a critical look not at existent things (which are *noumena*, that is, unknowable) but at one's notion of things, or at most at the phenomena which, as modified sense impressions, are taken to have been indirectly produced by those unknowables. Such a proposition is patently contradictory, and therefore fundamentally uncritical. Apart from this, it should be obvious that one of those two philosophies begins with objectively existing things, which provoke knowledge in the knower, whereas the other begins with the subjective thinker in union with the mere phenomena of things. To graft one on the other is no more profitable than to try to fuse two entities, such as a fly and a horse, just because the two are often seen together. The product would be no more than a horsefly.

Ever since Lucifer, who wanted to become like God, the centering of thought on the self has been the great lure for created minds. While this self-centeredness can be as lofty as the Platonic realm of ideas, its subjectivist strain gave itself away already in Plato. The rigid, if not cruel subjection of the state to idealist and transcendental philosophers in Plato's *Republic* anticipated the celebration of wilfulness by such direct students of Kant as Fichte and Hegel whose transcendental Thomist admirers are blissfully ignorant of the famed prophecy of Heine about the long-range impact of those two.[16] The subjectivism (from its refined phenomenological kind through its ever-shifting interpretations to the arbitrariness of situation ethics) of countless books written on philosophy, theology, and ethics by Catholics in the wake of Vatican II is the fruit of that rather uninformed transcendental Thomism, a euphemism for what should have been named Aquikantism.

The chief driving force of Aquikantism is the mistaken resolve to unlock the riddle of the age-old problem of how the universal can be seen in the particular. This problem is not resolvable in the sense in which solutions are often taken nowadays under the impact of physical science. There solutions means strict one-to-one reducibility of a proposition to another. This works smoothly in the exact sciences only because they deal exactly with the quantitative aspects of existence, all of which are univocal notions and therefore strictly reducible to one another. Kant's mistaken belief was that philosophy can be turned into an exact science so that all the propositions of philosophy could have that reducibility which in turn would have signified their "exactness" and therefore their certitude. The philosophical topic which is most refractory to such a procedure is the fact of objective existence. It appears in so many and widely different forms as to make them only analogous to one another. This is why the analogy of being is the opening chapter of any good account of Thomist philosophy, a chapter which cannot be consistently grafted on transcendental Thomism or Aquikantism.

Consistency is the decisive word here, because philosophy is a field of intellectual activity where logic is remorselessly at work, a good many philosophers notwithstanding. In other words, once a starting point is chosen it will impose consequences which can be avoided only at the price of flagrant inconsistencies. The true nature of the starting point may not be immediately transparent. Thus if the Kantian or Aquikantian starting point is taken in the form of the classic question of critical philosophy, "Is knowledge possible?", the retort can readily be made that the question, being some knowledge in itself, simply disqualifies the question. Yet it is not so transparent that the question as a starting point implies the thinking subject as the first step in philosophy and by doing so can lead only to subjectivism. If, however, the Kantian (or Aquikantian) starting point is located in the thinking subject's sensory impressions, which the same subject's mind infuses with intelligible content, the road to subjectivism becomes more obvious. At least to anyone who has the elementary insight that sensory impressions, as meant by Kant, are strictly *in* the subject and are not factors impressing that subject from the outside. Hence Kant's and the Aquikantists' hapless efforts to secure objective reality, including, in the latter's predicament, the flesh and blood reality of the Word Incarnate. The growing perplexity of an ever larger number of Aquikantists about the Incarnation should have seemed long ago a foregone conclusion.

If the Thomistic doctrine of the analogy of being is not *the* insight which governs the thinking of the Catholic philosopher and theologian, he will for all his good intentions contribute only to a decay of his respective field of investigation. The decay will evidence itself first in subtle non-sequiturs, noticeable only by a relatively few. The opening of the Church to all cultures, her transformation from a heavily Italian into a supranational force, from a largely European cultural factor to a transcultural leaven, are undoubtedly noble aspirations which all honest minds should share and support. But is it logical to aim at a supracultural philosophy if there are no truths that transcend all cultures in the sense of being equally valid for all of them? Is it not a *non sequitur* to repeat knowingly or unknowingly the father of positivism, who wanted a Catholicism without Christianity, that everything is relative and this is the only absolute truth? Does the truth of *being* become irrelevant for Buddhist subcontinents just because existence vanishes in the Nirvana of the Blessed One? Is the coherence of events and things—so marvelously displayed by modern science from fundamental particles to galaxies and beyond—not valid for the vast Muslim realms just because it is incompatible with the occasionalism lurking between the lines of the Koran? Is objectivism, preached by that divine master, who set as the condition of his following the parting from one's self, to be declared merely optional when dealing with Protestants, just because Protestantism was born in a nominalist atmosphere, the most subjectivist philosophical milieu of them all? And are Catholics, from America to Australia, to be raised on theological models, instead of the sacred truths of revelation defined by popes and councils over two millennia, just because a secular culture has undercut credibility in objective truth and allows only patterns? If, indeed, the insight held high by transcendental Thomists is so much the decisive part of man's drive for understanding, why is it that at the end of the first decade following the conclusion of Vatican II—a decade which boasted, almost *ad nauseam*, of spiritual renewal everywhere—an insightful cardinal–archbishop, and as good a theologian as any of the Aquikantist camp could boast of, had to admit that mostly decadence was produced in the Church during that decade?[17] And was not that decadence caused by letting the claimants of "insight" go unchecked in their studied oversight of original sin and did not that oversight call for a simultaneous slighting of the infallible Magisterium?

That the unfolding of these two trends is simultaneous, because they are most logically connected, had been pointed out by that Newman whom the "insightful" have been wont to claim for their patron saint. He did so in many contexts, among them in the great concluding chapter of his *Apologia*, hardly a document to be overlooked. There he predicated on the disastrous effects of original sin, both on will and intellect, his conviction about an absolute need for an infallible Magisterium. Newman's self-styled followers never quoted a Newman paraphrasing the message of the Magisterium with pointed reference to what is to be done to man's intellect: "Ye must be born again; . . . your whole nature must be reborn, your passions, and your affections, and your aims, and your conscience, and your will, must all be bathed in a new element, and reconsecrated to your Maker, and, the last not the least, your *intellect*" (Italics added).[18] Much less did they quote Newman's full and unconditional approval of a Magisterium which

> claims to impose silence at will on any matters, or controversies, of doctrine, which on its own *ipse dixit* it pronounces to be dangerous, or inexpedient, or inopportune. It claims that whatever may be the judgment of Catholics upon such acts, these acts should be received by them with those outward marks of reverence, submission, and loyalty, which Englishmen, for instance, pay to the presence of their sovereign, without public criticism on them as being in their matter inexpedient, or in their manner violent or harsh.[19]

Newman would be astonished if not utterly shocked by the liberals' relentless efforts which turn him into the inspiration of the "theological revolution" of Vatican II, as if he had not identified the scepticism and relativism of liberals as the chief evil to be relentlessly combated. Courageous as he was as a theologian and a churchman, he would be deeply troubled by that courage which is nowadays demanded of the Church of Rome "still scared by its own courage at Vatican II."[20] Champion as Newman did the laity and a greater voice to be accorded to non-Italian or non-Latin nationalities in the Church and in particular to the English and the German, he hardly meant thereby that the tone of the Church be set by that Anglo-Saxon pragmatism which he bemoaned: "It is not at all easy (humanly speaking) to wind up an Englishman to a dogmatic level."[21] He would brand dishonest the "scholarship" which continually recalls his quip about drinking a toast "to conscience first and to the pope afterwards,"[22] and ignores his denouncing its "miserable counterfeit . . . which now goes by the name."[23]

Who of the latter-day advocates of conscience cared to

quote Newman's gripping portrayal of that counterfeit conscience and its virulent support in academia, not only secular but also theological? That portrayal included such features as "the right of thinking, speaking, writing, and acting, according to their judgment or their humor, without any thought of God at all," and "the freedom of conscience to dispense with conscience, to ignore a lawgiver and judge, to be independent of unseen obligations," and "the license to take up any or no religion, to take up this or that and let it go again, to go to church, to go to chapel, to boast of being above all religions and to be impartial critic of each of them."[24] It was in fact very dangerous to quote Newman even as he cited popes and councils about the absolute supremacy of consciences and held high the rights of the Catholic, who after long prayer could not see the moral goodness of a particular papal command given for a particular case (in which the pope is never infallible), to disobey the pope in the name of conscience. For in the same breath Newman also declared that the Catholic was not entitled to oppose his conscience to general declarations of the pope in matters of faith and morals. In invoking Thomas Aquinas about conscience as a supreme judge on what *hic et nunc* is to be done or be avoided, Newman observed that "since conscience is not a judgment upon any speculative truth, any abstract doctrine . . . it cannot come into direct collision with the Church's or the pope's infallibility, which is engaged only on general propositions, or the condemnation of propositions simply particular."[25] There could be no collision because in such matters the individual conscience did not enjoy the divine guidance promised to the pope.

To that supreme papal forum in matters of faith and morals Newman was able to transfer his full allegiance precisely because his notion of conscience was not tainted with subjectivism. He would therefore, in all good conscience, find deceitful the scheme in which his going over to Rome counts for nothing and in which everything is so construed that Rome be forced to submit to the scheming and very subjectivist architect of that pseudo-theological construct. He would hardly find anything novel in that scheming. In his own days he saw that kind of scheming force the famed Döllinger, for whom he had great sympathy though never a blind spot, to remove himself from Rome. He quite possibly thought at that time of a page in Disraeli's *Lothair* where a brilliant but self-admiring Anglican theologian, rumored to go over to Rome, pours cold water on such expectations with the remark: "Rome may come to me," said the Reverend Dionysius Smylie, "and it is perhaps the best thing it could do."[26] Newman would today find signal justification for his going over to Rome in that baffling inconsistency which saw print on the occasion of the visit of John Paul II to England. For if Archbishop Runcie was right in saying that Rome "can give a great deal to us in terms of doctrinal coherence," then he could not also be right in declaring "impossible the idea that you have to go to Rome for ethical decisions, for doctrinal clarifications."[27]

The Keys of Truth and Life

Not only is doctrinal coherence inconceivable without decisive doctrinal clarity but the latter, insofar as it is Rome's possession, rests entirely with the papacy. To think differently is to take lightly both logic and history. In the emancipation from ecclesiastical authority, which that intellect, as described by Newman, claimed to itself in the name of Vatican II, he would readily recognize the reason why the fruits of Vatican II are so different from its seeds. Nor would he be reluctant to recall in this connection the truth of the parable about the sowing of very different seeds by the enemy under the cover of night (Mt 13:25). Such a conjecture should seem very natural in view of what Newman said about the deceit of the Antichrist. Its signs

> may not be a persecution of blood and death, but of craft and subtlety only—not of miracles, but of natural wonders and powers of human skill, human acquirements in the hands of the devil. Satan may adopt the more alarming weapons of deceit—he may hide himself—he may attempt to seduce us in little things, and so to move Christians not all at once but by little and little from their true position ... It is his policy to split us up and divide us, to dislodge us gradually from off our rock of strength. And if there is to be a persecution, perhaps it will be then; then, perhaps, when we are all of us in all parts of Christendom so divided, and so reduced, so full of schism, so close upon heresy. When we have cast ourselves upon the world and depend for protection upon it, and have given up our independence and our strength, then he may burst upon us in fury, as far as God allows him.[28]

If this may be too frightening an outcome—an outcome of harvesting mostly bad fruits—it may be very well to recall the fact well known to any gardener (including the divine pruner): bad fruit grows in large number on any tree whose branches are allowed to grow freely in every direction and at any point. To be sure, the Church is not going to set up a new Inquisition; but the time will come when purely pastoral approaches to patently doctrinal issues will plainly display their inadequacies. Time will come when the obituary of Pius x written by Chesterton will reveal an eery timelessness:

> As has been pointed out, with subtle power and all proper delicacy, in numberless liberal and large-minded

journals, the great and good priest now dead had all the *prejudices* of a peasant. He had a prejudice to the effect that the mystical word "Yes" should be distinguished from the equally unfathomable expression "No" . . . The pope never pretended to have an extraordinary intellect; but he professed to be right—and he was. All honest atheists, all honest Calvinists, all honest men who mean anything or believe anything or deny anything, will have reason to thank their stars (a heathen habit) for the peasant in that high place. He left people to agree with his creed or disagree with it; but not *free* to misrepresent it. It was exactly what any peasant taken from any of our hills and plains would have said. But there was something more in him that would not have been in the ordinary peasant. For all this time he had wept for our tears; and he broke his heart for our bloodshed.[29]

So wrote Chesterton in the *Illustrated London News* on August 29, 1914, with World War I already a month old, and to last, contrary to all expectations, four full years more.

The strictures which Pius x issued against modernism have become targets of snide remarks and even of ridicule in many seminaries, theological faculties, and diocesan chanceries. Many Catholics, clergy and laity, feel free today of the heaviness of Peter's keys. They are, indeed, heavy to bear and even heavier to carry. In connection with his famed decision against artificial birth control, Paul vi confessed that much to none other than Karl Barth.[30] In this age of the wildness of human intellect, which is more enthralled by the intellect of extraterrestrials, about which nothing is known, than about its own powers of which already all too much is known, Paul vi is still quoted only because he once said: "The pope, as we all know, is undoubtedly the gravest obstacle in the path of ecumenism."[31] That this phrase is invariably taken out of its context is a sign of the wild fruits appearing in ever greater number on the tree of ecumenism unable to come to terms with the keys of Peter and for which an inclusion of those keys in a "model" of the Church, means a closed model.³² This inability is a piece of subjectivism, which in its refined form allows the pope the use of keys only in the case when everyone else resorts to the same keys, that is, solutions. Such is the old error which makes papal authority dependent on the consensus of the faithful. In its newfangled form it is equivalent to the rising consensus among the faithful that private confession, or one's subjecting oneself to the power of keys in terms of sacerdotal absolution, is no longer necessary.³³

Consensus is a most precious commodity, indeed, the most precious that the Church, the family of the faithful, and the family of nations can hope for. This is why the question of the best means of securing consensus is so crucial. As was already noted, the reading of no book leads to consensus. On the contrary, the more a book is read, the more opinions and interpretations it generates. The gesture with which the Reformers and so many reformers after them wanted to liberate Christians through restricting them to the Bible *alone* was equivalent to the kind of liberation to which a barrel is subjected when all the hoops holding it together are removed one by one. In that sense the truth of the Bible was not the kind of truth about which was written that it will make us free. Revelation was not meant to cause a fragmentation of the deposit of faith through freedom of interpretation which keeps fragmenting those who on that basis want to believe sincerely in revelation.

The truth of this received recently from a Protestant a most revealing formulation: "Ever again and always for Lutherans the greatest obstacle in the path of ecumenism is the gospel."³⁴ The statement is revealing as a variation on Paul VI's humble and humbling words on infallibility. It also reveals that any logic which undercuts the visible unity of Christians based on Peter's keys foments the divisiveness which attention focused exclusively on the Bible would produce. For the same Lutheran theologian, steeped in Luther's proverbial veneration of the Bible, added almost in the same breath: "The unity of the Church is not an end itself. The unity of the Church is important only for the sake of the gospel."[35] What is truly revealing in such reasoning is not so much its countering the emphasis of Jesus' agonizing prayer: "That they may be one, as you Father and I are one," as its giving a glimpse of the gospel-alone logic insofar as it counters unity.

Nothing would be more mistaken than to see in that gospel-alone stance an infatuation with the written word and nothing else. The real inspiration of Protestantism is genuinely spiritual and goes far deeper than what is usually seen in the contrast between Scripture and Magisterium. Indeed, as was already noted, Protestants have, ever since Luther and Calvin, seen their chief aspiration in grasping what is hidden in the written word. In that respect they are not at all different from Catholics aware of the ultimate ineffability of divine truth. No less a Romanist and a saint than Thomas Aquinas kept insisting on the ultimately negative character of man's knowledge of God, be it a knowledge fully informed by revelation.[36] Undoubtedly, the ever-fresh source of man's religious instincts lies in a negative glimpse of what is most positive, namely, the reality of God.

The real difference between Protestants and Catholics concerns their judgment as to what is the most reliable means of securing and holding fast to that truly ineffable tie with the divine. Their difference is real in spite of the fact that both have to satisfy the same human nature which is a composite of the tangible and the intangible. At the risk of oversimplifying a problem on which long volumes could be and have been written, the Protestant answer implies an effort to go from the intangible to the tangible; whereas the Catholic answer implies the opposite course. It would be tempting to judge the merits of these two opposite approaches in terms of the respective fruits they produce, as if that judgment would not be fraught with dangers. It is possible to make much of the frustrating efforts within Protestantism to set up an unequivocally tangible ecclesial structure. A Catholic may, indeed, make much of the ability of Roman Catholicism to survive the Reformers, who found nothing good in it, and indeed of the fact that, to quote a well-known utterance of Karl Barth, Vatican II has stolen the thunder of the Reformation. The same Catholic, who points at the Protestants' inability to explain the inner resources which Roman Catholicism keeps finding within herself, should think twice. The missionary zeal displayed by Protestant churches for the past hundred years has done more than to offset the perplexity which a Protestant may feel on considering the missionary inactivity of much of Protestantism during its first three hundred years.[37]

The breaking of that impasse can only come from a careful reflection on the fact of Incarnation. Christ clearly referred to his flesh and blood reality as he instructed Philip: "He who sees me sees the Father" (Jn 14:9). Indeed, the Word would have become flesh in vain if God had not expected man to follow the logic which starts with the tangible in order to reach the intangible and which expects man to fall back again and again on the tangible so that his surge toward the intangible may be replenished with fresh vitality. The logic of the Word become flesh was true to itself insofar as its message was to be carried on by specially chosen flesh and blood beings, the twelve. It should be therefore no surprise that the most spiritual, though not spiritualist, ecclesiologies written by Catholics were always about a Church of the Incarnate Word.[38] Such a notion of the Church is a far cry from the Church of the Word alone which in the form of the gospel-alone logic now plays havoc inside the Catholic Church. Its protagonists have for some time reveled in their position, whereas hardly anyone in the field recalls any more Paul vi's agonizing warnings about those bent on Protestantizing the Catholic Church from within. Rather, statements are being put in his mouth such as that "the Roman Catholic Church seems destined to die."[39] A dime a dozen are those Catholic ecumenists who prophesy about a future Catholic Church with a petrine office void of all power worthy of that name.

While the time has not yet come to speak openly about the wresting of the keys from the hands of Peter's successors, the time is ripe in the eyes of many to conjure up such an eventuality. Ecclesiastical superiors are not yet simply written off, perhaps because it is written in the Scriptures: "Obey your leaders and submit to them for they keep watch over you as men who must render account" (Heb. 13:17). But it is also instinctively realized that on the basis of the gospel-alone logic one remains always entitled to question anyone, who presents himself as the leader or superior, with the words: "That is the question," words almost as old as Christianity, according to the observation of St. Ignatius of Antioch. Debates about the keys of the kingdom will go on forever unless Christians steep themselves not so much in reading the Bible as in the attitude invariably urged there, the attitude of loyal adherence to those who were sent to speak with authority. Such adherence was conjured up by Christ who said to the twelve after having washed their feet: "I solemnly assure you, he who accepts anyone I send accepts me, and in accepting me accepts him who sent me"

(Jn 13:20). Giovanni Perrone, S.J., one of the influential theologians blamed by some nowadays for Vatican I, was therefore on most biblical grounds when he pointed out that Christians must adhere to the pope not because he is infallible; but since they must, on divine command, adhere to the pope, he has to be infallible.[40]

Solidarity with the Keybearer

The point made by Perrone could not be to the liking of an age engrossed with the celebration of subjectivist individualism, the chief hallmark of modernism. The same point was, however, most welcome to a Church ready to resist modernism on all levels. Her half a thousand bishops assembled in Rome in June 1867 to celebrate the 1800th anniversary of the martyrdom of Saints Peter and Paul provided the best preparation for the dogma of infallibility by putting special emphasis on their solidarity with the pope, Pius IX.[41] In doing so they merely echoed an old theme, though a theme which even today awaits a full study. The impact, which such a study would make, may be gathered from the persuasiveness of two memorable witnesses who put that solidarity in focus in patristic times. In the case of both, the standing for solidarity with Rome meant a painful resistance to the advocates of local autonomy.

The tortures and lengthy imprisonments would have deserved the crown of martyrdom for St. Theodore, the Studite, to whom monasticism in the East owes so much and who appealed to Rome both in matters of morals and of doctrine. In resisting the adulterous emperor Constantin VI he put matters to Pope St. Leo III in a letter which opened with the following words: "Since Christ the God gave to the great Peter also the dignity of supreme pastoral rule after having given him the keys of the kingdom of heaven, to Peter and to his successor must be referred any innovation made in the universal Church by those who part with truth."[42] A decade or so later, in the midst of the iconoclast controversy, he urged steadfastness on his nephew and spiritual heir, Naveratius, with a statement in which reference to the keys held by Peter and his successors was prominent: "I witness before God and men that the iconoclasts departed from the body of Christ and from the supreme heavenward throne in which Christ placed the keys of the faith, against which the gates of hell, that is, the mouths of heretics, have not so far prevailed and shall not prevail because the promise was made by the One who does not deceive. Let therefore the most blessed and apostolic [pope] Paschal, worthy of his name, rejoice because he had fulfilled the function of the office of Peter."[43] That function, according to St. Theodore, implied the final word in disciplining the erring patriarch of Constantinople, Nicephor I, who sided with the iconoclasts. The eastern patriarchs, St. Theodore insisted, must submit their judgment of Nicephor I not to the emperor of Constantinople but to the one "who presides over the first see; . . . both parties must therefore send a delegation to Rome and from there should the certainty of faith be received."[44]

This act of receiving through adherence to the source was a pivotal point for St. Augustine engaged in a lifelong battle against the Donatists who with an eye on personal holiness insisted on rebaptising anyone baptised by "unworthy" prelates. Among the many writings which Augustine composed against them is the "psalm against the party of Donatus," a poem certainly destined for popular consumption. No theological learning was needed to follow its rhyming lines which peak with Augustine's call for solidarity with Rome:

> You know what is the Catholic Church and to be cut off the vine.

> Let the withered among them come and live from the root,
> For before they become too dry they are already consumed by fire.
> We do not rebaptize because there is one sign for faith, [but]
> Because you, though not saints, have the mere form of that sign.
> The branch retains its form though cut off the vine.
> Of what profit is to him to have that form if not living from the root?
> Come brethren if you want to be grafted on the vine,
> It is painful to see you cut off and lying on the ground.
> Count the priests only from Peter's very seat
> And in the line of those fathers as they succeed one another, see:
> It is the rock which is not conquered by the proud gates of hell.
> All you who want to enjoy peace, consider but what is true.[45]

In times resounding with the word "solidarity" as the road to freedom, the tying of infallibility to solidarity may help conjure up the true spiritual freedom of Christians, the sole purpose and God-given role of the pope's infallibility. Debates, however learned, about infallibility[46] will remain futile, indeed, at times equivalent to the putting of the cart before the horse, unless solidarity with the see of Rome is seen as the existential precondition to perceiving in its true light the infallibility of its occupant. It has become an old pattern that professional critics of the pope's infallibility are never among the promoters of solid loyalty to the pope. In fact, they all too often turn into festering sources of dissension. In their much publicized learnedness there is never room for remembering, say, a St. Anselm of Canterbury, who praised in the following words Count Robert of Flanders for complying with Rome in the crucial matter of investiture: "In doing so you are obeying not man but God and show yourself to be one of the sheep entrusted to the holy apostle Peter to whom God gave the keys of the kingdom of heaven. For it is certain that he who does not obey the Roman Pontiff's rulings made for the safeguarding of Christian religion, is disobedient to the apostle Peter, whose vicar he is, and is not of the sheep entrusted to him. Let him therefore look for other doors of the kingdom of heaven, because he will not enter through those doors whose keys are carried by Peter."[47]

Almost a hundred years ago when modernism made its first inroads into the Church, Hyppolite Taine, an agnostic himself but a keen observer of Christianity, wrote as he journeyed through Italy: "If Catholicism resists this attack, it seems to me that it will forever be safe from all other attacks."[48] Contrary to expectations the attack was not over with the antimodernistic oath, an oath dispensed with just before its updating would have become more needed than ever. The attack has returned even more vigorously and its front waves are well inside the walls. The chief target is the papacy which finds today as many detractors from within as from without. Their chief grievance relates to what is most difficult to bear for modern man who thinks that all arguments about everything under the sun can and should go on forever. Yet, even in the second half of the 20th century, the papacy has not stopped claiming to itself the right to pronounce the last word in matters both doctrinal and disciplinary. Resentment on this point can affect not only well-meaning journalists[49] but very insightful minds as well.[50] In fact, even among those in the Church whose glory and strength has been for centuries a special solemn vow of obedience to the pope, there are many whom even the extraordinary personality of John Paul II could not persuade to give him the benefit of doubt, let alone display plain submission to him, when in their own matter and to their greatest benefit he decided to intervene. The emancipation claimed by modernists was reverberating in Karl Rahner's letter,[51] in which the autonomy of the Society of Jesus was upheld against its professed supreme head, the pope, certainly the head of the Church, or the society of believers established by Christ.

The personal charisma of John Paul II took some of the wind out of the neo-modernist storm, which, however, may rise to full strength once his pontificate comes to an end, or should he decide on issuing a decree whose wisdom will be evident only in a century or two. The coming of that storm is all the more likely because the Church was not promised a steady supply of popes with personal magic. The Church was not even promised an exemption from bad popes, to say nothing of unreformed reformers. The Church was, however, promised that prayers would always be answered in God's good time, which, unfortunately, is hardly ever good enough for humans fomenting decay under the pretext of "renewal." The "ultimate weapon" against bad popes and bad prelates is ultimately prayer alone, hardly to be considered inappropriate either to the gospel or to a reform genuinely steeped in conformity to it.[52]

The Church, to last to the end of times, was promised an endless supply of shepherds holding and wielding the keys, because Christ, the door of the sheepfold, wanted it to remain under watchful eyes, lest the unauthorized, including ravaging wolves, should freely roam inside its walls.

Two thousand years of turbulent history produced no evidence that those keys had been mishandled in any substantive manner. Being keys, they will always work in most specific ways. Those ways are the very opposite to the studied haziness cultivated by the new spokesmen of the new "collegiality" which they leave unspecified so that doctrine and discipline may even more readily be manipulated by special groups within the Church. The pope and his keys will necessarily be resented by those expert in producing ever new smokescreens about anything obviously specific and specifically obvious, that is, the ever valid truths available to mere common sense. In fighting off the obvious in the name of their "genius," those experts make themselves the target of a line of Goethe struck by the blindness of a true genius to the obvious. Goethe wrote *Tasso* with an eye on his *faux-pas* in the court of Weimar where, so he felt, his greatness should have reduced to a small matter his transgressions of marital norms of greatest and obvious importance. Tasso, who stands for Goethe, is unable to appreciate common sense even when described as the highest refinement in thinking. Yet, great pagan though he was, Goethe also conveys something of his grudging admiration for papacy and Church as he lets Alphonso convey to Tasso, with a reference to the pope, the wisdom he has to learn: "The lofty sense of the pope! He sees the small as small and the great as great!"[53]

Such sense should seem to be the highest virtue to a keymaker and to anyone reflecting on the accurate match that has to exist between a key and the lock it operates. Only small keys can operate small locks and only big keys will make big locks click. Keys, big and small, have been a common property for a time even longer than the long past of the Church. Very old, indeed, may be that proverb according to which "all keys hang not on one man's girdle."[54] The moral of that proverb is not at all different from the one which St. Paul enjoined in speaking of the many different members needed to make one body. Indeed, the Spirit of God dispenses its gifts in manifold ways and to many. Decisively different has been the divine dispensation about the keys of the kingdom. Whatever the number of those keys (Christ spoke of them in the plural), they were all deposited by him in the hands of one single individual, Simon, the son of Jonah, whom in the same act he designated as the rock on which he was to build his Church.

Those keys, the entire history of Church and dogma is a witness, have been looked upon as real only as long as they were seen held in the hands of the successors of Peter as bishop of Rome. The head of the twelve, an impetuous and imaginative man he was, must have often thought of the words according to which he would, in his old age, no longer be free to go where he wanted to because someone else would "tie him up." Only when Nero's madness suddenly sought scapegoats in Christians may Peter have taken those words for a prophecy about the specific form of his impending martyrdom. As he agonized, being tied head down to a cross, he could hardly be concerned about the place where his tortured body would be laid to rest. Much less could he foresee his burial place to be along the road which, near Nero's circus, followed the slope of Mons Vaticanus.

His tomb there soon turned into the nucleus of a small Christian place of worship adjoined by a baptistry. The faithful flocking there, often in great secrecy, could hardly dream that Peter's tomb would one day anchor an axis dashing toward heaven through the pinnacle of the most stunning cupola ever built. Nor could they foresee that in front of that cupola there would one day stretch a vast square. Nor is there any evidence that Bernini, whose famed colonnades made that square look like a gigantic keyhole, had thought of Peter's keys as he drew its sketches. But no sooner had Bernini's masterpiece been completed than it began to be spoken of as a huge keyhole most appropriately located. After all, the square not only led to the tomb of the first keybearer but was also flanked by the residence of his living successor giving his blessings *urbi et orbi*, to the city and the whole earth. Thus the entire scene became symbolic of a huge lock serving the globe so that something beyond it might be opened and closed with keys of no human make.

Se non è proposto, è ben prodotto (though not planned, certainly well produced) might be the best comment on such a lucky match of archeology, theology, architecture, and history. As if by sheer luck, a square which a colonnade makes appear as a vast keyhole, matches the keys of the kingdom held over it. But when luck defies all human probabilities, divine Providence ought to be conjured up. Those familiar with the vicissitudes which in 1900 years could have time and again turned Peter's tomb and his body inside it into mere dust, will indeed think of Providence also in connection with the acumen and perseverance of a distinguished Roman archeologist, Dr. Margherita Guarducci. Had it not been for her, the daring excavations under St. Peter during the 1940s would have been deprived of their two great finds. One of them, the bones of St. Peter, is vouched for its genuineness by the other, a reddish plaster on the wall, just above the cavity in which those bones were found.

When first noticed in the early 1940s the wild variety of scratches (graffiti) on that plaster of about a square yard in size was judged to contain nothing worth looking at. The three magnificent volumes, in which Dr. Guarducci published her painstaking deciphering of those graffiti, tell a very different story. The graffiti are signs, names, and words witnessing to belief in eternal life, Christ, Trinity, Mary, the Saints—and to belief in a close unity of Christ and Peter.

The latter belief is conveyed through a sign[55] in which an *E* is combined with the Greek monogram of Christ (Illustration xi). But there is more to that sign than a double use of *P* as the Greek *rho* and the Latin *P* so as to stand both for Christ and for Peter. For the same combination also appears as a key in obvious reference to Peter's role as *the* key-bearer. This interpretation is amply confirmed by the combined appearance of the two letters as a carving into a stone from the catacomb under the Forum Romanum[56] (Illustration XII).

Those unwilling or unable to see that sign in such fortunate light still have to ponder luck, a luck very human in comparison. It is symbolized by a huge pillar-like stone in the same area. For as if by sheer luck Bernini's colonnades had for their center an obelisk which carries the words: *stat crux dum volvitur orbis* (the cross stands while the earth revolves). That stone and those words are a striking evocation of the biblical description of the Church as the column of truth (1 Tim 3:15). But such a description is valid only for a Church which is conscious of her built-in indefectibility, symbolized by that column of truth, in preaching the gospel infallibly.

Similar lucky coincidences abound, it is well to recall, in the history of the papacy. They are so numerous and obvious as to make commonplace such phrases as "the wisdom of Rome" and "the genius of the Vatican." It is far less obvious why that wisdom or genius should last for so many centuries and outlast so many popes who as individuals were not paragons of wisdom, let alone geniuses. The endurance of a wise and genial policy which defies all the projections and parameters of historians, including their latest brand known as psycho-historians, should seem outright perplexing. The solution to that greatest of all historic puzzles will be on hand once Christ is seen in his greatness far surpassing all the greats of history. But then logic demands that one should face up to the obvious face-value of all his words, not the least of which are the ones on the keys of the kingdom.

NOTES

Chapter 1

1. The following illustrations are the harvest of a few months' attention to headlines, captions, and phrases—mostly in *The New York Times*.
2. The subject/title catalogue of any major library contains a long list of books that carry the words key or keys in their titles. The examples given were gathered from the card catalogue of Firestone Library, Princeton University.
3. Published in Dallas by the Associated Locksmiths of America Inc.
4. Written by J. Blum and E. L. Blum (New York: Gordon & Breach, 1975). "The Key to the Universe" was the caption not too long ago of a two-hour TV report on modern cosmology. Of course, those who know the solution to all problems would readily come up with works such as *The Master Key* (1916), a heavy volume (reprinted in 1919 and 1933) which, tellingly, offers no clue to its author's identity.
5. The foldout may be obtained from the publisher, Mansell Publishing, 3 Bloomsbury Place, London. Here, too, the pattern is old. Some elderly readers of this book may recall from their school days "Kelly's Keys to the Classics," so many thin booklets ("ponies") to help in the reading of Greek and Latin authors. In their title pages the drawing of a key stands for the word itself.
6. Quoted in TIME, Oct. 25, 1982, p. 88, in a full-page report, the basis of this paragraph.
7. D. Hartley, *Observations on Man, His Frame, His Duty and His Expectation* (London: J. Leake and Wm. Frederick, 1749), vol. 1, pp. 15–16.
8. The picture of a key looms large in an Avis-folder which connects car rental with reduced rates for vacations in German castles transformed into hotels. The picture of a castle with its ornate and fortified main door inevitably conjures up the image of a big key.
9. The charge of "elitism," especially handy at a time of economic depression, can, of course, turn even a Phi Beta Kappa key into a possession

of dubious merit. The owner of one received a mere $5 for it in a pawnshop; see TIME Dec. 28, 1981, p. 67, and Jan. 18, 1982, p. 9.

10. The account on the early history of Yale locks in *The Lure of the Lock* by Albert A. Hopkins (New York: The General Society of Mechanics and Tradesmen, 1928; reprinted in 1954), pp. 60–66, has since served as the major source of information for a number of more recent books that offer an all too often spotty and almost invariably improperly documented history of lock-making. One of these, L. Zara's *Locks and Keys*, a title in the Collector's Blue Books series (New York: Walker and Company, 1969), deserves mention for its wealth of illustration. For an easily accessible brief history of Yale keys, together with very good diagrams of the locks they operate, see "Lock and Key" in *The World Book Encyclopedia* (Chicago: Thorndike Barnhart, 1965), vol. 12, pp. 366–68. Less accessible, but very informative for all its brevity, is *Keys: Their History and Collection* by E. Monk (Aylesbury, Bucks. U. K., Shire Publications, 1974; reprinted 1979), 64 pp. The July 1984 issue of *Smithsonian* contains (pp. 35–38) fine illustrations of old and modern keys, so many challenges to burglars and safecrackers.

11. The authority in question is Vincent J. M. Eras, one-time Managing Director of Lips' Safe and Lock Manufacturing Company Banking Engineers, who stated in his excellent *Locks and Keys throughout the Ages* (Folkstone, England: Bailey Bros and Swinfen Ltd, 1974): "The design of the key predetermines the design of the lock mechanism, which means that the key is made first and afterwards the lock. Subsequently the key bit constitutes the principal part of the key since this part brings about the locking and unlocking of the mechanism. A complicated key bit besides precision as regards the axial movement of the key on its pivot is a determinant of the degree of security in the lock" (p. 96).

12. See M. Alth, *All About Locks and Locksmithing* (New York: Hawthorn Books, 1972), p. 71.

13. Quoted in Zara, *Locks and Keys*, p. 67. The claim was certainly appropriate for an Englishman. In the portrait of Lord Heathfield by Sir Joshua Reynolds, since 1924 in the National Gallery (London), the hero, who as General Eliott defended the Rock for four years (1779–1783), is painted with a key in his right hand and with the fortress of Gibraltar in the background.

14. Including the Bramah lock. It was then that the Bramah Company paid the promised sum of 200 guineas; see Hopkins, *The Lure of the Lock*, p. 50.

15. For an excellent illustration, see Zara, *Locks and Keys*, p. 43.

16. Ibid., 44.

17. Ibid., 11.

18. See *The Devil's Dictionary* (1911; Cleveland: World Publishing Company, 1948, p. 196) of Ambrose Bierce (1842–1914) who aimed his sardonic wit at the proliferation of crime (and of prisons) in modern "enlightened" society.

19. *The Correspondence of Marcus Cornelius Fronto*, edited and for

the first time translated by C. R. Haines (London: W. Heinemann, 1919–20), vol. 2, p. 17.

20. It was so good a phrase as to find entry into the famed *Adagiorum . . . epitome* of Erasmus (see edition, Oxford: typis W. Hall, 1666, p. 20).

21. In his *Natural History* (Bk. vii, ch. lvi, par. 198) Pliny credits Theodorus with the invention of the square, the plummet, the lathe, the lever, and the key. In the standard modern translation of that work by H. Rackham (Loeb Classical Library; Cambridge, MA: Harvard University Press) the key is missing (see vol. 2, [1961], p. 641).

22. See lines 421–23; quoted from *Aristophanes* with the English translation of B. B. Rogers, vol. 3 (London: W. Heinemann, 1924), p. 167.

23. As suggested by a bas-relief representation of such a key in the Temple of Karnak.

24. The best account is in ch. ii, "Antike Türen and Schlüssel," in H. Diels, *Antike Technik. Sechs Vorträge* (Leipzig: B. G. Teubner, 1914), pp. 41–48. Also very useful is the article "Sera" by R. Vallois in Ch. Daremberg *et al* (eds.), *Dictionnaire des antiquités grecques et romaines d'après les textes et les monuments*. Tome 4, Partie 2 R-S (Paris: Hachette, n. d.), pp. 1241–48.

25. Bk. xxi, lines 5–8 and 42–50; quoted from *The Odyssey of Homer*, translated with an introduction by R. Lattimore (1965; New York: Harper and Row, 1975), pp. 309–10.

26. The remark is from *Phaenomena*, a brief account of the constellations by Aratus, a Stoic author (fl. 270 b.c.); see *Arati Phaenomena*. Introduction, texte critique, commentaire et traduction par Jean Martin (Florence: La Nuova Italia, 1956), p. 38.

27. See *Nineveh and Its Palaces—The Discoveries of Botta and Layard Applied to the Elucidation of Holy Writ*, by J. Bonomi (London: Office of the Illustrated London Library, 1852), p. 150.

28. See Eras, *Locks and Keys Throughout the Ages*, pp. 24–26.

29. As illustrated in *Nineveh and Its Palaces*, p. 150.

30. W. Eton, *Survey of the Turkish Empire* (1798; New York: Arno Press, 1973), p. 224. Almost a hundred years later, the French traveler and explorer, Louis Lortet, registered his surprise at the ingenuity of such keys still in usage in the Mideast with a drawing; see his *La Syrie d'aujourd'hui: Voyages dans la Phénicie, le Liban et la Judée, 1875–1880* (Paris: Hachette, 1884), p. 352. By then the Louvre had one such key from Palestine, described by H. de Villefosse, *Notice des monuments provenant de la Palestine et conservées au Musée du Louvre* (4th ed.; Paris: Librairies-imprimeries réunies, 1876), p. 21.

31. On these details, see "Sera" by R. Vallois (note 24 above), "Schlüssel" in Pauly's *Real-Encyclopädie der classischen Altertumswissenschaften*, Zweite Reihe R-Z, Dritter Halbband (Stuttgart: J. B. Metzler, 1921), cols. 565–69, and "kleis" in H. G. Lindell, *A Greek-English Lexicon* (new ed.: Oxford: Clarendon Press, 1925), vol 1, p. 957.

32. In Book xxiv, ch. 23 of *The History of Rome by Titus Livius*,

Books Nine to Twenty-Six, literally translated, with notes and illustrations by D. Spillan and C. Edmonds (London: H. G. Bohn, 1854), p. 923. Six years later, in 209 B.C., as Livy relates (ibid., bk. XXVII, ch. 24, transl. cit., *Books Twenty-Seven to Thirty-Six*, p. 1125), Terentius Varro, commander of the Roman army that captured Arretium (Arezzo), let new locks be put on all the doors in the walls of that city when its magistrates claimed that they had lost the keys. Complete re-keying of the doors of a place is not a modern procedure.

33. Such was the gold-plated Moorish key (now in the Treasury of the Cathedral of Sevilla) which Axataf yielded to Ferdinand in 1248 when Seville was reconquered (for its illustration, see Zara, *Locks and Keys*, p. 48). Another such key, the one presented in 1624 by Justin of Nassau to the Spanish general, Ambrosio Spinola, is the center piece of Velasquez's great painting, "The Surrender of Breda." Of no less historic importance was the key, though only figurative, which carried the gist of the uncompromising reply of the Turkish Sultan, Suleiman I, "I shall hang the keys of Hungary from my shoulders," given to the envoys of Ferdinand I who desperately sought to keep at least a part of that country. On this detail, see D. Palmieri, *De Romano pontifice* (new ed.; Prato: Giachetti et Co., 1891), p. 334. Last but not least, one must recall Rodin's monumental sculpture showing the six leading citizens of Calais surrendering in utter agony the keys of their city.

Chapter Two

1. The following discussion owes much to the section, "The master of the palace," in R. de Vaux, *Ancient Israel*, tr. J. McHugh (New York: McGraw Hill, 1961), pp. 129–31. To a lesser extent this is also true of O. Kaiser's *Isaiah 13–39: A Commentary* (Philadelphia: Westminster Press, 1974), pp. 151–57. These two works are in accord in their emphasis on the exclusive power symbolized by the keys in question and on the high status of Sebna's office. Very meager, by comparison, is what is offered in *The International Critical Commentary*. Concerning the occurrences of *mapathah* (key) in the Hebrew Bible, the standard reference is *A Hebrew and English Lexicon of the Old Testament with an Appendix containing the Biblical Aramaic* of W. Gesenius as translated by E. Robinson and edited by F. Brown *et al* (Oxford: Clarendon Press).

2. O. Cullmann, *Saint Pierre. Disciple-Apôtre-Martyr* (Neuchâtel: Delachaux et Niestle, 1952), see especially pp. 161–66.

3. Bultmann's rejection of the authenticity of the passage has nowadays a very diminished appeal compared to its erstwhile impact in the 1930s. In fact Bultmann himself insisted on the Palestinian provenance of what he called a logion; see Cullmann, *Saint Pierre*, pp. 151 and 167.

4. Cullmann's emphatic insistence, at the end of his book, on the ac-

tual historical Peter as the one who will forever remain the foundation of the Church, was in fact referred to by none other than Paul VI as something of enormous significance for the cause of ecumenism. The pope's words in *The Pope Speaks: Dialogues of Paul VI with Jean Guitton*, tr. Anne and Christopher Fremantle (London: Weidenfeld and Nicolson, 1968, pp. 188–92) may not, of course, be his exactly spoken words in spite of being in quotation marks.

5. It is enough to think of Simeon's prophecy, of Herod's plan, and of the immediate sequel to Jesus' crucial appearance in the synagogue of Nazareth which, humanly speaking, could have resulted in his death.

6. *Saint Pierre*, pp. 165–66.

7. Cullmann himself offered nothing specific as to where exactly the dialogue between Jesus and Peter should be located in the context of the Last Supper.

8. It is difficult not to see Jesus' supernatural power behind the troops falling to the ground after their first confrontation with him (Jn 18:7).

9. Lk 22:61. Christ in fact had to turn around to be able to look at Peter.

10. The reference in Matthew (16:23) is to *skandalon* whose derivation is uncertain, but there is no uncertainty of its being taken not only for a trap but for anything, such as a stumbling block or stone, that may trip up somebody. Hence the Latin usage of *petra scandali*.

11. Lk 21:37–39 and 22:1–3. The preparation (with no microwave or electric oven and gas range at their disposal for the roasting of the paschal lamb) could easily take a good part of the day even with the room being prepared. There is no indication that Peter and John returned to the Mount of Olives to tell Jesus about the Supper's being ready.

12. Mt. 17:24–27.

13. A. Oepke, "Der Herrnspruch über die Kirche in der neuesten Forschung," *Studia theologica* (Lund) 2 (1950):149.

14. Cullmann's brief reference to that background in the second edition was in its own way just as puzzling as his complete silence in the first. For details, see my *And on This Rock: The Witness of One Land and Two Covenants* (Notre Dame, In.: Ave Maria Press, 1978), p. 121, or its French translation, *Et sur ce roc: Le témoignage d'une terre et de deux testaments* (Paris: Téqui, 1983), p. 68, note. The first to point out in convincing details Cullmann's slighting of that background was M. Overnay, "Le Cadre historique des paroles de Jésus sur la primauté de Pierre. Saint Matthieu 16:17–19," *Nova et Vetera* 28 (1953):206–29. Overnay was not emphatic enough in calling attention to a similar slighting by prominent Catholic biblical scholars, including the Père Lagrange himself.

15. In my *And on This Rock* the entire ch. 1 is devoted to the significance of that geographic background.

16. Psalm 41 is particularly explicit in that respect.

17. In his *The Cessation of Oracles* (see *Plutarch's Complete Works*.

Essays and Miscellaneous. vol. 1 [New York: Thomas Y. Crowell, 1909], pp. 443–44) Plutarch (fl. 90 A.D.) makes Cleombrotus oppose spurious reports about the mortality of gods with a story whose accuracy is not suspect in the eyes of Cleombrotus (or of Plutarch for that matter) who begins with a reference to false apparitions of gods. But with respect to the gods' mortality, Cleombrotus continues, "I have heard a tale from a man who is neither a fool nor an idle talker—from that Aemilian the rhetorician, whom some of you know well; Epitherses was his father, a townsman of mine, and a teacher of grammar. This man [Epitherses] said, that once upon a time he made a voyage to Italy, and embarked on board a ship conveying merchandise and several passengers. When it was now evening, off the Echinad Islands, the wind dropped, and the ship, carried by the current, was come near Paxi; most of the passengers were awake, and many were still drinking, after having had supper. All of a sudden, a voice was heard from the Isle of Paxi, of some one calling 'Thamus' with so loud a cry as to fill them with amazement. This Thamus was an Egyptian pilot, known by name to many of those on board. Called twice, he kept silence; but on the third summons he replied to the caller, and the latter, raising yet higher his voice, said, 'When thou comest over against Palodes, announce that the great Pan is dead.' All, upon hearing this, said Epitherses, were filled with consternation, and debated with themselves whether it were better to do as ordered, or not to make themselves too busy, and to let it alone. So Thamus decided that if there should be a wind he would sail past and hold his tongue; but should there fall a calm and smooth sea off the island, he would proclaim what he had heard. When, therefore, they were come over against Palodes, there being neither wind nor swell of sea, Thamus, looking out from the stern, called out to the land what he had heard, namely, 'That the great Pan is dead': and hardly had he finished speaking than there was a mighty cry, not of one, but of many voices mingled together in wondrous manner. And inasmuch as many persons were then present, the story got spread about in Rome, and Thamus was sent for by Tiberius Caesar; and Tiberius gave so much credence to the tale that he made inquiry and research concerning this Pan; and that the learned men about him, who were numerous, conjectured he was the one that was born from Hermes and Penelope." This story inspired many modern literary works of which the best remembered are a section in Schiller's *Götter Griechenlands* and Elizabeth Browning's poem, "The Dead Pan," in which all the 39 strophes come to an end with the cry "Pan is dead" or a slight variation of it. As to the neopagan resurrecting of Pan's cult in modern society, a full page report in TIME (Aug. 6, 1979, p. 84) makes for an eye-opening reading. Long before that, Chesterton made incisive observations on the naturalness with which post-Christian society turns instinctively to Pan and the accuracy with which the logic of that turn is in evidence. Thus in *Orthodoxy* he wrote: "Pantheism is all right as long as it is the worship of Pan. But Nature has another side which experience and sin are not slow in finding out, and it is no flippancy to say of the god Pan that he soon showed the cloven hoof'' (p. 139).

18. Following that fleeting discussion of the keys, about which Cullmann recognizes that they are expressive of power and authority (*Saint Pierre*, pp. 183–84), he analyzes in much detail "construction" and "people of God" as concepts also contained in the idea of keys. As one would expect, he fails to emphasize that, if such is the case, then the only biblical notion of constructing the people of God is the one which is done with the power of authority, deposited in a concrete individual.

19. J. S. Exell, *The Biblical Illustrator* (Grand Rapids, MI: Baker Book House, 1964), p. 345.

20. As invariably noted in any standard (old and new) collection of Talmudic sayings that can be related to New Testament phrases, such as the ones written by Lightfoot, Wünschle, Strack and Billerbeck, and Dalman.

21. *The Jewish Wars*, 1, 5, 2. Quoted from *The Works of Flavius Josephus*, tr. W. Whiston (Auburn and Rochester: Alden & Beardsley, 1857), p. 560.

22. This can easily be gathered from a brief look at the texts in H. L. Strack and P. Billerbeck, *Das Evangelium nach Matthäus erläutert aus Talmud und Midrasch* (Munich: Beck, 1922), p. 737.

23. Ibid.

24. *Apocalypse of Baruch* 10:18.

25. In particular by J. M. van Cangh and M. van Esbroek whose essay, "La primauté de Pierre (Mt 16. 16–19) et son contexte judaîque," *Revue théologique de Louvain* 11 (1980): 310–24, is closely followed in the following pages.

26. I have repeatedly found Protestant friends, including theologians and other sedulous readers of the Bible, greatly surprised when I brought this passage to their attention.

Chapter Three

1. See English translation, *The Diatessaron of Tatian* in *The Anti-Nicene Fathers*, vol. 10, p. 80. This multivolume collection of patristic works in English translation and its sequel, *The Nicene and Post-Nicene Fathers*, will be quoted from its reprinting by W. B. Eerdmans, Grand Rapids, Michigan.

2. Next to that often quoted passage in St. Irenaeus' *Adversus haereses* (lib. 3, cap. 3, art. 1) one finds the emphatic recall by the bishop of Lyon of the fact that the holy apostles Peter and Paul "handed over to Linus the episcopal office" in Rome and that when during Clement, who succeeded Linus' successor, Anacletus, "no small dissension arose among the brethren in Corinth, the church in Rome sent a powerful letter to the Corinthians,

urging peace on them and rekindling their faith, and reminding them of the apostolic tradition it had recently received."

3. A. N. Whitehead, *Modes of Thought* (1938; New York: Capricorn Books, 1958), p. 235. The fallacy derives partly, according to Whitehead, from the presupposition "that human language, in single words or in phrases, explicitly expresses these fundamental ideas" (ibid.).

4. Quoted from P. Batiffol, *Primitive Catholicism*, tr. H. L. Brianceau from the fifth revised edition of *L'Eglise naissante et catholicisme* (London: Longmans, Green and Co., 1911), pp. 135-36. Needless to say, the pre-Nicene part of this chapter owes much to that still capital work of Batiffol whose incisiveness was acknowledged by Harnack himself (ibid., pp. viii–x).

5. *Primitive Catholicism*, p. 135.

6. One of Harnack's criticism of Batiffol's thesis was that he had already demonstrated twenty years prior to the publication of Batiffol's *L'Eglise naissante* that "Roman and Catholic are identical" (quoted in *Primitive Catholicism*, p. viii). From that period one may mention R. Sohn, a specialist in the history of ecclesiastical law, who also had concluded to the identity of Roman and Catholic. Needless to say, both Harnack and Sohn raised caveats against identifying Roman and Catholic with Christian without strong reservations.

7. My discussion of Tertullian follows closely the one in *Primitive Catholicism*.

8. Tertullian, *De pudicitia*, ch. 21; quoted from J. T. Shotwell and L. R. Loomis, *The Sea of Peter* (New York: Columbia University Press, 1927), p. 302. See also *Anti-Nicene Fathers*, vol. 4, p. 99.

9. Ibid.

10. Ibid.

11. Ibid., pp. 303–04.

12. Ibid.

13. Quoted from *Primitive Catholicism*. p. 220.

14. Tertullian, *On Prescription against Heretics*, ch. 22; quoted from *Anti-Nicene Fathers*, vol. 3, p. 253.

15. Ibid., ch. 42; p. 264.

16. Clement of Alexandria, *Stromata*, vii, 16; *Primitive Catholicism*, pp. 259–60.

17. Ibid., vii, 17; pp. 260–61.

18. Ibid., vii, 16; p. 258.

19. Ibid., vii, 16; p. 260.

20. Ibid., vii, 15; p. 257.

21. Origen, *Commentaria in Mattheum* (PG 13:1011); *Anti-Nicene Fathers*, vol. 10, pp. 458–59.

22. Ibid., 13:1014; for a partial translation, see *Primitive Catholicism*,

p. 308; for a rather different translation, see Shotwell and Loomis, *The Sea of Peter*, p. 321.

23. Ibid., 13:1015.

24. St. Cyprian, Epistula 27:1 (PL 4:305–06). While I owe to Batiffol's *Primitive Catholicism* most of the subsequent references to Cyprian's letters, the latter are quoted here in their order as given in the Migne edition and not in the earlier and much less accessible Oxford edition used by Batiffol.

25. St. Cyprian, *De unitate* 5 (PL 4:516).

26. *De unitate* 10 (PL 4:523).

27. He did so with the assertion that none of us sets himself up as a bishop of bishops. For the Latin context, see *Primitive Catholicism*, p. 391.

28. St. Cyprian, Epistula 55:14 (PL 3:844–45). Once more St. Cyprian could not have been closer to recognizing the factor which alone would have provided coherence to his ecclesiology. The latter evidenced in the most striking way its need for that coherence precisely when Cyprian spoke (Epistula 69:8) of the "mutual agglutination of the bishops" as the safeguard of the unity of the Church. Tellingly, in the same context Cyprian clearly perceived that his assertion, "he who is not with the bishop is not in the Church," could secure the unity of the local church but not of the universal Church. The latter required the agglutination of bishops about which it would have been more logical for Cyprian to state that it was secured by agglutination to the bishop of Rome, because he began the same paragraph with a recall of Peter's words to Christ that the twelve would not abandon him though everyone else should do so: "Christ is spoken to by Peter upon whom the Church was to be founded, and He in turn teaches and shows by using the word "Ecclesia" [gathering] that, although the stubborn and proud crowd of those unwilling to listen should secede, the Church will not secede from Christ to whom the Church is the people united to the bishop and the sheep adhering to its shepherd" (PL 4:418–19).

29. *Primitive Catholicism*, p. 368, where the problem of that "conflated" version is fully discussed.

30. St. Cyprian, Epistula 68:5 (PL 3:1064).

31. Ibid., 76:10 (PL 3:1191–93).

32. Ibid., 71:2–3 (PL 3:423).

33. Ibid., 60:3 (PL 4:372).

34. *Primitive Catholicism*, p. 390.

35. St. Cyprian, Epistula 52:9 (PL 3:799). Such comments on the authoritative behavior of early popes by their contemporaries witness the primacy of facts, life, and conduct over explanation as far as the reality and implementation of the supernatural are concerned, a primacy wholly inconceivable for theologians tainted, however slightly, with German idealism. That primacy was forcefully emphasized by John Henry Newman in the

wake of Vatican I and with an eye on the dispute between St. Cyprian and Pope St. Stephen, as if the dispute contradicted papal infallibility:

> 'As to St. Cyprian's quarrel with the Pope, strong letters came from the Pope to him. He certainly did not think the Pope infallible in those letters. I cannot tell without hunting them up, whether they look like *ex cathedra* letters. I should think not. I doubt very much whether the point of the Infallibility of the Pope was clearly understood, as a dogma, by the Popes themselves at that time; but then I also doubt whether the Infallibility of a General Council was at that time understood either, for no General Council as yet had been. The subject was what Vincentius calls "obscurely held." The Popes acted as if they were infallible in doctrine—with a very high hand, peremptorily, magisterially, fiercely. But when we come to the question of the *analysis* of such conduct, I think they had as vague ideas on the subject as many of the early Fathers had upon portions of the doctrine of the Holy Trinity. *They acted in a way which needed infallibility as its explanation.*'

From Newman's letter to Mrs. H. Froude (March 1871), quoted in full in W. Ward, *The Life of John Henry Cardinal Newman* (London :Longmans, Green and Co., 1912), vol. 2 pp. 378–79.

36. St. Hilary, *In Mattheum*, 16:7 (PL 9:1010).

37. St. Optatus, *De schismate Donatistarum*, lib. vii, cap. 3 (PL 11:1087).

38. For the classic locus of that indecision, see *Saint Augustine, The Retractationes*, tr. M. I. Bogan (Washington DC: Catholic University Press, 1968), pp. 90–91 (ch. 20).

39. Sermo 131, 6:10 (PL 38–39:734). This celebrated sermon was preached on Sept. 23, 417.

40. *De agone christiano*, 31 (PL 40:308).

41. *Quaestiones Veteris et Novi Testamenti*, 75 (PL 35:2270).

42. Epistula 53 (PL 33:195–97).

43. *Contra epistolam Manichaei*, 5 (PL 42:176).

44. *Contra epistolam Parmeniani*, 2:11 (PL 43:69). Not that Augustine had no idea about the gravity of some potential cause or justification for schism. In speaking about the wheatfield into which the enemy sowed cockles, he pointedly referred to bad rulers or prelates: "The heavenly master went so far in forwarning them [his disciples] that he even warned his people against bad rulers, lest, on their account the saving chair of doctrine should be forsaken, in which even the wicked are forced to utter truth; for the words that speak come not from themselves but from God, and he has placed the teaching of truth upon the chair of unity" (Epist. 105); quoted

from *Saint Augustine, Letters. Vol. 2 (83–130)*, tr. W. Parsons (New York: Fathers of the Church, 1953), p. 210. The "chair of unity" could only be Rome in the parlance and thinking of St. Augustine, who in the same context also emphasized that our Lord's warning related to rulers whose works were "manifestly evil."

45. St. Augustine, *De agone christiano*, 30 (PL 40:308).

46. St. Ambrose, *De poenitentia*, lib. 1, cap. 7 (PL 16:496).

47. J. H. Newman, *An Essay on the Development of Christian Doctrine* (new ed.; London, 1878), p. 11.

48. St. Ambrose, *Commentaria in epistolam ad Corinthios* II, cap. 11 (PL 17:320).

49. Ibid., cap. 12 (PL 17:332).

50. St. Ambrose, *Enarratio in Psalmum 40*, 30 (PL 14:1134). The remarkable spontaneity with which Ambrose moves from any incident connected with Peter to Peter's special standing and in particular to his holding the keys is well illustrated in Ambrose's reflections on Peter's cutting off the ear of the high priest's servant: "Peter strikes off his ear; and why Peter? Because he it is who received the keys of the kingdom of heaven; for he condemns and absolves, since he received the power of both binding and of loosing. He strikes off the ear of him who sins by his hearing, but by the spiritual sword he will cut off the inward ear of him who sins by his understanding." *In Lucam*, lib. 10, n. 67 (PL 14:1913).

51. St. Jerome, *Adversus Jovinianum*, lib. 1, cap. 26 (PL 23:258). Curiously, this capital and most enlightening text is not quoted in the otherwise excellent chapter "Jerome and Rome" in *Studies on the Early Papacy* by Dom John Chapman (London: Sheed & Ward, 1928), pp. 99–132.

52. Quoted as translated in *Nicene and Post-Nicene Fathers*, vol. 6, p. 18.

53. St. Damasus, Epistula 2 (PL 13:425). The genuineness of this letter is doubtful.

54. Pope Julius I, Epistula 2 ad Eusebianos (PL 8:981). As one could expect, the antipope Felix II (355–65) emphatically sought support for himself during the papacy of St. Liberius (352–66) with a reference to Peter's keys: "We absolve and restore those with the authority of our keybearer Peter; to him did our Lord say that whatever you loosed on earth shall be loosened in heaven as well." Epistula 1, cap. 18 (PL 13:22).

55. Subsequent quotations are translations from the text as given in PG 1:463 and 473.

56. Quoted in the translation of Shotwell and Loomis, *The Sea of Peter*, pp. 663–64.

57. St. Ephrem, *Adversus haereses*, Sermo 56, in *S. Patris nostri Ephraem Syri opera omnia quae extant Graece, Syriace, Latine* (Rome: Typographia pontificia Vaticana. 1732–46), vol. 2, p. 559. Needless to say, Ephrem urged the erring sheep to return to the true fold.

58. St. Gregory of Nyssa, *Adversus eos qui castigationes aegre ferunt* (PG 46:311–12).
59. St. Gregory Nazienzen, *Carminum liber* I. *Theologica. Sectio* II *Poemata Moralia,* lines 488–89 (PG 37:559).
60. St. Basil, *De judicio Dei*. Proemium, n. 7 (PG 31:671).
61. St. Epiphanius, *Ancoratus* (PG 43:33–34). It is only fair to add that the passage in question ends with a reference to Peter's giving his hand to Paul and Barnabas "together with James and John so that the matter should rest with three witnesses as should all matters." Yet, for all his spontaneity to invoke collegiality, St. Epiphanius never suggests a collegiality of which Peter would not be the point of cohesion.
62. St. Cyril of Jerusalem, *Catechesis*, 6 "De Deo Uno," (PG 33:563). In catechesis 17 "De Spiritu Sancto", in which St. Cyril recounts men filled with the Holy Spirit, Peter is described as "the keybearer of the kingdom of heaven" (PL 33:598).
63. The following paragraphs on St. John Chrysostom are much indebted to ch. 4 "St. Chrysostom on St. Peter" in Chapman's *Studies on the Early Papacy* quoted in note 51 above. His meticulous documentation makes references unnecessary to Chrysostom's works except in connection with the longer quotations.
64. Homilia 82 in Matthaeum; see Chapman, p. 84.
65. See Chapman, p. 88, who justly adds: "So far is Chrysostom from imagining that Peter held a primacy of honor like that of the Duke of Norfolk among English peers!"
66. Homilia 21 in I Cor; see Chapman, p. 94.
67. Homilia in S. Ignatii M. 4; see Chapman pp. 95–96.
68. See P. Batiffol, *Le catholicisme de Saint Augustin* (4th ed.; Paris: Gabalda, 1929), p. 425.
69. St. Leo, Sermo 2 De natali ipsius (PL 54:143).
70. Sermo 3 De natali ipsius, (PL 54:145).
71. Ibid., 145–56.
72. Sermo 3 quoted as translated in *The Nicene and Post-Nicene Fathers*, vol. 12, p. 117.
73. Sermo 4 De natali ipsius, (PL 54:149–51).
74. Sermo 5 De natali ipsius, (PL 54:155).
75. Sermo 4 De natali ipsius, (PL 54:150). A generation or so before Leo the Great, his predecessor in the chair of Peter, Pope St. Celestine, introduced his third letter to the Illyrian bishops with words that witness his full awareness of the universality of his office in terms of Peter's keys: "We have special anxiety about all persons because on us, in the holy apostle Peter, Christ conferred the necessity of making all men our care, when he gave him the keys of opening and shutting" (PL 50:428).
76. St. Maximus of Turin, Homilia de eodem Petro apostolo (PL 57:353).

77. Homilia 68, de natali SS Petri ed Pauli I (PL 57:393). St. Maximus repeatedly voiced this theme of participation in connection with Peter and Peter's keys. He did so, for instance, as he explained in a Lenten exhortation to his flock why both Christ and Simon can be rightfully called "rock" (Homilia 113, PL 57:518). In another Lenten sermon he explained to them his power to absolve as an act in which a recourse is made to Peter's keys because "the closed heaven cannot be opened otherwise . . . for our Lord himself said: I give you the keys of the kingdom of heaven" (PL 57:588). The keys of Peter, as St. Maximus added in the same breath, were not just the faith of someone, "but the strength of apostolic faith." While the twelve shared that faith with Peter, he possessed it in so eminent a degree that "nothing can be more magnificent than that Peter who as a reward for his magnificent confession was permitted, while still being in a corruptible body and not yet in heaven, to close and open that heavenly kingdom!" (Homilia 70, PL 57:397).

78. *St. Francis of Assisi: Writings and Early Biographies. English Omnibus of Sources*, edited by Fr. Marion A. Habig, O.F.M. (Chicago: Franciscan Herald Press, 1973), pp. 31, 46 and 57.

79. A declaration made by Sabatier in London on April 4, 1908. Quoted in *British Society for Franciscan Studies. Publications*. Extra Series, vol. 1, p. 9.

80. Quoted from O. Englebert, *St. Francis of Assisi: A Biography* (2d English edition revised and augmented by Ignatius Brady, O.F.M. and Raphael Brown [Ann Arbor, MI.: Servant Books, 1979]), p. 227.

81. *The Ecclesiastical History of the English People by the Venerable Bede*, tr. T. Stapleton, ed. P. Hereford, with an introduction by B. Jarrett (London: Burns Oates & Washbourne, 1935), p. 175 (bk. 3, ch. xxv).

82. St. Bernard, Sermo in festum SS apostolorum Petri et Pauli, 1 (PL 183:406).

83. St. Bernard, *De consideratione libri quinque ad Eugenium Tertium*, lib. ii, cap. 8 (PL 182:751).

84. *Inferno*, 15:76–78. On Dante's celebration of St. Peter with his keys, see *Paradiso*, 23:139, 24:21–54, 25:12–15, 32:124–26.

85. Quoted from J. Jörgensen, *Saint Bridget of Sweden* (London: Longmans, Green and Co., 1954), vol. 2, pp. 212–13.

86. Quoted from *Avignon in Flower 1309–1403* (London: Victor Gollancz, 1966, pp. 105–06) whose author, Marzieh Gail, daughter of a Persian diplomat, never wonders throughout her leery portrayal of a corrupt papacy the problem of the survival value of that very "human" institution.

87. Quoted in J. Maritain, *The Peasant from the Garonne*, tr. M. Cuddihy and E. Hughes (New York: Rinehart, Holt, Rinehart and Winston, 1968), p. 3.

88. M. Grisar, *Martin Luther: His Life and Work*, adapted from the second German edition by F. J. Eble, edited by A. Preuss (St. Louis: B. Herder Book Co., 1935), p. 256. The German original is the summary of

Grisar's six-volume treatise (see note 5 to ch. 4).

89. Ibid., pp. 515–25. A few years earlier Luther and Melanchton had already condoned the tie between Henry VIII and Ann Boleyn, a bigamy, on seeing the king's shifting toward their side (ibid., pp. 414–15).

90. Ibid., p. 522.

91. Such was at least a main charge by Sebastian Castellio, professor of theology at the University of Geneva and a prominent adversary of Calvin. Quoted from Stefan Zweig, *The Right to Heresy: Castellio against Calvin*, tr. E. and C. Paul (New York: The Viking Press, 1936, p. 179), an impassioned narrative, but based for the most part on unimpeachable sources.

92. Ibid., p. 139. Zweig had, of course, in mind the centuries preceding the burning of Joan of Arc and John Hus.

93. Such is the gist of Castellio's question addressed to Calvin: "Will you dare, in the last resort, to say that Jesus himself taught you to burn your fellowmen?"; quoted ibid., p. 181.

94. Such as P. A. Henry, W. Walker, W. Koehler, F. Wendel, E. Doumergue, and J. D. Benoit.

95. See Zweig, *The Right to Heresy*, p. 62.

96. Though not all, and hardly the most genuine of them. It was in the circle of the latter that were jotted down the finest gems of early Franciscan spirituality, "The Life of Brother Juniper," "The Life and Sayings of Brother Giles," "Considerations on the Stigmata of Brother Francis," and above all that collection of episodes in the life of Francis which became a world-classic under the title, *The Little Flowers of St. Francis*. While members of that circle were deeply pained by certain developments in the Order, they heeded some memorable pleas on behalf of unity. One such plea came from Jean Pierre Olieu (Olivi), a leader of Franciscan spirituals in Southern France: "Did the holy Brother Giles or Brother Leo or Brother Masseo or the other companions of St. Francis ever leave the Order because of *such things*?" (Italics added). Another plea was the statement of Blessed John of Alverna, made shortly before his death in 1322: "Sons, you did not come to raise yourselves up as judges of others but to offer your wills to God . . . When I came into the Order, I received this grace from God, that for all the things I saw in the Order I gave praise and thanks to God. And as a result I always lived in peace." Quoted from *The Little Flowers of St. Francis* (First Complete Edition. An Entirely New Version with Twenty Additional Chapters). *Also the Considerations on the Holy Stigmata—The Life and Sayings of Brother Giles—The Life of Brother Juniper*. Modern English translation from the Latin and the Italian with Introduction, Notes and Biographical Sketches by Raphael Brown (Garden City, N.Y.: Hanover House, 1958), pp. 24–25.

Chapter Four

1. For documentation, see the references given in H. Grisar, *Martin*

Luther: His Life and Work, adapted from the second German edition by F. J. Eble, edited by A. Preuss (St. Louis: B. Herder Book Co., 1935), p. 424. To quote Grisar as an authority on Luther will, of course, displease many in this ecumenical age which has witnessed the publication of a host of "learned" works that fall far behind the scholarship of Grisar, whose six-volume monumental study of Luther (quoted below) is the basis of the work here quoted.

2. *Luther's Works*. vol. 16. *Lectures on Isaiah*. Chapters 1–39 (St. Louis: Concordia Publishing House, 1969), p. 180.

3. *Luther's Works*. vol. 40. *Church and Ministry* II (Philadelphia: Muhlenberg Press, 1959), p. 329.

4. Ibid., pp. 365–66.

5. H. Grisar, *Luther*, authorized translation from the German by E. M. Lamond, edited by L. Cappadelta, (St. Louis: B. Herder, 1915), vol. 3, pp. 9–11. In the one-volume compendium, *Martin Luther: His Life and Work*, see p. 267. Behind Luther's readiness to dismiss baptism there lay not the traditional doctrine of baptism by desire, but that radical subjectivism which Newman, still an Anglican, rendered with classic conciseness in the conclusion of his *Lectures on Justification*: "Luther adopted a doctrine original, specious, fascinating, persuasive, powerful against Rome, and wonderfully adapted, as if prophetically, to the genius of the times which were to follow. He found Christians in bondage to their works and observances; he released them by his doctrine of faith; and he left them in bondage to their feelings."

6. For their statements, see Grisar, *Martin Luther: His Life and Work*, p. 169.

7. Ibid., p. 170.

8. John Calvin, *Commentary on the Book of the Prophet Isaiah*, translated from the original Latin and collated with the latest French version by the Rev. William Pringle, vol. 2 (Edinburgh: The Calvin Translation Society, 1851), p. 136.

9. Ibid., p. 137.

10. Ibid.

11. John Calvin, *Commentary on a Harmony of the Evangelists, Matthew, Mark, and Luke*, translated from the original Latin and collated with the author's version by the Rev. William Pringle, vol. 2 (Edinburgh: The Calvin Translation Society, 1845), p. 292.

12. Ibid., p. 295 note, where the passage is given from the French version of the work produced by Calvin, who obviously felt that the much milder "something different" of the original Latin version did not properly reflect his thinking.

13. Ibid., pp. 296–97.

14. St. Francis de Sales, *Les controverses*, Partie II, chap. vi, art. iii, in *Oeuvres de Saint François de Sales* (Lyon: E. Vitte, 1892–1937), vol. 27, pp. 240–41. There is also a memorable graphic touch, characteristic of the times, in the reply which the Blessed Richard Gwynn, a Welsh schoolteacher, gave shortly before his execution in 1594 to a Protestant minister

with a large red nose, who tried to sway him from the Catholic faith with the claim that Peter's keys were also his own: "There is a difference, namely, that whereas St. Peter received the keys of the kingdom of heaven, you appear to have received those of the beer-cellar." Quoted from *Butler's Lives of Saints*, revised and supplemented by H. Thurston and D. Attwater (New York: P. J. Kenedy and Sons, 1962), vol, IV, p. 203. The reply, certainly *ad hominem*, was touched off by Gwynn's exasperation on being subjected to lengthy exhortations by a group of ministers.

15. After pointing out that neither the prophets, nor our Lord and the apostles had separated themselves from the Synagogue in spite of the many faults in it, Calvin concludes: "Let the following two points, then, stand firm. First, he who voluntarily deserts the outward communion of the church (where the Word of God is preached and the sacraments are administered) is without excuse. Secondly, neither the vices of the few nor the vices of the many in any way prevent us from duly professing our faith there in ceremonies ordained by God. For a godly conscience is not wounded by the unworthiness of another, whether pastor or layman; nor are the sacraments less pure and salutary for a holy and upright man because they are handled by unclean persons." *Calvin: Institutes of the Christian Religion*, ed. J. T. McNeill, tr. F. L. Battles (Philadelphia: Westminster Press, 1960), vol. 2, p. 1033 (bk. 4, ch. 1, par. 19).

16. G. K. Chesterton, *All Things Considered* (New York: John Lane, 1909), p. 221.

17. See Grisar, *Martin Luther: His Life and Work*, p. 166.

18. It reveals a great deal of Luther's self-centeredness that he saw in Pope Adrian's German nationality a threat to his own cause which he always identified with the rights of the German people. He was not reluctant to refer to himself as "the German pope," and was looked upon as such especially by those erstwhile allies whom he had banished from Wittenberg for insubordination. See Grisar, *Martin Luther: His Life and Work*, pp. 413 and 502.

19. Quoted from L. Pastor, *The History of the Popes*, vol. 9 (London: Kegan Paul, Trench, Trubner & Co., 1910), pp. 134–35.

20. Ibid., p. 133. The quote is a shortened paraphrase of St. Ambrose's declaration in his *De fide* (lib. 1, cap. 13): "Non creditur philosophis, creditur piscatoribus; non creditur dialecticis, creditur publicanis" (PL 16:548). In the context St. Ambrose referred to the fact that by his time pagan philosophers had largely lost all their students, whereas catechetical teachers had an overflow audience.

21. Pastor, *History of the Popes*, vol. 9, p. 145.

22. Ibid., p. 142.

23. Grisar, *Martin Luther: His Life and Work*, p. 55.

24. For a series of such utterances, see ibid., pp. 206 and 506.

25. To be sure, St. Augustine emphasized the spirit of love and understanding in which the superior was to exercise his authority over the bre-

thren. But Augustine was never for a moment so unmindful of the weakness of human nature as to dream about "mature religious life" wherein the right and duty of the religious superior to "correct and punish" would cease, because the precepts of religious life would never be "poorly observed." See chapter 11 on "The Reverence due to Prelates and their Office" in *The Rule of Saint Augustine* with a commentary by A. Zumkeller, translated by J. S. Resch (Du Père, Wisc.: St. Norbert Abbey, 1961), pp. 57–58.

26. Reginald Pole, *Pole's Defense of the Unity of the Church*, translated with Introduction by J. G. Dwyer (Westminster: The Newman Press, 1965), p. xiv. Whatever the usefulness of Dwyer's introduction concerning Pole's life and the background of his *Defense*, his presentation of its gist is characteristic of those one-way-vision Catholic ecumenists who systematically fail to perceive three points: 1. Even in the time of Luther and Calvin there were a great many good Christians who refused to look at the vices of popes and prelates as a justification of revolt against them. 2. Vices of all sorts were not at all absent in the reformed camps. 3. Obedience to ecclesiastical superiors, as predicated in the New Testament, was quickly requested by ecclesial authorities set up by the Reformers, who certainly claimed it to themselves.

27. *Pole's Defense*, p. 321.

28. Ibid., p. 83. Augustine did so in his Epistula 53 (PL 33:196) in which he also points out that not a single Donatist bishop could be found in that list of succession.

29. *Pole's Defense*, p. 246.

30. Ibid., p. 121.

31. Ibid., p. 122.

32. Ibid., p. 123.

33. Ibid., p. 93.

34. Ibid., pp. 97–98.

35. Ibid., pp. 245–46.

36. Ibid., pp. 104–05.

37. Melanchton was one of those very few. In fact, he was the only one among the forty-three signatories of the Smalcald Articles to add to his signature this qualification which left wholly intact the radical rejection in them of the papacy as something intended or foreseen by Christ. Nor were the keys given to the Church taken by those Articles as standing for power in the traditional sense. While endorsing the practice of confession, those Articles (see part 3, art. viii) gave the right to the penitent to be selective in the listing of his sins. None of these additional details are mentioned by A. Burgess in his contribution, "Lutherans and the Papacy," to *A Pope for All Christians: An Inquiry into the Role of Peter in the Modern Church*, ed. P. J. McCord (New York: Paulist Press: 1976), where (p. 23) the qualification by Melanchton is quoted as being of great ecumenical significance.

38. *Pole's Defense*, p. 44.

39. Ibid.

40. *Luther's Works. Volume 35. Word and Sacrament I*, ed. E. T. Buchman (Philadelphia: Muhlenberg Press, 1960), p. 395.

41. Ibid, pp. 396–97.

42. As done at the very outset in the enormously learned work, *De clavibus Petri. Opus in IV libros divisum* (Romae: Typis Philippi Mariae Mancini, 1660, p. 1), by Franciscus Macedo, a minorite friar, who set forth in two massive volumes the vast impact which a proper interpretation of the keys of Peter has on dogmatic and moral theology as well as on sacramental discipline and missionary practice.

43. Ibid., p. 2.

44. The story was told with obvious relish and in great detail by the Abbé Fleury, confessor of Louis XIV and instructor of his children. See *Nouveaux opuscules de M. L'Abbé Fleury* (Paris: Vve Nyon, 1807), pp. 146–61.

45. K. Barth, *The Word of God and the Word of Man* (New York: Harper Torchbooks, 1957), p. 124.

46. Ibid., pp. 125–26.

47. As I have argued through the second part of my Gifford Lectures, *The Road of Science and the Ways of God* (Chicago: University of Chicago Press, 1978).

48. He did so, tellingly enough, in a most programmatic way in the introduction to the first part of the first volume of his major work, *Kirchliche Dogmatik* (1932).

49. Thus in his *Church Dogmatics*, Vol. IV, *The Doctrine of Reconciliation*, Part Two (Edinburgh: T. & T. Clark, 1958) Barth stated that "certainly we must calmly consider and accept that Mt 16:18 does speak of an absolutely extraordinary authority, power and mission of the apostles, and of its ultimate concentration specifically on Peter" (pp. 717–18). Barth does not explain why such an authority was needed for the few decades during which many eyewitnesses of Christ's mission were around, but not for the subsequent times deprived of those witnesses. Contrary to Barth, Mt 16:18 refers to Peter alone.

50. And all the more so as Cullmann himself contributed the articles "petra" and "petros" that first appeared in the German original in 1959 and in English translation in 1968.

51. O. Cullmann, *Saint Pierre, Disciple-apôtre-martyr* (Neuchâtel: Delachaux & Niestle, 1952), a work already discussed in ch. 2.

52. Cullmann's reference (ibid., p. 183) is to T. Zahn's commentaries on the Gospel of St. Matthew.

53. Cullmann, *Saint Pierre*, pp. 183–84. One could only wish that the falsity of the traditional Protestant exegesis of the meaning of the keys given to Peter had been pointed out by Cullmann who rejected the same exegesis of Peter the rock in the following words: "The solution of Reformers, that the rock is only the faith of Peter, does not satisfy. The text offers no real

support for this interpretation" (ibid., p. 184).

54. Ibid., p. 184.

55. Ibid.

56. Tellingly, Cullmann sees the reason for this in the fact that only in Peter's case is the conferring of the power of loosing and binding "connected to the role of being the rock foundation of the *ekklesia*" (ibid). It is also important to note that for Cullmann Peter's role as a representative of the twelve never degenerates into the role of a mere figurehead who simply announces the others' majority opinion.

57. P. S. Minear, *Christian Hope and the Second Coming* (Philadelphia: Westminster Press, 1954), p. 186.

58. Ibid., p. 187.

59. Cullmann, *Saint Pierre*, p. 186. As to the break, it implies the complete dismissal of the possibility of any ministerial succession whatever. Discouraging as such a position may be from the ecumenical viewpoint, ecumenists desirous of clarity should feel most indebted for a remark of Cullmann made in the same breath. According to Cullmann (*Saint Pierre*, p. 189), the decisive factor in his interpreting in such a manner the relation of the apostolic to the post-apostolic church lies "on the borderline of exegetical study." Such is as clear a warning as one could expect from an exegete that the ultimately decisive factor in his *métier* is a philosophical option. It takes no special expertise to see the utterly nominalist conditioning, inherited from the general Protestant tradition, in Cullmann's presentation of biblical events as *once-for-all unique events*. But so are all other events. The destructive consequences of that nominalist position for the continued significance and even for the lasting reality of Cullmann's book itself, just another unique event, should not be difficult to guess.

60. These statements of Harnack are quoted in Batiffol's Introduction to the fifth edition of his *L'Eglise naissante*. See English translation, *Primitive Catholicism* (London: Longmans, Green and Co., 1911), pp. xii–xv.

61. Which, however, essentially consists in a more or less recent adoption of the title "bishop" for superintendents or moderators, and is rightly resisted by Calvinists interested more in substance than in semantics.

62. Quoted by Batiffol, *op cit.*, p. xxi (note).

63. *Peter in the New Testament*, ed. R. E. Brown and others (Minneapolis: Augsburg Publishing House, 1973).

64. Ibid., pp. 96–98.

65. Ibid., p. 97.

66. Ibid., pp. 97–98. Such recourse to the "gates of hades" as a means of making the reference to the "keys of the kingdom of heaven" intelligible should seem rather expressive of a tacit reluctance to face up to the obvious meaning of such plain objects as keys. A mere reference to the house-keys or car-keys of any participant of that distinguished panel should have been more than enough.

67. *A Pope for All Christians: An Inquiry into the Role of Peter in the Modern Church* (see note 37 above).
68. Ibid., p. 25. The contributor in question, Joseph A. Burgess, did not, however, say much more about the keys given to Peter in an entire dissertation, *A History of the Exegesis of Matthew 16:17–19 from 1781 to 1965* (Ann Arbor, MI: Edwards Brothers, 1976).
69. *A Pope for All Christians*, p. 54. The contributor was Fr. Avery Dulles, S.J.
70. Ibid. Clearly such has to be the case with a modern mind, even if theologically oriented, once it is steeped in Hegelianism or its even more treacherous version, transcendental Thomism.
71. For details, see ch. 15, "Paradigms or Paradigm," in my Gifford Lectures, *The Road of Science and the Ways to God* (Chicago: University of Chicago Press, 1978).
72. Joseph S. Exell, *The Biblical Illustrator. Matthew* (Grand Rapids, MI: Baker Book House, 1964), p. 345. The words, quoted, were spoken by the Rev. M. McCheyne.
73. *The Interpreter's Bible*. Volume vii, *Matthew, Mark* (New York: Abington Press, 1951), p. 452.
74. The quotation from Chesterton's *Heretics* (New York: John Lane, 1905, p. 67) is a classic case of omitting something essential given explicitly in the immediate context.
75. Had the lines, "He chose for its cornerstone neither the brilliant Paul nor the mystic John, but a shuffler, a snob, a coward—in a word, a man," been included in the quotation, the subsequent comment, which allows to Chesterton a "partial truth," would have revealed its tendencious character. Two decades before he became a Catholic, Chesterton clearly perceived the full bearing of Christ's words to Peter as will be evident from another statement of Chesterton to be quoted shortly.
76. *The Interpreter's Bible*. Vol. 7, p. 452.
77. G. K. Chesterton, *The Poet and the Lunatics: Episodes in the Life of Gabriel Gale* (New York: Dodd, Mead & Company, 1929), p. 26.
78. G. K. Chesterton, *Orthodoxy* (London: John Lane, 1908), pp. 149–50.

Chapter Five

1. *The Pope Speaks* 9 (1963–64), pp. 139–40.
2. Ibid., p. 134. It is only fair to add that Paul vi did not have in mind any compromise on dogmatic matters: "What We have to say is spoken in friendship and complete sincerity. We are not trying to lay a trap for them [non-Catholic Christians] or to get the better of them in any worldly sense. We adhere most firmly and openly to our faith, as We must, for We fully

believe it to be divine" (p. 136).

3. Ibid., p. 132.

4. *The Documents of Vatican* II, ed. W. M. Abbott (New York: Guild Press, 1966), p. 43.

5. Ibid., p. 44.

6. Ibid.

7. Ibid.

8. Ibid., pp. 99–101.

9. Indeed, the phrase, "The Vatican Council has firmly repudiated Nehemiah's solution: the walls are down," is followed by the warning, "No doubt from time to time we shall hear the Curial trumpet sounding the alarm," in *Our Dialogue with Rome* by George B. Caird (London: Oxford University Press, 1967), p. 91.

10. M. Novak, *The Open Church: Vatican* II, *Act* II (New York: The Macmillan Company, 1964).

11. In fact, within a month of the conclusion of Vatican II Maritain completed, on January 18, 1966, the first two chapters of his book.

12. *The Open Church*, p. 70.

13. One must think in a very novel way about the philosophies of Fichte, Schelling, and Hegel, if one is to see in them, with Father Maréchal, the spokesmen of a metaphysics compatible with Thomism. See his *Le point de départ de la métaphysique. Cahier* v. *Le thomisme devant la philosophie critique* (Paris: Félix Alcan, 1926), p. 436. Enthusiasm for Maréchal (or for German idealists for that matter) could only generate startling claims, such as J. Donceel's statement that "Maréchal was one of the great pioneers of the Neo-Thomistic revival at the beginning of our century" (*A Maréchal Reader* [New York: Herder & Herder, 1970], p. xi). Just as the adjective "Neo-Thomistic" amounts to a practical equivocation in the foregoing sentence, the word "fair" is left deliberately vague in Donceel's categorization of Cahier III or Maréchal's *magnum opus* as the "first fair evaluation of the philosophy of Kant by a Catholic author" (ibid., p. x).

14. Quoted from Father Rahner's autobiographical talk, broadcast by Radio Austria and printed in *Entschluss*, 1977, no. 10.

15. G. K. Chesterton, *St. Thomas Aquinas* (New York: Sheed & Ward, 1933), p. 206.

16. In his *Concerning the History of Religion and Philosophy in Germany* (see *Heinrich Heine. Selected Works*, translated and edited by H. M. Mustard [New York: Vintage Books, 1973], pp. 417–18) Heine conjured up Kantians "with sword and axe" who "will mercilessly rummage around in the soil of our European culture in order to eradicate the last roots of the past." He also foresaw the day when the Cross, "that last restraining talisman," would be broken to pieces.

17. Quoted from Mgr. E. Kevane, "The Rule of Faith in Catechesis," in *Reflections*. Fall 1982, p. 2. The same archbishop (Cardinal Ratzinger)

spoke in much the same vein in his famed *Report* published last year.

18. J. H. Newman, *Apologia pro vita sua* (Garden City, NY: Doubleday Image Books, 1956), p. 325.

19. Ibid., pp. 326–27.

20. A remark by W. A. Visser't Hooft, co-founder of the World Council of Churches, and chief advocate of a non-Roman Catholicism, made in connection with John Paul II's visit to Great Britain; quoted in TIME, June 7, 1982. Quite similar was the gist of a quasi-editorial comment in *Times* (London) (Aug. 18, 1983, p. 8, cols. 2–5) concerning the very early retirement of Archbishop Emmanuel Milingo of Lusake (Zambia) who practised faith healing with the assistance of voodoo priests and advocated a "native African theology."

21. J. H. Newman, *Apologia pro vita sua*, pp. 290–91.

22. J. H. Newman, *A Letter Addressed to His Grace the Duke of Norfolk on Occasion of Mr. Gladstone's Recent Expostulation* (London: B. M. Pickering, 1875), p. 66.

23. Ibid., p. 63.

24. Ibid., p. 58.

25. Ibid., p. 62.

26. B. Disraeli, *Lothair* (New York: D. Appleton, 1870), p. 177.

27. TIME, June 7, 1982, p. 51.

28. Such is Newman's closing meditation in his four lectures on "The Patristical Idea of Antichrist," in his *Discussions and Arguments on Various Subjects* (New ed.; London: Longmans, Green & Co., 1897), pp. 105–06. Such meditation will act, he added, "as a curb upon our self-willed, selfish hearts to believe that a persecution is in store for the Church, whether or not it comes in our days."

29. *A Selection from the Uncollected Writings of G. K. Chesterton*, arranged and edited by A. L. Maycock (London: Dennis Dobson, 1963), p. 107.

30. "In the meantime," wrote Karl Barth to Paul VI on September 28, 1968, "many unusual things have happened in both the world and the church to lay upon the whole of Christianity ever new cares and questions and tasks. Kyrie eleison! Believe me, Holy Father, that as I have reflected on these things from my own restricted corner, the power of the keys, whose transmission to the church and to Peter our Lord spoke of, has not been the last thing on my mind. In our meeting almost two years ago one thing that made a lasting impression on me was the seriously troubled way in which Your Holiness mentioned the burden which this in particular laid upon you. You may rest assured of the sympathy with which, as I follow Roman Catholic matters with ever-increasing attentiveness, I continually think of the way of your special Peter-ministry, confident that it will be given to you, and given to you again and again, to fulfill this ministry with joy, no matter how great the burden may be . . . As concerns your encyclical *Humanae vitae* . . . you may be assured of my great respect for what

might be called the heroic isolation in which, Holy Father, you now find yourself along with your closest advisers." *Karl Barth Letters 1961–1968*, edited by J. Fangmeier and H. Stoevesandt, translated and edited by G. W. Bromiley (Grand Rapids, MI: W. B. Eerdmans, 1980), p. 314. Barth's most respectful reference to *Humanae vitae* sharply contrasts with the failure of liberal Catholic newspapers, such as *The Tablet* (London), to recall, following the death of Patriarch Athenagoras of Constantinople, the latter's immediate endorsement of *Humanae vitae* as the "only possible Christian teaching." See I. T. Ker's letter to *The Tablet*, August 12, 1972, p. 769.

31. From Paul vi's Speech to the Secretariat for Promoting Christian Unity, April 29, 1967, in *The Pope Speaks* 12 (1967), p. 101. Since all too often this statement of Paul vi has been quoted with the innuendo that he had doubts or misgivings about his infallibility as the successor of Peter, what he said in the same breath deserves to be quoted in full: "What are We to say? Shall We appeal once again to the evidence that validates Our mission? Shall We try once again to spell out exactly what it purports to be: the indispensable fountainhead of truth, charity and unity; a pastoral mission of direction, service and brotherhood which does not challenge the freedom or dignity of anyone who has a legitimate position in the Church of God, which rather protects the rights of all and only claims the obedience called for among children in the same family? It is not easy for Us to plead Our own case. You are the ones who, with gentle and sincere words, will know how to do this when the proper opportunity presents itself. As for Us, right now we prefer to keep silent and pray calmly." To what extent that request of the Pope has been implemented by members of that secretariat, or by Catholic theologians in general, is another matter.

32. Far less harmful than a studied resolve against speaking one's mind openly, should seem plain outspokenness. On hearing, say, a Hans Küng charge the pope with an absolutist rule in the Vatican, where he allegedly deprives his own subjects of those human rights which he claims for people elsewhere (see interview given to *Newsweek*, Aug. 8, 1983, p. 10), one should at least feel content that Küng's frame of mind stands now wide in the open. The same profit may also be gathered from the statement of those who openly speak of the institutionalized Church as a "closed model," and one should be even more grateful to those among them who identify the source of that closedness in the role of Peter's keys. Such was certainly the case with the 178 signers (mostly affiliated with Mundelein, Loyola, and Rosary colleges in the Chicago area) of a declaration made in the wake of John Paul II's visit to the United States in October 1979. In their view (see *Beyond the Mountain*, Nov. 1979) the pope communicated a vision of a "closed model of hierarchical authority." Openness is bound to be absent when in imitation of the Aquikantist Lonergan, one writes a "theological dialectic" which subtly serves as a substitute for "doctrinal theology." One could only wish that this all-important distinction had been stated in boldface letters in the opening page of the work, *Models of the Church* (1974:

Doubleday Image Books, 1978, p. 197), by its author, Fr. A. Dulles. Typically, even in discussing the institutional model he fails to refer to Peter's keys as if the Roman Catholic Church, the obvious embodiment of that model, could be conceivable without those keys. The only time Fr. Dulles speaks of keys in that book is in referring "to religious experience" which provides "a vital key force for the evaluation and interpretation of symbols" (p. 25). No less telling should seem the fact that, in speaking of the sacramental model, Fr. Dulles translates the phrase *ex attrito fit contritus, vi clavium* as "the experience of sacramental confession and absolution itself transforms the attitude of the sinner so that his initial aversion from sin becomes a sorrow motivated purely by the love of God" (p. 70). The disappearance of "by the power of the keys" (*vi clavium*) in that passage matches the equivocation latent in Fr. Dulles' use of the word experience. He seems to suggest that the absolution gives the penitent the subjective experience of being sorry for his sins out of the love of God and not merely out of fear of God's punishment, which is hardly ever the case. The sacrament of confession turns the fear of God into a love of God only in a *sacramental* way, that is, a way essentially supernatural and mysterious. The quotations given earlier in this chapter from the official texts of Vatican II should be enough of a warning about the true merit of Fr. Dulles' statement: "Vatican Council II . . . cannot be fairly accused of institutionalism, though some traces of institutionalism may no doubt be found here and there in the conciliar documents" (p. 40). Vatican II fully and unequivocally restated the institutional character of the Church.

33. The faithful into whom such consensus has been fed for some years by bishops, parish-priests, and theologians have almost entirely stopped going to confession in some parts of the Church and go far less frequently in most parts than was the case only twenty years ago. The same faithful find now rather perplexing the tenacious resolve with which John Paul II, the chief holder of the keys, keeps reaffirming the enduring necessity of sacramental confession as defined by the Council of Trent. As to the outsiders, such as the markedly secularist Italian daily, *La Repubblica*, the spectacle of empty confessionals triggering the pope's agonized concern is worth such a headline as "Ma il Cattolico non si confessa più" (Jan. 29, 1982). Those outsiders are as a rule more mindful, than are many present-day Catholic theologians, of the enormous though grudging admiration in which a Nietzsche and a Jung held private sacramental confession. The foregoing newspaper found it also significant that for the first time the agenda, mostly dealing with confession, for the synod of bishops for the fall of 1983 had been made available in full long before the deliberations of the synod began.

34. J. A. Burgess, "Lutherans and the Papacy: A Review of Some Basic Issues," in P. J. McCord (ed.), *A Pope for All Christians? An Inquiry into the Role of Peter in the Modern Church* (New York: Paulist Press, 1976), p. 21.

35. Ibid.

36. On the central role of negative theology in St. Thomas' thought, see E. Gilson, *The Spirit of Thomism* (1964; New York: Harper Torchbooks, 1966), pp. 78–79.

37. One such Protestant was the Reverend Dr. James McCosh, a Scottish Presbyterian minister by training, who in the 1870s singlehandedly turned the College of New Jersey into what it later became rightly called, Princeton University. The surge of Protestant missionary activity was in fact so great as to make some Catholic students of foreign missions take the view that "if we fail in our efforts to impress vividly and clearly upon Catholics their missionary obligations, . . . the future supremacy of Protestantism in Asia is an assured fact." Fr. Frederick Schwager, S.V.D., quoted in *The Conversion of the Pagan World*, translated and adapted from the Italian of Rev. Paolo Manna, by Joseph F. McGlinchey (Boston: Society for the Propagation of the Faith, 1921), p. 99.

38. Such as *L'Eglise du Verbe Incarné* by Charles Cardinal Journet and, earlier, *La Sainteté de l'Eglise christoconforme* by S. J. Tyszkiewicz. For details, see ch. 4 "Recherches systématiques sur l'Eglise," in my *Les Tendances nouvelles de l'ecclésiologie* (Rome: Casa Editrice Herder, 1957; Esseti Reprint, 1963).

39. Paul VI allegedly made that statement during the synod of bishops held in October 1974. "Pope Paul was widely quoted as having said . . ." was, however, the only documentation given in what may be the first printed appearance of that statement, the unscholarly sketch, "The Church Untriumphant: Say it Ain't So, Paul," by J. Carroll, in *National Catholic Reporter* (December 13, 1974, p. 14), an organ hardly noted for its accuracy.

40. This perspective emphatically reappeared in L. Billot, *De ecclesia Christi* (Rome: Universitas Gregoriana, 1921), p. 677, and in C. Journet, *L'Eglise du Verbe Incarné: Essai de théologie spéculative. I. La Hiérarchie apostolique* (2nd ed., revised and augmented; Paris: Desclée de Brouwer, 1955), p. 577. The same perspective also transpires in a contemporary Protestant theologian's remark about the respective closeness of Catholic and Reformed positions to the attitude of Old Testament prophets: "Catholics—like the prophets and unlike the Reformers—do not envision the possibility, if expelled by the authorities, of establishing alternate ecclesiastical orders or new churches. This unshakable Roman Catholic loyalty to a concrete and empirically specifiable people of God, even when it is unfaithful, is similar to that of the biblical prophets." G. A. Lindbeck, "The Reformation and the Infallibility Debate," in *Teaching Authority and the Infallibility Debate: Lutherans and Catholics in Dialogue* VI, ed. P. C. Empie et al (Minneapolis: Augsburg Publishing House, 1980), pp. 117–18. Lindbeck asserts in the same breath that, unlike Catholics, the Reformers "shared the prophets' refusal to set any limits to the possible errors of the leadership of the people of God." No effort was made by Lindbeck to show how the prophets themselves could be exempt from the possibility of erring if the

latter had no limits. The problem loudly cries for the Catholic solution of papal infallibility when one considers the case of a Moses, a David, and even of a Caiaphas, who at the same time and in the same person were both very fallible religious leaders and truly infallible prophets. That solution should amount at least to balancing one's dissent on infallibility with a passionate affirmation of loyalty, as was the case with Lord Acton. Curiously, it took an Anglican, O. Chadwick, Regius Professor of Modern History in Cambridge, to recall in our times that in addition to making virulent anti-infallibilist statements, Lord Acton also kept stating that for him union with Rome was dearer than life. See O. Chadwick, "The Challenge of Acton," *The Tablet* (London), January 28, 1984, p. 77.

41. The drafting of that declaration, whose importance is duly noted in *Ecumenical Councils of the Catholic Church: A Historical Survey* (New York: Herder & Herder, 1960, p. 194) by H. Jedin, was assigned to Louis Haynald, Archbishop of Kalocsa (Hungary). The Archbishop, one among those hundred-fifty or so fathers who left the Vatican Council shortly before the solemn declaration of papal infallibility, signed, together with the other dissenters, a declaration, addressed to Pius ix, which ended with the words conveying full solidarity with him: "Meanwhile, with our whole heart, we commend the Church of God and your Holiness, to whom we avow our unaltered faith and obedience, to the grace and protection of our Lord Jesus Christ, and are your Most devoted and obedient . . ." For the full text, see W. Ward, *The Life of John Henry Cardinal Newman* (London: Longmans, Green, and Co., 1912), vol. 2, p. 303. One wonders whether such and similar texts have ever been meditated upon by leading modern Catholic critics of papal infallibility.

42. Epistula 33 (ad Leonem papam), PG 99:1018.

43. Epistula 63 (ad Naveratium), PG 98:1281.

44. Epistula 129 (ad Leonem sacellarium), PG 99:1420. The letter is also interesting because it contains a "pentagonal" theory of the Church, as based on the five patriarchates. But St. Theodore insists even in that context on the priority and primacy of the see of Rome.

45. Psalmus contra partem Donati, PL 43:30.

46. As illustrated more recently by the debate between A. P. Martinich and P. McGrawth in *Religious Studies* 16 (1980): 15–27, 16 (1980):469–79, and 18 (1982): 81–86. This is not to suggest that epistemological presuppositions play no part in such debates. Martinich could imply for convincing reasons that McGrawth's criticism of infallibility had in it the kind of Hegelianism which can gladly live with patent self-contradictions.

47. Epistula 248 ad Robertum comitem Flandriae, in F. S. Schmitt (ed.), *S. Anselmi opera omnia*, vol. 4 (Edinburgh: Thomas Nelson & Sons, 1949), p. 158. Whatever the genuineness of Anselm's comments on Mt 16:18, "Christ granted the power of loosing to Peter alone in a special way and invited us to unity so that the Church may have one principal vicar of Christ to whom all the particular churches of the universal Church ought to

come together, should they perchance disagree among themselves," it certainly reflects convictions and views most sacred to him.

48. Quoted in V. Giraud, *Essai sur Taine, son oeuvre et son influence d'après des documents inédits* (2d rev. ed.; Paris: Hachette, 1901), p. 75.

49. The preference of journalists for fashionable clichés and easy contrasts receives, however, support time and again from people who are supposed to speak with appropriate nuances. "The Kremlin thinks of itself as being like the papacy: Infallible in the top ranks of leadership. It's very difficult to admit error . . .," stated Mr. Sewryn Bialer, director of Columbia University's Research Institute on International Change, to *Newsweek* (Sept. 26, 1983, p. 36) following the shooting down of the Korean airliner over the Sea of Japan.

50. It must, however, be added that in his last years M. Polanyi expressed regrets for his juxtaposition of Communism and the Catholic Church in his *Personal Knowledge: Towards a Post-Critical Philosophy* (1958; New York: Harper Torchbooks, 1964), p. 153, and less directly on pp. 271 and 297.

51. A half a year after the writing on October 27, 1981, of that letter which, because it was co-signed by several Jesuits, had almost of necessity to fall into the hands of the media, Rahner openly pleaded for papal respect for the Society's democratic rights (for the full text see the Austrian weekly, *Präsent*, March 11, 1982, pp. 1–2). He found nothing disturbing in the existence of considerable differences between the thinking of the pope and a segment of the Society. Rahner identified the Society with those confrères whose thinking was similar to his. One wonders whether Rahner and other "progressive" theologians of our times have ever had second thoughts on finding that their judgmental attitude toward the papacy may prove so contagious as to issue in a call, in the front page of an archdiocesan weekly, to rank-and-file Catholics to evaluate the pope: "How Would You Grade the Pope after Four Years in Office?" Curiously, no such questionnaire was suggested about the local archbishop, let alone about the editor of the weekly. Such is the new-fangled democracy in the Church.

52. Contrary to what seems to be suggested by E. L. Mascall in his *The Recovery of Unity: A Theological Approach* (London: Longmans, Green and Co., 1958), p. 205.

53. *Tasso*, act 1, scene 4, lines 615–16.

54. Quoted in L. Zara, *Locks and Keys* (New York: Walker and Company, 1969), p. 19. May I be allowed to recall a small 18th-century fresco in the refectory of my abbey, Pannonhalma (Hungary), which shows a dozen or so different keys hanging from a ring with the inscription above it: "non omnia possumus omnes" (none of us is capable of everything—Virgil, *Eclogue*, viii, 63).

55. For the photograph and deciphering of the entire context of that sign, the primary source will forever remain Dr. Guarducci's monumental work, *I Graffiti sotto la Confessione di San Pietro in Vaticano*, 3 vols (Citta

del Vaticano: Libreria Editrice Vaticana, 1958); see especially vol. 2, pp. 129–32. A popular, but still well documented account is found in Dr. Guarducci's *The Tomb of St. Peter* (transl. from the Italian; New York: Hawthorn Books, 1960). Heavily indebted to both works is the very readable book by John E. Walsh, *The Bones of St. Peter* (Garden City, NY: Doubleday & Company, 1982).

56. It is my pleasure to thank Dr. Guarducci for the reprint of her article (sent to me through the good services of the Rev. Paul Haffner), "Il fenomeno orientale del simbolismo alfabetico e i suoi sviluppi nel mondo cristiano d'Occidente," (Quaderno nr. 62 of *Problemi attuali di Scienza e di Cultura* [Roma: Accademia Nazionale dei Lincei, 1964], which contains a photograph of that carving. Its drawing as it appears here as Illustration xii is the art work of Mr. Henry L. Tucker of the Walt Disney Studios in Burbank, California, who has also done all the art work implied in the other illustrations.

Note on the Author

Stanley L. Jaki, a Hungarian-born Catholic priest of the Benedictine Order, is Distinguished Professor at Seton Hall University, South Orange, New Jersey. With doctorates in theology and physics, he has for the past twenty-five years specialized in the history and philosophy of science. The author of sixteen books and over seventy articles, he has served as Gifford Lecturer at the University of Edinburgh and as Fremantle Lecturer at Balliol College, Oxford. He is a recipient of the Lecomte du Nouy Prize and has lectured at major universities in the United States, Europe, and Australia. He is also *membre correspondant* of the Académie Nationale des Sciences, Belles-Lettres et Arts of Bordeaux.

ILLUSTRATIONS

Sources for the Illustrations

I. Drawing by Mr. Henry L. Tucker, based on diagrams in *All about Locks and Locksmithing*, pp. 69-70, see note 12 to Ch. 1.
II. Drawing by Mr. Tucker.
III. Drawing by Mr. Tucker, based on diagram in *All about Locks and Locksmithing*, p. 67.
IV. Photographic reproduction from *Antike Technik*, p. 49, see note 24 to Ch. 1.
V. Photographic reproduction from *Dictionnaire des antiquités grecques et romaines*, vol. 4, pp. 1244-45, see note 24 to Ch. 1.
VI. Photographic reproduction from *Antike Technik*, p. 46.
VII. Photographic reproduction from *Locks and Keys throughout the Ages*, p. 20, see note 11 to Ch. 1.
VIII. Photographic reproduction from *Antike Technik*, p. 45.
IX. Photographic reproduction from *Nineveh and its Palaces*, p. 150, see note 27 to Ch. 1.
X. Photographic reproduction from *Locks and Keys throughout the Ages*, p. 39.
XI. Drawing by Mr. Tucker after photograph (Tav. 3) in *I Graffiti sotto la Confessione di San Pietro in Vaticano*, vol. 2, p. 130, see note 55 to Ch. 5.
XII. Drawing by Mr. Tucker after photograph (Tav. II. Fig. 4) in "Il fenomeno orientale del simbolismo . . .," see note 56 to Ch. 5.

Illustration I

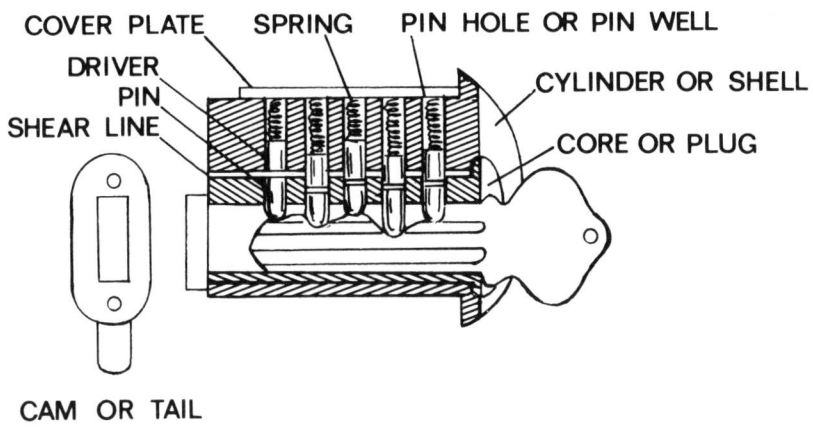

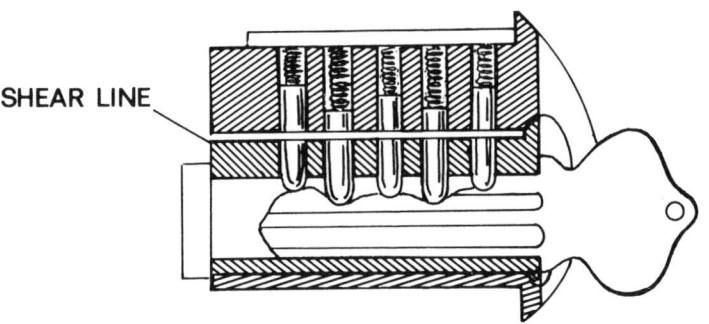

The structure of Yale lock with a non-matching and a matching key

Illustration II

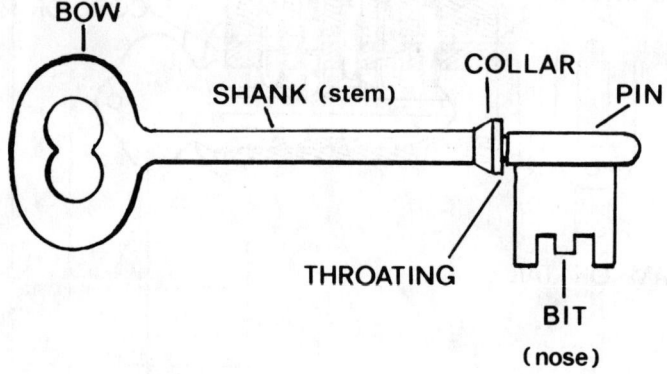

The stem, nose and other parts of a typical key

Illustration III

BARROWS	
BEST	
BRIGGS & STRATTON	
CORBIN	

NORWALK	

PENN	
SCHLAGE	

YALE	

Cross sections of the Yale key used by its chief manufacturers

Illustration IV

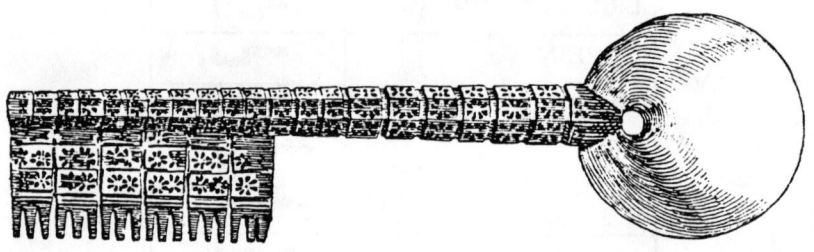

Door-key from Pompeii (c. 50 A.D.)

Illustration V

Laconian key (c. 300 B.C.)

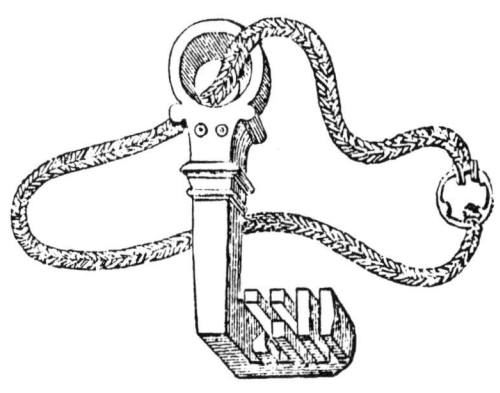

Its improved Roman type with rotary motion (c. 50 B.C.)

Illustration VI

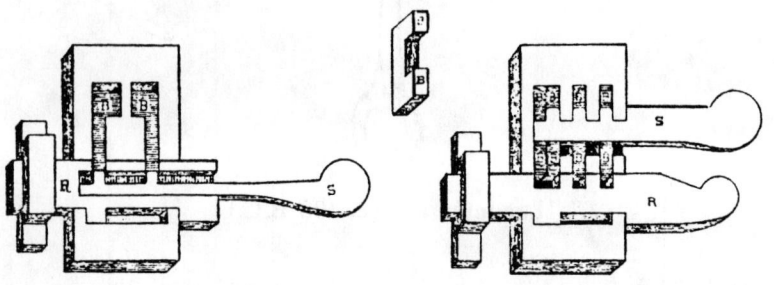

Reconstruction of ancient key

Illustration VII

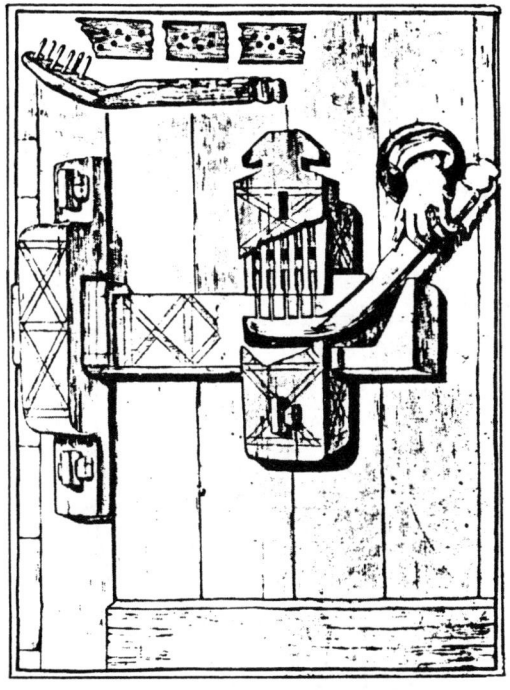

The actual use of ancient key

Illustration VIII

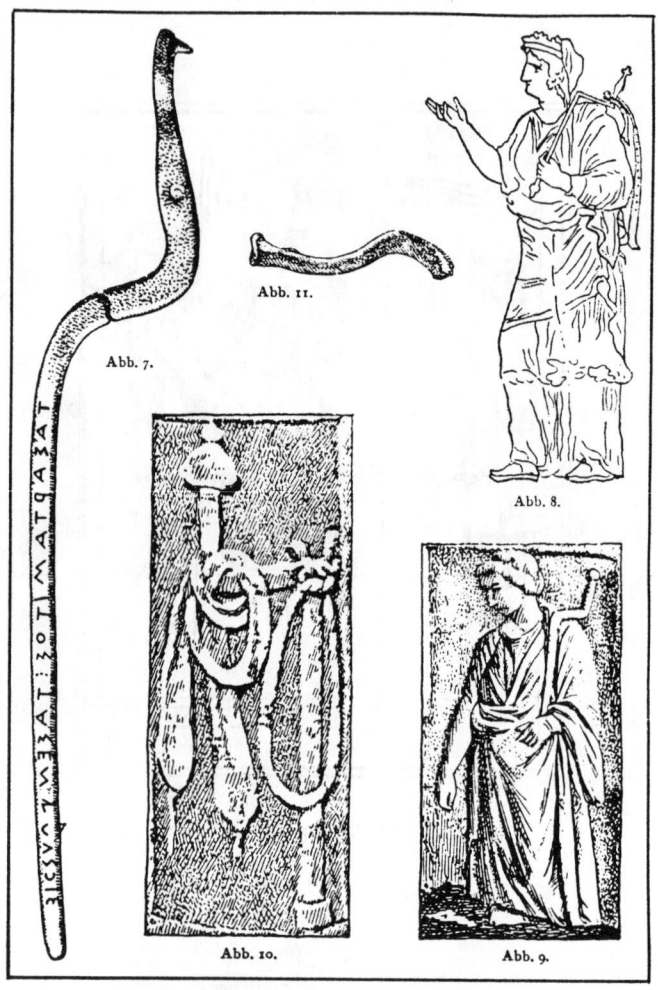

Simplest forms of ancient keys
7. Key of Artemis' temple at Lusia, Arcadia
8. Detail of Greek vase with a priestess carrying the temple key
9. Funeral bas-relief with a priestess carrying a key
10. Temple key from Habryllis   11. Left keybone of man

Illustration IX

Cairo merchant carrying keys on his shoulder
a hundred and fifty years ago

Illustration X

**Key of King Ptolemy's sarcophagus, Egypt.
(c. 250 B.C.)**

Illustration XI

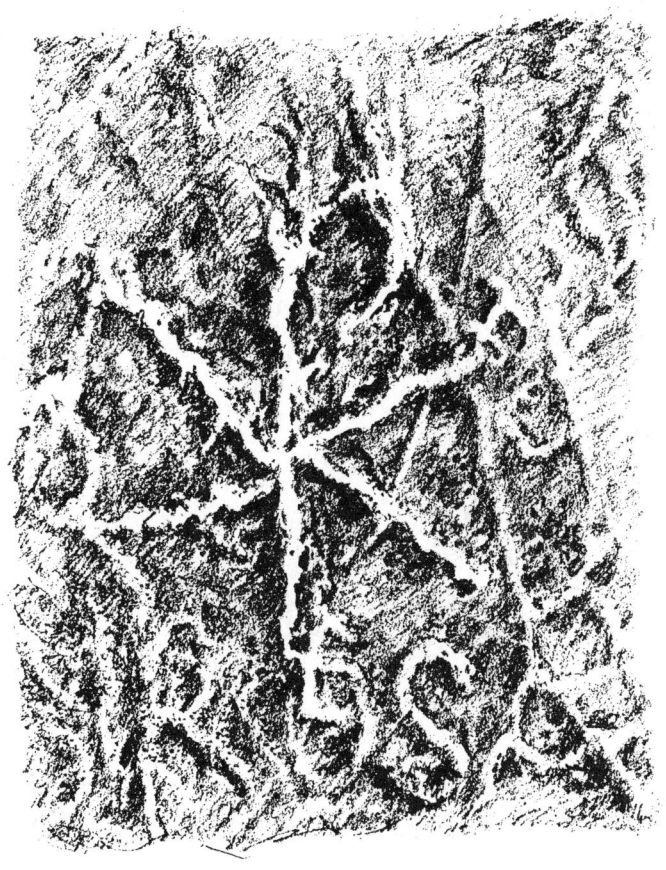

Detail from the red-stucco graffiti wall above the tomb of Peter, showing the combination of P and X (Christ) with E into a sign for Christ-Peter and a key

Illustration XII

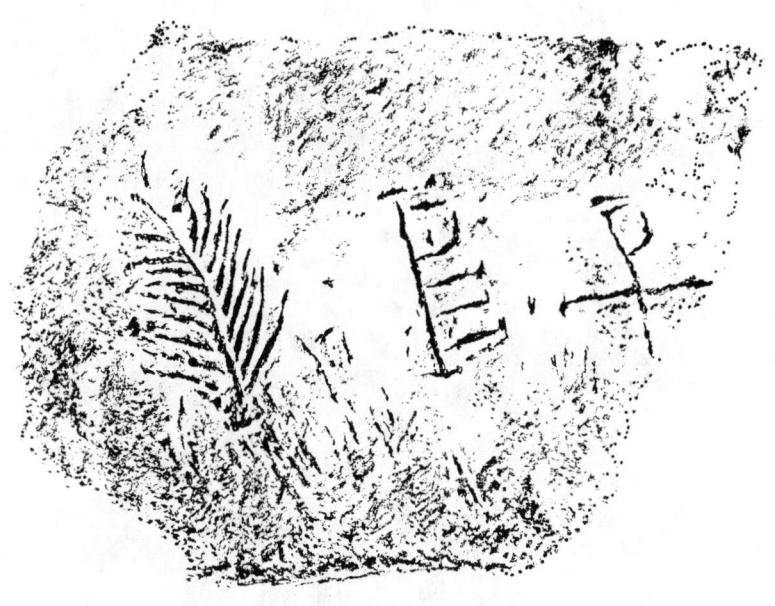

Stone from the catacomb under the Roman Forum
showing the combination of P and E into the shape of a key.

INDEX OF NAMES

Acton, J. E., Lord, 204
Adrian VI, Pope, 117, 119, 194
Alexander VI, Pope, 117
Alth, M., 180
Ambrose, Saint, 78–80, 119, 189, 194
Anacletus, Saint, Pope, 185
Anastasius I, Saint, Pope, 76
Anselm, Saint, 172, 204
Aratus, 21, 181
Aristophanes, 20
Arius, 74
Athanasius, Saint, 74, 81–82
Athenagoras, Patriarch, 201
Augustine of Hippo, Saint, 75–78, 89–90, 92, 121–122, 171, 188–189, 194–195
Augustus, Emperor, 39
Axataf, 182

Bardesan, 85
Barron, R., 17
Barth, K., 135–136, 165, 168, 196, 200
Basil, Saint, 85
Batiffol, P., 186
Bede, Venerable, 94
Benedict XII, Pope, 97
Benoit, J. D., 192
Bernard of Clairvaux, Saint, 95
Bernini, G. L., 176
Bialer, S., 205
Bierce, A., 180
Billerbeck, P., 185
Billot, L., 203
Blum, E. L., 179
Blum, J., 179

Boleyn, A., 192
Bonomi, J., 181
Bossuet, J. B., 134
Botta, P. E., 21
Bramah, J., 17
Bridget, Saint, 96
Browning, E., 184
Bultmann, R. K., 182
Burgess, J. A., 198, 202

Caird, G. B., 154, 199
Callistus I, Saint, Pope, 59–60
Calvin, J., 101–103, 110–115, 120, 137, 167, 192–194
Cangh, J. M. van, 185
Carroll, J., 203
Castellio, S., 116, 192
Celestine I, Saint, Pope, 190
Chapman, J., 189–190
Chesterton, G. K., 117, 146–147, 164, 184, 198–199
Chieregati, F., 118
Choiseul-Praslin, G. de, 134
Chrysostom, John, Saint, 86–89, 190
Clement I, Saint, Pope, 53, 82–83
Clement of Alexandria, 62–63
Columba, Saint, 94
Cullmann, O., 31–34, 38, 40–41, 136–140, 143, 182–183, 185
Cyprian, Saint, 55, 67–73, 187–188, 196–197
Cyril of Jerusalem, Saint, 86, 190

Dalman, G. H., 185
Damasus I, Saint, Pope, 57, 81
Dante, A., 96

Decius, Emperor, 67, 73
Diels, H., 181
Disraeli, B., 163, 200
Döllinger, J. J. I. von, 163
Donceel, J., 199
Doumergue, E., 192
Dulles, A., 202

Englebert, O., 191
Ephrem, Saint, 85, 189
Epiphanius, Saint, 86, 190
Eras, V. J. M., 180
Erasmus, D., 88, 119
Esbroek, M. van, 185
Eton, W., 181
Eugenius III, Pope, 95
Exell, J. S., 185, 198

Felix, antipope, 189
Fichte, J. G., 110, 157, 199
Fisher, John, Saint, 121
Flavian, Saint, 89
Fleury, C., 196
Francis de Sales, Saint, 115
Fronto, Marcus Aurelius, 19

Gail, M., 191
Giraud, V., 205
Giulio di Medici, Cardinal, 117
Goethe, J. W. von, 110, 175
Gregory of Nazienzen, Saint, 85
Gregory of Nyssa, Saint, 85
Gregory the Great, Saint, Pope 57
Grisar, M., 191–193
Guarducci, M., 177, 205–206
Gwynn, Richard, Blessed, 193

Hadrian, Emperor, 62
Haffner, P., 206
Harnack, A., 57, 72, 110, 135, 140–141, 186, 197
Hart, T., 17
Hartley, D., 12
Haynald, L., 204
Hegel, G. F. W., 157, 199
Heine, H., 157, 199

Henry VIII, 121–122, 126, 130, 192
Henry, P. A., 192
Hilary, Saint, 74
Hobbes, A. C., 17
Homer, 21
Hopkins, A. A., 180
Hus, J., 192

Ignatius of Antioch, Saint, 53, 56–57, 169
Innocent I, Saint, Pope, 75, 89
Innocent VIII, Pope, 117
Irenaeus, Saint, 55, 185

Jaki, S. L., 183, 196, 198
Jedin, H., 204
Jerome, Saint, 81
Joan of Arc, Saint, 192
Jörgensen, J., 191
John of Alverna, Blessed, 192
John XXIII, Pope, 3, 153
John Paul II, Pope, 163, 173–174, 201–202
Josephus Flavius, 43
Journet, C., 203
Julius I, Saint, Pope, 81–82, 189
Jung, C. G., 202
Justin, Saint, 54
Justin of Nassau, 182

Kaiser, O., 182
Kant, I., 103, 110, 156, 158–159
Ker, T., 201
Kevane, E., 199
Koehler, W., 192
Küng, H., 116, 201

Lagrange, J. M., 183
Leo I, Saint, Pope, 57, 90–92
Leo III, Saint, Pope, 170
Leo X, Pope, 117
Liberius, Pope, 189
Lightfoot, J. B., 185
Lindbeck, G. A., 203
Linus, Saint, Pope, 185
Livy, 24, 182

Index of Names

Lonergan, B., 155–156, 201
Luther, M., 73, 98–103, 105–109, 112, 116–117, 119–121, 131–133, 137, 141, 167, 192–194

Macedo, F., 196
Marcion, 85
Marcus Antonius, Emperor, 19
Maréchal, J., 156, 199
Maritain, J., 155, 191, 199
Martinich, A. P., 204
Mary Tudor, Queen, 128
Mascall, E. L., 205
Maximus, Saint, 92, 191
McCord, P. J., 195
McGrawth, P., 204
Melanchton, P., 100, 192, 195
Meletius, Saint, 89
Milingo, E., 200
Minear, P. S., 138–139, 197
Monk, E., 180
Montanus, 58, 61
More, Thomas, Saint, 121
Münzer, T., 98, 100

Naveratius, 171
Nero, Emperor, 176
Newman, J. H., 79, 160–162, 164, 187–188, 200
Nicephor I, Patriarch, 171
Nietzsche, F., 202
Novak, M., 155, 199

Oepke, A., 183
Olieu (Olivi), J. P., 192
Optatus, Saint, 75
Origen, 64–66
Overnay, M., 183

Paschal I, Saint, Pope, 171
Paul IV, Pope, 128
Paul VI, Pope, 3, 98, 149–150, 153, 165–166 169, 183, 198–201, 203
Pelagius, 89
Perrone, G., 170
Philip of Hesse, 99

Pius IX, Pope, 170, 204
Pius X, Saint, Pope, 164–165
Plato, 66, 157
Pliny, 20
Plutarch, 19, 40, 184
Polanyi, M., 205
Pole, Reginald, Cardinal, 121, 124–126, 128–131, 195
Pope, A., 9
Ptolemy II, 24
Pyke, J., 116

Rahner, K., 156, 174, 199, 205
Ratzinger, Joseph, Cardinal, 200
Reynolds, J., 180
Risenfeld, A., 45
Robert, Count of Flanders, 172–173
Runcie, R., 163

Sabatier, P., 93
Sampson, R., 122, 124–125
Sargon II, 22
Schelling, F. W. J., 199
Schiller, F. von, 184
Schwager, F., 203
Servetus, M., 102
Sohn, R., 186
Spinola, A., 182
Stephen I, Saint, Pope, 69, 71–73, 188
Strack, H. L., 185
Suleiman I, 182

Taine, H., 173
Tatian, 53–54
Terentius Varro, 182
Tertullian, 58–62
Theodore, Saint, 170–171, 204
Theodorus of Samos, 20, 181
Thomas Aquinas, Saint, 162, 167, 203
Tucker, H. L., 206
Tyszkiewicz, S. J., 203

Vaux, R. de, 182

Vallois, R., 181
Velasquez, D. R. de Silva y, 182
Villefosse, H. de, 181
Vincent of Lerin, 188
Virgil, 205
Visser't Hooft, W. A., 200

Walker, W., 192
Walsh, J. E., 206
Wendel, F., 192
Whitehead, A. N., 55, 186

Wolsey, Thomas, Cardinal, 121
Wünsche, A., 185

Yale, L., Jr., 15
Yale, L., Sr., 14

Zahn, T., 136, 196
Zara, L., 180, 205
Zosimus, Saint, Pope, 90
Zweig, S., 101–102, 192